NORTH

CAROLINA &

OLD SALEM

COOKERY

A

CHAPEL HILL

BOOK

North Carolina & Old Salem Cookery

NEW & REVISED EDITION

Beth Tartan

The University of North Carolina Press : Chapel Hill & London

© 1955, 1992

The University of

North Carolina Press

96   95   94   93   92

5   4   3   2   1

Library of Congress

Cataloging-in-Publication Data

Tartan, Beth, 1919–

  North Carolina and Old Salem cookery /

by Beth Tartan.—New and rev. ed.

    p.   cm.

"Chapel Hill books"

Rev. ed. of: North Carolina and Old Salem

cookery / Elizabeth Hedgecock Sparks (Beth

Tartan). 1955.

Includes index.

  ISBN 0-8078-2035-0 (cloth : alk. paper).—

ISBN 0-8078-4375-X (pbk. : alk. paper)

  1. Cookery, American—Southern style.

2. Cookery—North Carolina.   I. Sparks,

Elizabeth Hedgecock, 1919–   North

Carolina and Old Salem cookery.   II. Title.

TX15.2.S68T37   1992   91-50790

641.59756—dc20   CIP

Contents

Introduction

Before World War II ended, it was obvious that the life-style many of us enjoyed while growing up had vanished. That life-style included three meals a day and a magical Sunday dinner each week. The weekly menus that featured meat loaf on Wednesday and creamed dried beef on Thursday were not monotonous but rather offered security. At Thanksgiving, we traveled "over the hills to Grandmother's house." Today, Grandmother's house is no longer there and the road that went over the hills may be a superhighway.

Not only did we feel secure growing up, but also there was stability—as indicated by the number of recipes used in the 1920s and 1930s that called for a five-cent box of this or a ten-cent jar of that. Our mothers tended to wear frilly aprons around the house, their domain, and our fathers earned the living. Whatever else growing up was in the twenties and thirties, ours was truly a gentler, kinder life. A culinary guardian angel surely watched over us for our chocolate fudge, and pulled mints never turned to sugar, our pickles were not slippery, our kraut did not mold, and our salt-rising bread always rose.

Our mothers, grandmothers, and other ladies, especially in spring and summer—attired in their exquisite voile, crepe de chine, organdy, Irish linen, and pongee dresses—went off to or gave luncheons in homes decorated with a profusion of sweet peas and other flowers.

Men and boys who went to war came back talking about pizza and pot-au-feu. Many of the household servants who went to war never came back, at least not to their old jobs.

Gingerbread mix, the only mix we ever heard of—unless you can call self-rising flour a mix—was soon joined by more than enough cake mixes to fill a section in the supermarket, the form of food merchandising that replaced the neighborhood grocery store and butcher shop with a butcher who cut the meat.

Actually, it became apparent that there were enough changes to fill a book—this book. Not only did old favorites disappear from menus but so did the cooks with the knowledge and skill to prepare them.

Some information and sources of recipes that were scarce when this book first appeared in 1955 are nonexistent now. If someone had not written down the old recipes, many would be forever lost. *North Carolina and Old Salem Cookery* provides a picture of another culinary era. Soon after it first appeared, the Rotary Club of Wilmington selected the book as a gift for one hundred libraries around the world. And for several years it was used in social studies classes at the school in Granite Quarry.

This revised edition has the same basic purpose as the original one: to portray life in the home as an important part of our history. Some of the recipes have been included simply as a way of identifying a dish or a method of preparing it; the old recipes are often sketchy and list ingredients that are no longer available. Those recipes that deserve to be served for many generations to come have been tested and are so marked. Information has generally been updated; some recipes give better directions and newly discovered material has been added.

East Is East & West Is West

Based on topography, North Carolina has three sections—the coastal plain in the east, the mountains in the west, and the Piedmont in between. In the east, there is strong evidence of the early English settlers. The Piedmont was settled by the Quakers in Guilford County, the Moravians and Germans in Forsyth, the Pennsylvania Dutch in Rowan and Cabarrus, the Calvinists in Mecklenburg, and a good sprinkling of English Methodists, Scottish Presbyterians, and Baptist followers throughout. Here and there were scattered a few Mormon settlers. The traditions of the Scots who settled in Moore County have continued. The Irish, who located in Duplin County, part of which later became Sampson, have left their mark as well. In Burke County, we find the strong influence of the Waldensians from northern Italy. (The Waldensians are discussed later in this chapter.)

Many of the customs of the early settlers have been handed down. In Rodanthe, a small village on a windswept island near Cape Hatteras and in the neighboring village of Waves, Christmas or Little Christmas is still celebrated on the Twelfth Night Epiphany (January 6). The Twelfth Night celebration includes an exchange of gifts, the music of fifes, the beating of an ancient drum, and a visit by Old Buck, the legendary wild bull of Trent Woods. One of the villagers plays the part of Old Buck. He waves a cow's skull on a stick. Dinner is likely to be planned around roast turkey and plum pudding. In the village, families with names like Midgett, Meekings, Baum, Dough, and Basnights are believed to be descendants of Sir Walter Raleigh's Lost Colony.

Though the Quakers of the Guilford area have influenced religious life in the state, their influence on food has been slight. For years the old-time "thee and thou Quakers" frowned on the practice of preparing food on Sunday. The Quaker ladies cooked great quantities of food on Saturday but stopped at sundown. Unlike the Quakers, however, the Moravians and the Germans have had a significant impact on the culinary tastes of the Piedmont (see Chapter 6).

Overall, there has been a marked difference in the food habits of eastern, western, and Piedmont North Carolina, though gradually that distinction is decreasing. The difference is based not only on the customs of the early settlers, but also on the way of life in the three areas.

In the mountainous regions of the west, where travel was difficult, families lived pretty much to themselves. In the eastern part of the state, the existence of large plantations led to a great deal of visiting and numerous social occasions. Though plantations have dwindled in size and number, folks in the east have inherited that tradition of extreme hospitality. One reason for its continuance is that in almost every eastern community there are a number of "tobacco men" who follow the market. In other words, they buy during the season but are free to stay at home for several months out of the year.

Farms in the Piedmont have always been smaller, and it was in this area that the major industries in the state developed. Someone once said that the dividing line between eastern and Piedmont North Carolina is "where the sale of salt mullet stops and salt mackerel begins." Mullet is the eastern favorite.

Hot breads are favored throughout the state, but in the east you find a preference for corn bread or corn pone made without milk or eggs, and in the west biscuits are the choice. Western corn bread is made with milk and eggs and is like what the easterners call muffins.

Sweet potato biscuits are found a great deal more in the east. In general, sweet potatoes have a greater following in the east, where sweet potato pudding made with raisins is preferred to persimmon pudding.

Pinto beans are standard fare on western tables, while easterners prefer black-eyed peas or small dried beans that turn a blush-pink when cooked.

Preferences in barbecue also differ. Such preferences are described in Chapter 14.

Seafood is, of course, widely consumed along the coast. In the days before modern methods of refrigeration, seafood in inland towns was pretty much restricted to salt fish or to fish caught in ponds and streams.

Even the soil of North Carolina has gained world fame as an ingredient in fine dinnerware. Josiah Wedgwood, the English ceramic artist, heard about the state's pure white "Cherokee clay" and sent a man on an expedition for some. Wedgwood's agent left Charleston, South Carolina, on October 17, 1767, and traveled into the hills of North Carolina near present-day Franklin, where he dug about five tons of clay to send to England.

•　•　•　•　•

THE WALDENSIANS

A Waldensian festival held occasionally in Valdese in Burke County helps keep the customs of these settlers from northern Italy alive. At such a festival in 1974, Waldenses celebrated with a picnic of traditional food, folk songs, dances, and boccia playing (an Italian bowling game).

The Waldenses greeted each other in what seemed to be, at first sound, an unknown tongue. To this day, the Waldensians speak patois (pronounced pat-toy)—ask half a dozen Waldenses how to spell it and you will get half a dozen different spellings. One spelled it paqua; another, paquita.

Patois is a variety of the Provençal language spoken in southern France and northern Italy. It is not, as some believe, a mixture of French and Italian. Although patois has some French, Latin, and Italian words, it is a separate Romance language. That the Waldenses speak this strange tongue is natural because some emigrated here in their youth. Lena Bounous came when she was thirteen and her husband, Emilk, when he was twenty-one. The whole Waldensian settlement traces its heritage to the first immigrants who arrived here in 1893.

The Waldenses are a religious sect that traces back eight centuries to 1174 and perhaps even to the Apostles in the Bible. They had been driven from their farms in Italy by a religious persecution. A search by a couple of Waldenses prior to 1893 located several thousand acres in Burke County. According to most sources, the first settlers consisted of twenty-nine persons in twelve families. These settlers came to uncleared lands, where they had to endure a cold winter before the first crops could be planted and harvested.

In addition to a strong religious faith, the proud Waldenses brought their skills as wine makers, cheese makers, bread makers, and sausage stuffers, as well as their expertise in the preparation of spaghetti and other pasta.

Belle Femme (Strawberries in Wine)

Fresh peaches may also be prepared using this Waldensian recipe.

Prepare 1 basket of fresh strawberries. Combine a 6-ounce glass of wine, a 1-ounce glass of brandy, and 3 teaspoons of sugar. Pour over strawberries and chill overnight.

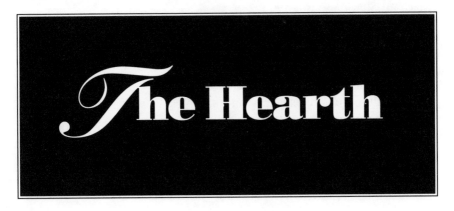

TWO

The Hearth

The typical North Carolina farmhouse is a T-shaped or L-shaped two-story structure with a one-story porch across the front. A hallway usually separates the two front rooms—one of which is the parlor. The other room is the master bedroom, which is the real family sitting room. There are, of course, many other types of houses, but this model is found more often than any other.

In the older homes, the kitchen was a separate structure; it was joined to the main portion of the house by a porch or by what has become the breezeway in modern architecture. The reason for this type of construction was to decrease the possibility of fire, which might originate in the kitchen, from destroying the whole house.

There was a well in the porch or under a small roof near the house. Before running water became a kitchen comfort, every drop of water used had to be pulled out of the well and carried into the house.

On the back porch, there was a shelf to hold tin or enamel wash pans in which "the hands"* washed up before meals. A towel in the shape of a fan belt was attached to a roller on the wall. Soap was of the homemade lye and fat variety. There was also a bucket for freshly drawn drinking water. The dipper in the bucket was used by the whole family.

The woodshed and the woodpile were important parts of the home place. Sometimes the logs were cut into stove-length wood with a handsaw. After the Model T Ford became so widely used, there was always a pair of men in the village who went from house to house with a motor-

---

*The hands were employees who worked in the fields.

ized saw to cut the wood. The sound of that saw buzzing in the backyard was a familiar one.

After the logs were cut into stove lengths, they had to be chopped to make stove wood and kindling. Knotty pine pieces or "lightnin' pine" were carefully hoarded for kindling fires.

The woodpile was quite an institution. The chopping block was an ideal spot for cracking black walnuts and hickory nuts. Some cooks were adept at wringing the heads from chickens; others chose to chop off the heads on the chopping block.

Somewhere near the woodpile stood a big black wash pot. The pot was used for boiling clothes and scalding chickens. If there was a large crowd to feed, it was used for making chicken stew or Brunswick stew.

• • • • •

BOTTLE TREES

Outside the back door of a farmhouse, you will occasionally see a bottle tree. A bottle tree did not grow bottles; rather, it was used to dry them. The trunk of a tree with several low branches was cut down to a height of about six or seven feet. The branches were cut off to a length of about a foot or so. These branches make spikes to hold bottles and jars so they could dry. In the old days, people liked the idea of drying their bottles and jars in the fresh air and hot sun.

• • • • •

INSIDE THE KITCHEN

Inside the kitchen of these old homes, the furnishings follow a similar pattern. Before the introduction of the wood stove early in this century, there was an open fireplace with cranes for swinging pots into place over the fire. Skillets on legs stood on the hearth ready to be used for frying meat or making corn pone. The skillets had heavy lids, and hot coals were placed on the lids to hasten the cooking.

Sweet potatoes, Irish potatoes, and onions were roasted in the ashes. It was even possible to make a pound cake on the hearth in a pound cake baker, which stood on short legs and was covered with a heavy top.

If you think baking waffles for the whole family is a slow process, then you should have to do it over an open fireplace. The fireplace waffle iron had two handles about a yard long and looked like a giant pair of scissors. At one end was a small box about the size of a slice of thick bread. The batter was poured into this little flat box, which was held over the open fire to bake the waffles. A cooky or wafer iron, made in the same scissorlike design as the waffle iron, was used to bake cookies over an open fire.

Of course, for baking the family's supply of breads, pies, and cakes, many kitchens had Dutch ovens, which were built in the chimney. Sometimes these ovens were outside the house or in the village.

THE BIG BLACK WOOD STOVE

When cooking was finally transferred from the fireplace to the big black wood stove, the range became the center of the kitchen. (In those days, the kitchen was more qualified to be called the family room than the room given that title in modern architecture.) In most cases, gas and electric ranges have now replaced the wood range.

In the winter months, the firebox of the wood range operated continually—no less often than the furnaces of Pittsburgh's steel mills. Many a child dressed on a winter's morning standing next to the hot stove. On nippy days in the fall and early spring, the warmth of the stove made the kitchen as inviting as a mountain stream on the Fourth of July.

Of course, hot as the old wood stove was on winter mornings, it managed to be even hotter in the good old summertime. If the outside temperature climbed to 100 degrees Fahrenheit, the kitchen temperature must have been 125 degrees, but that never stopped a homemaker from putting a hot meal and hot bread on the table.

Yes, the old wood stove made a cozy room. If there was a cat in the house, it spent a good portion of the winter curled up under the stove. In the early spring, the first baby chicks were often brought into the kitchen in a box to spend the chilly nights by the stove.

In the days of the wood stove, there was no such thing as a reliable thermostat or push-button control. The proper management of a wood stove requires a bit of genius and a touch of intuition. The amount and kind of wood used and the opening and closing of the flue with the damper controls the blaze.

There were a few men who took charge of the stoking but it was mainly the women who stoked. The fires might be kindled in one of three ways—with paper and kindling or with lightning pine, or by pouring "lamp oil" (kerosene) on stove wood.

A quick, roaring fire was the kind folks built first thing in the morning, or for boiling a kettle of water or making coffee, but for real Tar Heel cooking, a slow fire burned down to hot coals was vital. That slow fire cooked a mess of beans or baked a cake the way they should be cooked or baked. Just before it was time to make up a batch of biscuits, the firebox was stoked with a good supply of fast-burning sticks to get the oven quite hot.

Some of the later-model wood ranges had an indicator on the front of the oven door, but the average cook tested the heat by laying a piece of paper in the oven or by putting a hand in it momentarily. With the paper, the heat was determined by how fast the paper turned brown. Another way to find out was by putting a spoonful of flour on an old dish and setting it in the oven. If the flour browned in sixty seconds, the heat was right for bread. If it browned in less time, the temperature needed to be lowered.

The top of the stove sometimes doubled as a broiler for steaks. A cook could spread a layer of coarse salt on the surface of the wood range. Steaks were laid on the salt and broiled. Getting rid of the salt was easy—it was brushed into the fire.

Though the modern range has everything from chimes to a dashboard lighted in four colors, few have warmers. A warmer was stock equipment and built into every wood range. The warmer is like a shelf and is usually covered with doors. The heat from the top of the range and the flue keeps it warm. In former times, warmers were also used for storing leftover foods. Children headed for the warmer the minute they arrived home from school. There they found fried pies or whatever happened to be left from dinner.

Another useful feature of the wood stove was that by opening "an eye" over the firebox, the scene was set for singeing a chicken. With home-killed and picked chickens, a coating of soft fine feathers is left. These have to be burned or singed off.

Standard equipment on every stove was the coffee pot, which stayed there from morning until night. Each homemaker had her special spot on the range where the coffee was placed for quick boiling. It is an old saying that when the coffee pot or tea kettle rocks as it boils, "company's comin'." Once the coffee was boiled and ready to serve, it was pushed to the back of the stove to stay until it was emptied and new coffee made.

Mention of the coffee pot brings to mind coffee that was "saucered and blowed." It was most often the man of the house who poured his steaming hot coffee into a saucer, gave it a hearty blow to help cool it, and then noisily enjoyed the cooled contents of the saucer.

Then there was the tea kettle, which was the source of hot water for scalding chickens and dishes. Most of the wood ranges had a hot water box. The box helped provide hot water for family bathing, which took place in a tin tub.

OTHER KITCHEN FURNISHINGS

In the days before modern containers, the standard vessel for holding foods was the old stone crock, some with lids and others without. Gourds were also widely used. Fresh gourds were carefully cut so there would be a lid to cover the bottom portion when the drying-out process was completed. Here and there you will find an old salt gourd that has been carefully preserved. Homemade salt boxes that hang on the wall are still fairly plentiful.

For years sugar was such a precious substance that it was stored with great care. In many homes it was doled out from homemade boxes or specially made bins.

Then there were the flatirons, which are now prettily painted to use as doorstops. The flatirons were heated on top of the stove and when one cooled during the ironing, another stood hot and ready.

In addition to the stove, other kitchen equipment included a table for family eating. Oilcloth was the usual covering for the table. Possibly, there was a kitchen cabinet with a tin front. The tin was used in place of glass in the doors. To allow air to circulate through the cabinet, tiny holes were punched by hand with the point of a nail. Anything from a hunk of salt pork to whole nutmegs might be found in these cabinets.

Few of the tin-front cabinets—sometimes called a pie safe—have been preserved. Original owners had little desire to keep the ugly old cabinets after cleanly painted modern cabinets became available. The fatback stored in the tin-front cabinet plus the continual practice of frying or boiling a hunk of fatback for cooking vegetables gave the old kitchens a distinctive odor. This odor is not particularly inviting for anyone visiting them for the first time.

A meal chest or "chist" was also standard equipment in the days before commercially built kitchen cabinets. A typical meal chest is shaped like a blanket chest. The lid of some slanted like the front of a desk. Other lids were flat. The interior was usually divided into two compartments with a wooden partition between. One side was filled with flour, the other with cornmeal. Both flour and cornmeal were used so abundantly in most families that the man of the house brought them back from the gristmill by the 100-pound sack. The contents of the sacks were emptied into the bins in the meal chest. Many a family used a 100-pound sack of flour every week in the year.

Standard kitchen equipment still includes the black, black skillet. Though all sorts of frying pans are now available at all sorts of prices, none appeals to a southern cook the way the black skillet does. A few mothers of prospective brides often see to it that a new skillet has been seasoned for the bride so food will not stick in it.

The way to season a new skillet is to add unsalted oil or fat and heat it hot, then allow it to cool gradually. That has to be done a couple of times but even after that treatment, food may be inclined to stick a little. The sticking will stop after the pan has been used for a while. In addition to the black skillets, there is an assortment of pots or kettles called stew pans, which refer to any type of pan used for stewing or boiling food.

The dishpan is another institution found in yesterday's kitchens. With the arrival of modern sinks and dishwashers, the dishpan has disappeared. But until then, washing dishes without a dishpan was unknown. A dishpan was a flared pan about twenty inches across the top and about eight to ten inches deep. It was usually made of tin or enamel. Most homes claimed at least two dishpans—one for washing and the second for piling clean dishes for scalding. Hot water from the ever-hot kettle on the stove did the scalding. The dishpan was also used to hold foods of one sort or another. A few of the old recipes, such as one for persimmon pudding, begins with "take a dish pan full of ripe persimmons." Strings of red pepper pods or onions with purple skins completed the kitchen scene, except for the cook.

In homes that could not afford a servant, the kitchen was run by the lady of the house, who wore her apron like a uniform from early morning until late at night. Women made full use of their aprons—I have seen them carry a load of kindling from the woodpile to the house or pick a mess of beans or corn in their aprons. When there was a crowd on hand to feed, the woman of the house might fill her apron with biscuits hot from the oven and take them to the table and pass them around.

So accustomed was she to wearing an apron that when dinner was finished, she would put on a clean apron before sitting down to do her needlework. Many is the woman I have seen finish the Sunday dinner dishes, take off her dirty apron, and then put on a fresh one before sitting on the porch or in the living room. When a woman went to the garden or outdoors, chances are she would cover her head with the traditional slat bonnet.

· · · · ·

THE COOK

"As we grew up as a nation, and after our pioneering days were over, people had a certain degree of prosperity. There was always a hired girl or cook. It was not just the minority. Practically everybody could afford it and people wanted to spend their time doing other things." That is from a speech made by the late James Beard, a pacesetter in the field of food. Not everyone had a "hired girl or cook," but many families did, certainly more than enough to qualify these people as an important segment of the work force.

Many kitchens in North Carolina and other states in the South were presided over by a woman called the cook, who was actually a phenomenon of the times. Although this person had incredible status in a household and community, little has been published about her work, her duties, and her training.

One of the few bits of information written about cooks is in a book entitled *Four Great Southern Cooks*, which was the subject of a food column written by Helen Moore for the *Charlotte Observer* in 1987. One of the four cooks, Beatrice Mize, was born in 1893. Her family worked on a large estate, where she began her training at age fourteen. "I was just tickled to death to get in that big kitchen with everything in it," she recalled. The lady of the house would take "me in the library and set me on a stool and tell me what she wanted me to fix for dinner. I would memorize everything and fix it like she told me. Lots of things she taught me to cook." Beatrice Mize went on to work in other homes. "I've never worked for anyone but the richest and the finest," she said in 1981 at age eighty-eight.

Good cooks sometimes went on to become distinguished caterers. An excellent example is Jessie Hargrave Payne, of Lexington, North Carolina, who left behind a cookbook entitled *Jessie Payne's Recipes*, published in 1955. Some of her menus and recipes are included in the present book.

Little cookbooks such as the one that came with the Majestic wood range and those for Rumford baking powder had rules for housekeeping, but these were of no help to most cooks, who not only had their own rules but also could neither read nor write. As for a cook's rules, it is the same as Tom Wicker said about North Carolina barbecue: "we are not taught, we are born knowing" about it. Surely, the cooks I have known were born to follow certain rules as if they were law.

The cook has been at the heart of a life-style called Southern Hospitality. An example of that hospitality was cited by the late Carlton Byrd, sports editor of the *Sentinel* in Winston-Salem. In a report on his visit to the Orton Plantation near Wilmington at the time of the 1951 Azalea Festival, Byrd wrote that Kenneth and Betsy Sprunt, plantation owners, invited sixty people to a buffet supper. More than one hundred guests appeared for dinner. Mrs. Sprunt said: "I don't know where they all came from but we tried to take care of them as best we could." The cooks had simply followed the old custom of cooking a little extra.

Here are some of the old-time rules for cooks:

- *The proper household sets its best foot forward.* With the running of an efficient household in the hands of the cook, she rather than the lady of the house competed with cooks in other households. If a cook was slothful in her duties, somehow knowledge of this quickly spread to other cooks.
- *If there is a possibility of "company comin',"* the house must be spotless. No one ever spelled out what would happen if a guest saw a speck of dirt.
- *Set a good table.* Anything less was unacceptable. That also meant having enough for everyone. No one ever spelled out what would happen if there was not enough food.
- *Have dinner "on" by eight in the morning.* That meant that some of the food—especially dried beans and chunks of salt pork for the greens—had to be on the stove cooking by 8:00 A.M. in order to serve dinner promptly at 12:00 noon.
- *After washing and drying the dinner dishes, wash and hang the towels to dry.* The towels were either 100 percent linen or cotton.
- *Sweep the kitchen.*
- *Sweep the yard.* If the yard consisted of only dirt or soil, the custom was to sweep it with a sagebrush broom. An unswept yard was a sign of "po' white trash."

The cook also had procedures for feeding the hired help. We did not have farm hands, but Cousin Julie Hendrix did at her home at the Old Mill in Oak Ridge. Just before noon each day, she rang the dinner bell as a signal for the hands to come in from the fields and eat dinner. The men washed their hands in water drawn from the well and dried them on a roller towel, a long towel (two yards or more) on a roller, which permitted it to be turned. When all of the towel was dirty, it was removed and a clean one was placed on the roller.

Because the hands at the Old Mill worked only in warm weather, they were served dinner on the back porch. They sat at long tables laden with food. The beverages consisted of cool water from the spring and milk or buttermilk from the springhouse. Butter for the loaves of hot salt-rising bread (for Cousin Julie's recipe see index) also came from the springhouse, a little wooden building constructed over a stream of springwater that was generally cooler than the water from the well.

The unwritten protocol of feeding men who worked in the yard, as well as hobos who came by frequently, was to give them a plate of food piled high and a large container of cool water. Sometimes they pumped their own water from the well. (Hobos were men who wandered from city to city, traveling primarily in empty railway boxcars. They were the nomads, vagrants, or homeless people of an earlier period, transporting their worldly belongings in a cloth sack tied to a stick carried over the shoulder.)

• • • • •

FLY BUSHES

Before screen wire, insecticides, and air conditioning, flies were an annoying problem in the spring and summer. An abundance of them had to be dealt with—especially at mealtime. Sheets of gummed flypaper and spiral coils of flypaper suspended from the ceiling were common in every home. Even with flypaper, swarms of flies seemed to appear from everywhere just as people were sitting down to enjoy their dinner. That is when the fly bushes appeared. Fly bushes were "going out" about the time I "came in," but I remember well my grandmother waving one over the table to shoo away the flies as she called the clan to eat.

There were a variety of fly bushes. The most common one was made on a long stick of lightweight reed. One end served as the handle. Folded newspaper cut in strips was placed on the other end. A needle and thread were used to stitch the newspaper and hold it in place around the stick. The newspaper was cut into strips about a half-inch wide that hung down from the sticklike fringe. The ends of the strips were curled with the fingers.

Quite likely for Sunday and company there was a special fly bush. Some of these were made from white tissue paper and were just like the newspaper ones. It was also possible to buy extra-special ones with thin, leather-covered handles that resembled an umbrella. At the "umbrella end," feathers from the colorful peafowl were fastened to resemble a fan.

· · · · ·

THE HEARTH ON A GRAND SCALE
Korner's Folly in Kernersville

There stands on Main Street in Kernersville, which is located on the highway between Winston-Salem and Greensboro, one of North Carolina's most fascinating houses—Korner's Folly. Jule Gilmer Korner, the original owner of the house, which looks like a castle, named it "The Folly." The story is that while the house was under construction (it was started in 1880), a farmer passed by on a mule and remarked to one of the workmen: "He'll live to see it called 'Korner's Folly.'" Fearing that he might not live that long, Mr. Korner began calling the house the Folly at once and had the name, Korner's Folly, put into tiles at the front.

Mr. Korner designed the house himself and tried to make all sides look alike so there would be no front and back. As it stands today, there are twenty-two rooms and the same number of fireplaces. There are three floors in the center and five on either side, with no two rooms on the same level. A hand-carved staircase winds all the way to the top on the left side.

Along one whole side of the dining room is a china closet, or breakfront, made of beautifully aged and intricately carved wood. The closet is so massive that it cannot be moved, which is true of much of the furniture in the house.

The shelves in the kitchen and the table tops are marble. The convenience of the built-in cabinets suggests that they were a modern innovation rather than a part of the original building. The kitchen had an ice closet and a method of refrigerating foods in winter—the unit consisted of shelves outside a wide window. The house was air-conditioned with the aid of a tunnel through the basement, a carefully worked out plan of cross-ventilation, and pivoting windows.

To help end vandalism and other destructive elements, a group of twenty-seven interested citizens purchased the Folly in the early 1970s and formed Kerner's Folly, Inc. The Folly is open to the public on a limited schedule and by special arrangements. To arrange for a tour, contact the Kernersville Chamber of Commerce.

Sufficient culinary aspects of the Folly came to light after its purchase to produce *The Korner's Folly Cookbook*, which covers three eras: the Victorian period, when the home was built; the early twentieth century, when Dore Korner (Mrs. Lanier Donnell) was married; and the later twentieth century.

From this fascinating house comes an equally fascinating account of the food served there. It is the story of Aunt Dealy, as told by Mrs. Donnell, who grew up in Korner's Folly.

AUNT DEALY

Aunt Dealy was a slave and came to the home of my grandparents, Philip and Judith Korner, near Kernersville, about 1834. She was then in her early teens, a girl of light skin, gentle nature, and unusual intelligence. She was made a house girl and kitchen helper—that is how she learned the way of the "cook room."

She was a remarkable nurse, too. In 1853, when my grandmother died leaving a two-year-old son, Aunt Dealy became a mother to the little boy. That little boy was my father and he learned to love his mammy the way children did in those days.

When the war was over, the former slave became a free woman— she was about 50 years old then, but she did not want to leave her white folks.

When Jule Korner grew up and began building his future home, Korner's Folly, at the same time he built a house for Aunt Dealy in the back. Aunt Dealy continued to cook and look after the young bachelor. When he brought his bride to the new home, Aunt Dealy was put in charge of the kitchen.

Aunt Dealy died in 1896 in her cottage, which was known as "Aunt

Dealy's House." Her funeral, which was conducted by a white minister as well as a Negro one, was held at Korner's Folly. She was buried in the private Korner cemetery at the back of the Moravian Church cemetery.

She was known for her tasty cooking though, of course, the words *menu* and *recipe* were unknown to her. She cooked entirely by hand—a little bit of this and a little bit of that.

My memories of her are dim, but I remember that it was an accepted fact that no one could cook like Aunt Dealy. I do remember these things about her cooking.

Her vegetables were cooked perfectly. She seasoned them with bacon drippings, ham hock, or fatback. The bowl of turnip greens was always carefully topped with overlapping slices of hard-cooked eggs. Her turnips were light and fluffy. Her green snap beans that cooked for three hours with tender kernels of corn added the last 20 minutes were delicious.

Aunt Dealy was an expert hominy maker. A lye hopper was a permanent fixture in the backyard of her cottage. To make hominy, she made a lye solution strong enough "to eat a feather when boiling hot." Shelled hard corn was put in the lye water and boiled until the husks and "eyes" came off. Then there was much rinsing in water and more boiling until the kernels became white and juicy and tender. Sometimes, she cooked the hominy with bacon and served it with butter. Other times she fried it crisp and brown in a little fat.

Aunt Dealy's corn bread was relished by everyone who ate it. Sometimes she made it into pones or hoe cakes patted down into a black three-legged skillet which was placed on the hearth next to glowing coals. She turned the skillet around ever so often as the bread cooked.

The same corn bread with eggs added was cooked in a round pan in the wood stove. It was cut out in pie-shaped wedges. She made spoon bread, too.

Of all the corn bread she made, none was as popular as the little corn cakes cooked on top the stove in a black iron frying pan. She always served them with summer vegetables. My father was delighted when I learned how to make them. There was no recipe—Aunt Dealy taught me to throw them together just before it was time for them to go to the table.

For each cake, I pick up enough corn meal to fill my cupped palm. Salt and soda are added and then buttermilk, which is best when a little sour. The mixture is stiff. That is all there is to them. The following proportions will work but you may find them temperamental. In that case, you add a little bit of this and a little bit of that:

Aunt Dealy's Corn Cakes

2 cups corn meal
½ teaspoon salt
½ teaspoon soda
1½ cups buttermilk, more or less

Make the stiff batter into round balls—rather small ones—and flatten into cakes about ½-inch thick. Have bacon grease or lard deep enough in the pan to run back and forth—but not too deep. Have the pan medium hot.

When the cakes are brown (it will not take long), turn. They should rise and be light and happy. When both sides are brown, whisk the cakes to the table. They are best if slit across with a knife and filled with a slice of country butter. They're good, too, topped with black molasses in place of dessert.

Sunday dinner was not Sunday dinner without Aunt Dealy's boiled custard served in big thick heavy goblets. That meant a big serving of custard for which everyone was grateful. I still have one of these big goblets.

The custard was thin enough to drink from the glass after the sudsy egg white had been eaten off the top with a spoon. She often served it with thick slices of pound cake, which was truly an out-of-this-world combination.

This is the recipe I have developed for the custard. Better double this amount—Aunt Dealy used to make a gallon at a time:

Aunt Dealy's Custard

1 quart milk
5 tablespoons sugar (this is a little sweet, but the
refrigerator chill makes it just right)
4 to 6 eggs (the more the better)
2 teaspoons cornstarch
⅛ teaspoon salt
Vanilla

Instead of using a double boiler, which is too narrow for the whole operation, I put a wide saucepan on a rack (or some scrunched-up oil paper) in a large frying pan a third filled with water. Put the milk in the pan to warm up, keeping out a little for dissolving the cornstarch. Add the salt any time, only don't forget it.

Separate eggs. Beat yolks well and add sugar and beat some more. Add egg mixture to milk and stir, then add cornstarch. This is where the real stirring begins to keep everything smooth. When you are sure about that, turn on your electric mixer to beat the egg whites to a stiff froth and add a little sugar.

By that time the custard will be creamy—don't cook too long—just until it is nice and thick. Take it off the stove and let cool a few minutes before adding vanilla.

While still hot, pour the egg whites right on top without breaking too much. Dip the custard over it with a big spoon until the egg whites are "cooked."

That is what I remembered of Aunt Dealy.

Soul Food

About the time that the classic French cuisine appeared in a less rich, lower caloric version called nouvelle cuisine, interest in old American favorites increased. These old favorites were given the name *soul food*. Some, including meat loaf and mashed potatoes, are called comfort foods.

In 1984 the late Nina Hyde, *Washington Post* fashion editor, put fine southern cuisine on the "in" list and rich European cuisine on the "out" list. As to fine southern cuisine being in or out, the general southern reaction to the announcement that it was "in" was that it had never been out.

Soul food did take a step in the direction of the highfalutin when Viola McKee, a native of Winston-Salem, was in charge of the kitchen for the executive dining room for Halston, the designer, in Manhattan, where he entertained the likes of Liza Minnelli and Elizabeth Taylor. Each noon from four to twenty-four individuals gathered around Halston's table, which was filled with foods such as fried chicken, lima bean soup, and peach cobbler prepared by Ms. McKee. Halston named the offerings "Nouvelle Soul Cuisine."

John Robinson, writing in the *Boston Globe* in 1984, tried to identify soul foods but singled out only one: "One food that is unarguably associated with American black traditions is chitterlings, pronounced CHIT-lins, unless you are hopelessly refined." Chitlins, as he continued, are pigs' intestines. In the old tradition, black slaves in the pre–Civil War South ate them out of necessity.

"Chitterlings were once survival food for blacks," according to Knight-

Ridder writer Jane Snow. "They were part of the pig that plantation owners had no use for. Hungry blacks would labor for hours to turn these castoffs into tasty meals." That sounds as if only hungry blacks ate chitlins, but such was not the case. Others enjoyed them as well. (For example, see Commissioner Frank Crane's letter in Chapter 7.) Pigs' intestines still have their adherents, so in his article John Robinson included a recipe from *Spoonbread and Strawberry Wine*, by Norma Jean and Carole Darden (Fawcett Crest, 1978), one of the better books on soul food.

As the expression *soul food* turned up more and more often in print and as the food was more widely served in restaurants, I began to try to learn more about the subject. The list of soul foods tended to include the dishes we grew up on in our part of the country. One thing is for sure and that is we never heard of anyone sitting down to a meal of soul food. If my grandmother were living and I asked her the meaning of the term, she would probably answer: "Land sakes, I don't know. Must be something to keep body and soul together."

A certain mystique has been woven around soul food—the same way there is some mystery surrounding the southern woman and out-and-out consternation in the face of a card-carrying southern belle. When Walter Mondale and Geraldine Ferraro were running on the Democratic ticket for president and vice-president of the United States, the question of predicting how southern women would vote came up. The wise answer they received was that there is little chance of predicting or understanding a southern woman. To understand a southern woman, you have to be one. By the same token, to understand soul food, you have to grow up on it. Then it is no mystery.

Some years ago, to help define soul food for people who did not grow up on it, I interviewed Minnie Brown, whose work with the North Carolina home economics extension service took her all over the state. (Mrs. Brown is now retired.)

"I can't explain soul food, I have to cook it for you," she said. And so she invited me to one of her luncheons. Between the trips from the kitchen and the front door, she managed to stir up and bake a pan of corn bread. As the bread baked, she sliced cucumbers, tomatoes, and onions into a glass bowl. Soon after the bread came from the oven, she announced: "It's ready. Come sit down and eat."

The meal included fried chicken cooked to perfection and served from a baking dish on the dining room table. From pots on the range in the kitchen guests helped themselves to collard greens, dried navy beans, and stewed chitterlings. Another baking dish on the stove held candied sliced sweet potatoes.

Our hostess passed the corn bread in its metal baking pan. Butter for the bread was on the table, along with fruit jars of homemade chowchow to spoon over the beans and peppery vinegar to spoon over the chitterlings. She also served tomato juice made from home-canned tomatoes and for dessert, homemade pound cake. Every bite was superb. Three of her recipes appear below.

Soul Bread

2 cups sifted cornmeal
2½ cups boiling water
2 tablespoons bacon drippings

Put cornmeal in a mixing bowl. Add boiling water and 1 tablespoon bacon drippings. Place remaining drippings in a skillet and turn on medium heat.

Spoon the cornmeal mixture into the hot skillet; pat out flat. Cook for 10 minutes on each side. Spread with butter and serve with collard greens or turnip greens, or dunk in pot liquor or sop in molasses for dessert.

As for butter versus margarine, Mrs. Brown's gold standard was golden butter. "Margarine never comes into my house," she said. Her standard for napkins was linen. She did not believe in serving soul food the highfalutin way it was done when soul food restaurants became popular in the late 1960s. "They came out with chitlins on silver platters," she noted.

Bread is the most important item in a soul food menu. Bread, most often hot bread, is served at every meal, and when crumbled into buttermilk, it makes a favorite meal in itself.

Collard Greens

2 pounds meat (neckbones, ham hocks, or salt pork)
4 medium-size bunches greens, thoroughly washed
Salt and pepper to taste
1 red pepper or ¼ teaspoon ground red pepper (optional)
2 tablespoons cooking fat or bacon drippings

Parboil meat until tender; remove from pot. Add well-washed greens that have been cut into small pieces.

Place meat on top of greens; cover. Simmer over low heat until greens have cooked down. Add seasonings to taste and cooking fat or drippings. Cover and simmer until greens cut easily with a fork.

Note: Add a small amount of water occasionally to prevent sticking.

Mrs. Brown prepared collards by parboiling, simmering a few minutes in water. Drain and add to water in which slices of streak-of-lean* have been boiled for 1 to 2 hours. Simmer until done.

"I know that parboiling and pouring off that water puts some of the vitamins down the kitchen sink and that we frown on that practice," Mrs. Brown said. However, parboiling gives a better flavor and even if a few vitamins go down the sink, a pot of collards provides more of some vitamins and minerals than a family needs in a day.

Pickle Relish

3 large cucumbers
2 medium ribs celery, each cut in 1-inch pieces
1 green pepper, cut in 12 pieces
1 sweet red pepper, cut in 12 pieces
1 medium onion, quartered
Salt to taste
Water
1½ cups vinegar
1 cup sugar
1 teaspoon mustard seed

Remove seeds from cucumbers, if tough. Shred cucumbers. Process other vegetables coarsely and add to shredded cucumbers. Sprinkle with salt, then add enough water to cover vegetables and stir. Let stand for 1 hour. Drain well.

In a 3-quart saucepan combine vinegar, sugar, and mustard seed; bring to a boil and add vegetables. Simmer, uncovered, for 15 minutes. Place in hot sterilized jars. Cool, then refrigerate. Will keep in refrigerator for several weeks. Or, for home canning, seal sterilized jars tightly with a vacuum seal and process in a hot water bath for 10 minutes.

*Streak-of-lean is salt pork or fatback with thin ribbons of lean, like bacon.

A food processor turns fresh vegetables quickly and easily into a relish to spoon on top of pinto or other dried beans or over hot dogs.

. . . . .

A "MESS"

In olden times, the exact quantity of food that constituted a "mess" varied with the size of the family. A mess for one family would not cover the bottom of the "take-up" dish used in another household. Roughly, a mess seems to have been the amount of a food sufficient to serve the family and the hands at dinner with enough left over for supper. (A mess was about the amount the lady of the house gathered into her apron to carry into the house.) A mess more often refers to fresh produce than to other foods.

One thing is for sure and that is North Carolina produces many a fine mess of food. From the shores of the Outer Banks in the east to the hills in the west—as Bill Sharpe of *State Magazine* would say, "From Manteo to Murphy"—the fields and streams are full of fine foods, some that are wild or natural and others that must be cultivated.

. . . . .

MEATS

POULTRY

Just about every farm has its own flock of chickens. The chickens run around the yard until somebody grabs one up by the leg and takes it to market or wrings its neck. An older female chicken is a hen.

North Carolina has long been a leading chicken, especially broiler, producer. It is now the nation's largest producer of turkeys. Many of the old farms had a little flock of guinea or "potarack" hens and perhaps a flock of geese. The term *speckled as a guinea egg* comes from the fact that the little eggs are dotted or freckled. (Guinea hens and geese have virtually disappeared from the state.) Some of the geese eventually went into the pot to parboil until tender, which for an old goose is a very long time, but the main value of a flock of geese was their feathers made into feather beds and bolsters (a long pillow that went all the way across the top of the bed underneath the two regular pillows).

Anyone who has never sunk his or her weary body into a thick, fluffy feather bed has missed quite an experience. Of course, nowadays the theory is that the spine should be well supported during sleep. A feather bed would not support that theory or the spine either. Sleeping on an old-fashioned feather bed filled with goose feathers remains for some a warm memory.

PORK

Today, pigs and hogs are grown on fewer farms. Of interest to visitors is the Tar Heel term *to pig*, meaning to have young pigs. On many farms with pigs, hog killing begins after the first severe cold spell, which is usually around Thanksgiving and sometimes a little before. It is a messy business.

There are the hams, shoulders, and side meat to salt down; the sausage, liver pudding, and souse meat to make; and the fat to render into lard. The shoulders, side meat, sausage, lard, and cracklings can wait to be used, but that still leaves quite a mess of fresh pork to cook, can, or give away. In the eastern part of the state, some cuts are preserved by corning. Fresh pork is now often frozen for future use.

Leaf Lard

The choice lard is leaf lard. It is made from the thick sheaf of fat that encases the hog's viscera. Once the lard is rendered, the cracklings are placed in a lard press, which looks like a well pump on a stand like the one used to support a sausage mill. The press makes just about all the fat ooze out.

Cracklings

Cracklings are the small pieces that remain after most of the fat has been removed. These are used for making crackling corn bread—about the best bread ever to be put on a table.

Cured Hams

Hams are mostly treated by the salt cure or sugar cure rather than smoking. The sugar is brown sugar and sometimes includes molasses.

There are those, of course, who still smoke hams but not as many as when most farms had a smokehouse.

It takes a good while before a ham develops its full flavor. Experts claim that a ham should be a year old before it is eaten. After about a year, tiny little white flecks appear in the meat; these are thought to be the indication of a good ham. Because of research done in food science at North Carolina State University in Raleigh, the control of temperature, salt, and humidity produces cured ham of uniform quality.

Pork Sausage

Was there ever anything as tasty as homemade pork sausage? The bite is given by snippets of red pepper throughout the meat, which is redolent with sage and black pepper.

Liver Pudding

There are any number of ways to make liver pudding. This one is often used.

Cook the liver and head separately in salted water until tender. Cut the head in half and grind half with the liver. Season with salt, black pepper, red pepper, and rubbed sage. Add sufficient cooking broth to moisten well. Pour into pans and allow to become firm.

Liver Mush

Liver mush is similar to liver pudding except that cornmeal is cooked in the broth used to cook the liver and then added to the ground liver mixture.

Scrapple

A few of the old cooks made scrapple by simmering the hog jaw until tender. The meat from the jaw was mashed to a pulp and added to the "bree" (broth) in which it was cooked with red pepper and cornmeal to thicken. Then the mixture was poured into pans to harden so it could be sliced and browned in a little fat.

Souse Meat

Souse meat is made by allowing the cooked head, which has been ground or finely chopped and seasoned with salt, black pepper, and red pepper, to congeal in a mold with a little broth. It becomes firm because of the natural gelatin in the head. Sometimes, the pig's feet are added to the souse meat.

Souse meat is also made by mixing the chopped head and feet, seasoned with vinegar, salt, black pepper, and red pepper, and then allowing to gel.

Ann Geis's Souse

5 pig's feet, split
4 ½ pounds pork loin roast
1 teaspoon salt or to taste
¼ teaspoon black pepper
3 envelopes unflavored gelatin
½ cup cold water
1 cup vinegar
Several shakes of hot pepper sauce
2 cups diced pimento-stuffed green olives

Place pig's feet and pork loin roast in a large Dutch oven; cover with water. Bring to a boil; reduce heat to simmer and cook, covered, for 4 hours. Lift feet and roast from broth; strain broth and let stand, covered, in the refrigerator overnight. Remove grease from top and discard.

Dice meat and skin; add to broth with salt and pepper. Soften gelatin in ½ cup cold water. Heat broth and meat to boiling; use to dissolve gelatin. Remove from heat; add vinegar and hot pepper sauce. Allow to cool to room temperature. Add olives. Pour into loaf pans. Chill in refrigerator, agitating contents of pan occasionally. Makes 5 partially filled loaf pans.

BEEF

There was a time when fresh beef was to be had only when a neighbor killed an animal. More often than not, it was a cow whose milking days were on the decrease.

The farmer who killed a "beef" shared it with his neighbors or relatives, or he peddled it from the back of his wagon or truck just as he did fresh produce.

GAME

Rabbits

Cottontail rabbits were plentiful in North Carolina. In the fall and winter, trappers set rabbit gums to catch them. A rabbit gum is nothing more than a hollow log or a box to lure the rabbit. As the rabbit goes inside, it trips the catch that holds open the door and bing, it is trapped. Marsh rabbits are still fairly common in the swamps and marshes along the coastal plains.

Today, a number of rabbit breeders produce the animal commercially. The rabbits, cut up and packaged like frying chickens, are available in a few stores.

Squirrels

There were about as many gray squirrels as rabbits. Fox squirrels were seen but not in such abundance. The red squirrel or "boomer" was found in the mountains.

Possums

A possum is really an opossum, according to the dictionary, and belongs to the marsupial order of mammals—that means having a pouch to carry its young.

Rarely, if ever, does anyone still hunt possums. There was a time, however, when there were possum hunts. A possum hunt was not as fashionable as a fox hunt, for the only resemblance to pink coats would have been the red plaid wool shirts worn by some of the hunters to keep warm. Because the hunt was at night, there was no fancy hunt breakfast. Somebody in the crowd might have supplied a fruit jar of corn liquor, but certainly there was no fancy fare. But a possum hunt and a fox hunt did have one similarity—the catch of the possum hunt was relished by only a few more diners than the fox would be.

The ideal time for a possum hunt was from late October, when there was a nip in the air, on through the cold months. It seemed to me that the night selected was always a pitch black one. Apparently, after dark possums creep out of their tree hollows or dens in the ground to go looking for an evening snack, so night was the time for the hunt. The hunters traveled on foot. Their equipment included trained dogs, flashlights or lanterns, and tow sacks (burlap bags).

The success of the hunt depended on the dogs. A fairly well-trained dog could follow a newly made trail, but it took an expert hound to keep on a cold trail. Once the dogs got the scent of the possum, they were off and the chase was on. A long, throaty howl, known by every possum hunter, verified that the dogs were not fooling.

The hunters fell in after the dogs. Over a course of hills and hollows, through briar patches, bushes, and weeds and over fallen dead trees, they went, huffing and puffing all the way. And most likely a fellow in front would let a sapling fly back and slap the person behind him right in the face.

The dogs would get way ahead of the hunters and tree the possum. That means the dogs chased the scared possum up the tree. The first hunter on the scene flashed a light in the possum's eyes and the critter was done for. It would just sit there on a limb until some nimble-footed individual climbed up and fetched it down and then threw it in a tow sack. Sometimes when the possum fell to the ground, it appeared to be dead, but actually it was "playing possum." (What really happened was that the possum was seized by a nervous spasm, caused by fright. As soon as the danger passed, the possum regained its self-control and went hurriedly on its way.)

Unless a possum was plump, it was penned up for a few days and fattened before killing. Often the possum was turned loose for another hunt.

Groundhogs or Woodchucks

Groundhogs, those little creatures that see or fail to see their shadows on February 2, were once so plentiful in the state that there was no closed hunting season to protect them. In the mountainous regions of the west, seeing a groundhog scurrying across a field before diving into its subterranean home was a common sight. Some people cooked the prepared groundhog by parboiling and then roasting, but certainly groundhog consumption was not widespread.

Deer

At one time white-tailed deer were found throughout the state, but now they live in only a few counties. They are seen primarily in the eastern lowlands and in the western mountains.

Quail

The Bob White quail and the partridge are regarded as one and the same in this state. Quail thrives here, but there has never been half enough to satisfy hunters.

Wild Turkeys

Wild turkeys are native to the state and can still be found in some sections.

Ruffed Grouse and Pheasant

Natives call ruffed grouse pheasant. They are great favorites with hunters and gourmets. There are sufficient pheasant in North Carolina to be covered by the game laws.

Mourning Doves

Doves generally are found throughout the state.

Mud Hens, Rail, or Coots

These little creatures live in coastal areas. Even those who claim they like the flavor of the meat admit they had to learn to like it. Most hunters feel that these birds belong in the class of ducks that should be cooked on a board. When the duck is done, throw the bird away and eat the board.

Raccoon

A raccoon turns up every now and then. Some folks prepare them by parboiling and then roasting, just like they would a possum.

Wild Boars

The wild boar population in western North Carolina is the result of fifteen pairs that were brought to Graham County in 1912 from the Harz Mountains in Germany. If a boar is reasonably young, the meat may be cooked like pork. It is especially tasty if barbecued over an outdoor pit. It may also be butchered, brine-cured, and then smoked like ham. Those who have tasted it prepared in this manner claim that the flavor is as good as that of the finest country ham.

• • • • •

VEGETABLES

Although countless acres of land in North Carolina are planted in tobacco, cotton, and grain, there is still room for an abundance of vegetables. The list includes string beans, tomatoes, squash, lettuce, cucumbers, broccoli, lima beans, beets, artichokes, carrots, collards, egg plant, rhubarb or pie plant, green peas, black-eyed peas, crowder peas, kale, mustard, okra, green peppers, radishes, rutabagas, spinach, turnips, and watercress. Those described below deserve special mention.

ARTICHOKES

The Jerusalem artichoke, which is a knotty tuber, grows abundantly, especially in the eastern part of the state. The artichokes are used primarily for making relish and pickles.

BEANS

Almost every garden has a few rows of green, string, or snap beans. In some cornfields the farmer will drop a few bean seeds in with the corn. The beans come up and run up the cornstalk. These are called pole beans.

The commercial production of green beans is significant in many areas of the state. It is especially important in northwestern North Carolina, where the beans are noted for their succulent flavor and quality.

KOHLRABI

Kohlrabi is grown near Jonas Ridge in the upper part of Burke County, where the high altitude makes good growing for anything in the cabbage family.

LETTUCE

Lettuce (both iceberg and leafy) is an important commercial crop in Pender and New Hanover counties. Widely grown throughout the state, it is most often the leafy or garden variety. (Increasing quantities of hydroponic lettuce are now being grown.)

The practice on many farms was to plant a few seeds in the corner of the tobacco plant bed. The cloth covering the bed caused the seed to germinate quickly, and, in this way, lettuce reached the table much earlier than when it was planted in the open. Before lettuce was readily available, nasturtium leaves were sometimes used in sandwiches in place of lettuce.

IRISH POTATOES

There is a strong possibility that Irish potatoes originated in this state. The story goes that Sir Walter Raleigh's colonists, when they arrived here in the sixteenth century, found that the potato was being cultivated by North Carolina Indians. According to another account, however, the potato first was discovered among the Incas of Peru. Regardless of which story is true, it would seem that Irish potatoes originated in this hemisphere and were taken to Ireland, where they became a staple food.

"Arsh pertaters" grow well throughout the state. They are planted from seed potatoes in early spring. It used to be the woman's job to cut the eyes out of the seed potatoes for planting. If she was thrifty, she cooked the remaining portion of the potatoes. The Albemarle potato, a favored variety, is smaller than the Idaho potato and does not match the Idaho as a baking treat. Rather, the Albemarle's thin skin and excellent flavor make it superior for French frying and mashing.

Digging potatoes is an interesting job. In digging, you cover a good area around the vine to be sure you get all the potatoes—some are "biguns" and others are like marbles. In a good potato patch, it does not take long to fill up a bushel basket.

RAMPS

In the region around Haywood County, there grows an onionlike root called ramp. The natives regard it so highly that each year they have a ramp convention, complete with a ramp queen. Ramp is regarded as a delicacy in some quarters. Some people say that the odor of onions and garlic is nothing compared to that of a ramp.

SQUASH

The squash grown in North Carolina is of three kinds—the yellow crookneck, the greenish-white cymling or patty-pan squash with scalloped edges, and the butternut. White squash were once called soquots. Anyone who has never gone to the garden and lifted the big green leaves of a squash plant to pull off golden crookneck squash and feel the shiny, slick surface of a truly fresh squash will never know how fresh they can be. Certainly, the semiflabby ones often found in the grocery store never have that feel.

Butternut squash generally grow well throughout the state. They have been called "smooth as butter and sweet as a nut," the basis of the name. The butternut squash combines the best qualities of a pumpkin and a sweet potato. Shaped like a gourd, this winter-type squash has a firmly ridged skin like a pumpkin and flesh that is a cross between a pumpkin and a sweet potato.

SWEET POTATOES

Superior sweet potatoes are produced in this state. Tabor City, which celebrates each year with a sweet potato festival, is the center of sweet potato production. Some people prefer the pale yellow, almost mealy sweet potato, but I believe the greatest preference is for the deep orange, moist variety. Many old homes have a "sweet potato cellar," where potatoes are stored for use throughout the winter.

•   •   •   •   •

FRUITS

For the fruit basket, there are apples, peaches, plums, blackberries, dewberries, watermelons, cantaloupes, pears, cherries, persimmons, grapes, strawberries, figs, quince, blueberries, and huckleberries. Those named below are of particular interest.

APPLES

The principal varieties of apples grown in North Carolina are red delicious, golden delicious, red stayman, blacktwig, red Rome beauty, red winesap, black ben, and limbertwig. There are also the so-called June apples. These are green and have a delightfully tart flavor; they make superb fried apples and applesauce.

Crab Apples

Quite a few crab apple trees are scattered around the state. The tart little apples are pickled, made into jelly, and sometimes used for applesauce.

Apple Cider

One of the joys of driving through the mountains of western North Carolina in the summer is being able to stop at numerous spots to enjoy a glass of chilled apple cider. Making cider was once a common practice in the fall, when apples became plentiful. Many farms owned their own hand-operated cider press to squeeze out the apple juice, which is, of course, all cider is.

The best cider is made from a blend of several varieties of apples—the not-so-pretty apples are used. The flavor is superb the first day the cider is made; it stays sweet in the average autumn temperature for about ten days. Many a child has come down with "the green apple quick step" from drinking too much cider. Commercially, it may be preserved by pasteurization or by the addition of benzoate of soda. The old folks used to wrap a rag loosely around a stick and then coat the rag in sulfur. The rag was set afire and stuck into the cider. That procedure helped stop the action of the yeast.

Though freshly made cider is a treat and no method of preservation preserves its full, satisfying flavor, the real reason for making cider is to have vinegar. To make vinegar from cider, you simply let nature take its course. The sugar in the cider ferments or "works."

Between the apple cider and vinegar stages, cider gets "hard." During the fermentation, the alcohol content goes up to as much as 6 percent, sometimes more. There are those who drink hard cider but for most tastes, it is unpleasant to swallow. Once the alcoholic content of the fermenting cider reaches its limit, the mixture turns very sour—then, it is vinegar. The acid in the vinegar kills the yeast or bacteria that caused the fermentation, and this inactive yeast mats together to form a mass that settles at the bottom of the vinegar. That mass is called mother. In these days of commercially prepared vinegar, you never see the mother, but it was always present in the homemade variety.

BERRIES

Blackberries

Blackberries did grow wild and abundantly. With sufficient rain during the spring and early summer, the berries were big and luscious and ready to pick at least by the Fourth of July. With dry weather, they were apt to be scrawny and dried up. Sometimes they even dried up on the vine.

Blackberry picking is not much of a sport but you have missed something if you have never had the experience. I remember picking the berries as a child; it was a hot job. Blackberries are never ripe before the sultry, oppressive weather. It seemed that wherever the vines were located, the air around them was always so heavy that it was hard to breathe. Often the biggest field of berries was in bottomland. The most objectionable part was that it was impossible to pick a bucket of berries without getting scratched. Some berry pickers covered their arms with old stockings to avoid scratches. Children were warned to be careful because scratches were hard to heal in dog days.

The berries were picked in a lard bucket or wash bucket, and unless there was a good patch of wild blackberries "on the place," finding berry vines meant roaming the countryside. But despite the hot sun, the heavy air, the scratches, and the chigger bites, seeing the bucket fill up with fresh berries was fun. The child who grows up knowing blackberries only as they appear in the grocery store in neat square boxes has indeed been deprived of learning firsthand what it was like for early settlers to have to make use of all sorts of natural foods.

Not all the blackberries picked in the state went into pie or jelly— not by any means. Many a bucket was dumped into barrels in alternate layers with sugar. The sugared barrels of berries were shipped off to someplace like Baltimore, where the berries were made into wine. Sometimes the berries were dried and sent to the winery in that form.

Huckleberries and Blueberries

Huckleberries, sometimes called whortleberries, grow wild, especially in the mountains. Huckleberries, which are dark purple in color, are smaller than blueberries and have a more distinctive flavor. Blueberries are grayish blue.

Blueberry production is one of the most successful farm enterprises in the state. The berries are without rival as to size, color, flavor, and perfection of packaging. The berry belt is in Pender, New Hanover, Duplin, and Sampson counties. At the height of the season, when a truckload of berries pulls out of Burgaw, the driver may not know his destination. He heads northward on some main route and after driving about two hundred miles, he calls the Burgaw office for instructions. He is then sent to the markets offering the best prices for the berries.

Raspberries

The soil in many areas of the state produces excellent cultivated raspberries, but the supply is unable to meet the demand. In recent years the crop has become important around Dobson in Surry County.

Cranberries

According to the late Aycock Brown of Manteo, who no doubt knew more about the coast of North Carolina than anybody, the quantity of cranberries that grows in the natural bogs in Dare County is sufficient to make wives hand their husband cranberry scoops and send them out to gather a mess of berries.

Dewberries

Dewberries grow wild, though the supply has been diminishing for years. They may also be cultivated. Compared to a blackberry, the portion of fruit to seed is larger with the dewberry. In color, a dewberry is redder. The flavor is more fruity and tart. Dewberry jam and jelly are highly prized.

Currants and Gooseberries

The vines for currants and gooseberries, which used to be rather plentiful, especially in the mountains, have lost their popularity—apparently because they harbored the parasites or fungus growth that caused chestnut trees to die.

Mostly, gooseberries went into pies, which were made just like blackberry pies. Cooks put the gooseberries with flour and sugar into an unbaked pie shell. Before baking, they dotted the top with butter and poured over it egg beaten with a little milk and flavored with vanilla.

Strawberries

Both cultivated and wild strawberries grow well in North Carolina. The wild ones grow mainly in the western sections. Chadbourn is the largest strawberry market in the world and the site of an annual strawberry festival.

CHERRIES

Cherries range from light-colored sour pie ones to the deep red, meaty sweet cherries. The luscious sweet ones grow in great abundance around West Jefferson in central Ashe County.

Cherry Cider

There are areas in the mountains where cherry cider is available in summer and fall. Its ruby red color is beautiful.

Ground Cherries

Ground cherries, now practically nonexistent, are not cherries that have been put through a grinder but little yellow cherries that grow wild on low bushes. They are the color of yellow tomatoes and about the size of plump blueberries, with seeds similar to blueberries rather than the usual cherry pit. The flavor resembles that of gooseberries rather than cherries. Ground cherries were made into pies and preserves.

CITRUS FRUIT

The production of citrus fruit is not likely to become a major industry in North Carolina, though folks along the Outer Banks are able to grow oranges, grapefruit, lemons, and tangerines in very limited quantities.

FIGS

Fig bushes are rather common in the state. The figs are primarily of the Brown Turkey or Celeste variety, though other varieties grow in the vicinity of Dare County. It is a joyful event for a fig lover to be in Dare County about August, when fig supplies are most plentiful. A few women in that area continue to produce fig preserves in their own kitchens for sale.

An antique compote of whole preserved figs did not appear on the table daily but rather was reserved for slightly special occasions. Lifting a plump preserved fig out by its stem is a happy experience.

GRAPES

Grapes are certainly native to the state. That fact was supported by Captains Arthur Barlowe and Philip Amadas of Sir Walter Raleigh's expedition to the coast in the 1590s. On their return to England, they reported: "The land . . . so full of grapes, as the very beating and surge of the Sea overflowed them. . . . I think in all the world the like abundance is not be found; and my selfe having seene those parts of Europe that most abound."

Vines that produce Concord grapes and related varieties are common. The most famous grapes are those of the Muscadine family, of which the Scuppernong is the most prominent member. The Muscadine family also includes the Thomas, Eden, Munsoniana, Luola, Flowers, James, and Mish varieties. It seems that the Mish grape was developed in Beaufort County and named for a pioneer family there.

The best known Scuppernong vineyard is the Mother Vineyard in Dare County. William C. Etheridge, of the University of Missouri, an authority on the Mother Vineyard, said that he never learned its origin. Of the vineyard, he wrote: "The vine is a romantic and revered object and you should approach it with the imagination and respect due its dignity as the oldest living thing on the Island [Roanoke] and one of the oldest living fruit plants on earth."

Muscadine jelly is choice. Scuppernong jelly has a fragrant aroma, a beautiful golden color, and a delicate flavor. The Thomas grape yields a sweet, mild, bright red jelly, whereas the Eden gives a tart jelly that is perfect for serving with meats and game.

Then there are Fox grapes and possum grapes, which may very likely be the same type of grape. They grow wild. Fox grapes are found on large-leafed vines that run up trees. They make very good jelly. You hear about possum grapes in the mountains. No doubt the name comes from the fact that these grapes, along with persimmons, are a favorite food of possums.

Vines around Tryon bear what have become known as Tryon grapes, which, over a period of years, have been held in high regard. Tryon grapes are usually Niagaras, which are white, or Delawares, which are red. In this area you will also find the very distinctive grape catsup.

MELONS

The area around Candor and Pinehurst is the center of the vast growing section that produces top-quality watermelons and cantaloupes. Most of the cantaloupes grown today are the conventional rounded ones, but a few years ago some growers raised the banana cantaloupe, which was a foot or more long with tapered ends like a sweet potato. Its melon fragrance was such that you could smell it halfway across the garden.

Whatever the variety of cantaloupes, they were once all called mushmelons. When mushmelons were in season, a platterful of curved peeled strips usually appeared on the table for breakfast and other meals.

MOLLY POPS

A molly pop is the size and shape of a lemon. It is smooth-skinned and grows prolifically in low vines similar to those of cucumbers. Molly pops are green when underripe but turn yellow and become quite fragrant when ripe. They have numerous small seeds, and many like to eat them.

PEACHES

Peaches grow well in the central part of the state, with a few scattered orchards in both east and west. Commercial production is centered in the Sandhills, the area around Pinehurst.

Vine Peaches

This fruit, which once grew on vines on the ground, is about the size of a peach but is shaped more like a lemon. It is slick-skinned and yellow in color when ripe. Vine peaches, which are sometimes called mangoes, are quite fragrant. They do not have the same flavor as peaches but may be made into preserves or pickled just like peaches.

PEARS

Many a backyard has one or more pear trees. The pears are most often keiffers or seckels. Keiffer trees are vigorous, very productive, and more resistant to blight and insect attack than most varieties. For that reason, keiffer pear trees are likely to have more pears than you can eat or can but the trees do not bear well every year.

Keiffer pears are large, with green to burnished brown skin when ripe. Even when ripe, they would still be hard enough to raise a big knot if one fell on your head. The pears never ripen on the tree to the soft texture desirable in fresh fruit. The flesh is coarse, and the stone cells are more in evidence than in many varieties. Even after cooking, the pears are still coarse in texture. They are, however, delicious made into preserves, sweet pickles, ginger pears, pear relish, and pear mincemeat. The custom was to gather the keiffers before the first frost and to wrap each one in paper. The wrapped pears were covered with straw in the cellar, where they mellowed and were often still good at Christmas.

There are fewer seckel pear trees in the state. Seckel pears are small— about twice the size of a crab apple—and coarse textured. Pickled whole, they make a good accompaniment to meats.

PERSIMMONS

Persimmons are a wild fruit and grow on trees. The variety found here is different from the Japanese persimmon, which is larger and lighter in color. The North Carolina, or native American persimmon, is known as the *Diospyros virginiana*; the Japanese one is called *Diospyros kaki*.

Ours are small, rarely exceeding 1¼ inches in diameter. The color is a dull orange, which darkens as the fruit ripens and develops a purplish overcast. There are a number of large, darkly colored seeds in proportion to the pulp, and each persimmon is topped with a cap. The pulp is separated from the seeds and is used for making pudding. The usual procedure was to force the pulp through a colander, which is rather a tedious process. A food mill does a better job. The pulp is bright orange in color, almost as bright as pumpkin.

Of the persimmon it has been observed: "If it be not ripe, it will draw a man's mouth awrie with much torment." One variety ripens before, but it takes a heavy frost to sweeten the full-flavored ones. There is an old saying that if the trees are heavy with persimmons in the fall, a cold winter is ahead.

DAMSON PLUMS

These plums are different from other varieties in that they are smaller, quite tart, and have to be cooked to be tasty. They are about the size of large olives and are blue with a grayish look. Damson plum preserves are a great favorite, as is damson plum pie.

POMEGRANATES

Old gardens almost always had a pomegranate vine. Pomegranates were popular not so much for their fruit as for their fragrant odor. Thoroughly dried, the seeds inside rattled when shook and provided a way to amuse the baby in the days before celluloid (or plastic) rattles.

•   •   •   •   •

CULINARY HERBS

According to a horticulturist of the North Carolina Agricultural Extension Service, the state's soils and climate are suitable for the production of most herbs. Those that he suggests are angelica, anise, balm, basil, burnett, caraway, catnip, chervil, chives, cicely, coriander, cumin, dill, fennel, horehound, horseradish, hyssop, lovage, marigold, mint, parsley, perilla, rosemary, rue, sage, sesame, sorrel, summer savory, sweet marjoram, tarragon, thyme, and woodruff.

Angelica is not too well known in North Carolina but it will grow here. The seed is used in candy and cookies. The leaf stalks are used like celery.

Anise is easily grown from seeds. The seeds are used in cookies, candies, and sauces. The plant matures in about eight to ten weeks after sowing in early April. The seeds should be harvested before they are completely ripe, as they shed quickly when ripe.

Balm is frequently called lemon balm. It thrives here. A sprig is excellent in iced tea. It is easily grown from seeds or cuttings. Seeding is best in late March, and cuttings from old plants are taken after growth starts in the spring. An Arab proverb says that tea from this plant makes the heart merry and joyful.

Basil plants flourish here but do not sow until the danger of frost is past. Use in catsups and other tomato mixtures.

Burnett is easily grown from seeds sown in the early spring. The leaves have a taste resembling cucumbers and are used in flavoring salads or soups.

Caraway seeds should be planted in late March where the plants are to stand.

Catnip is propagated from seeds or by division.

Chervil is easily grown from seeds planted where the plants are to stand.

Chives rarely produce seeds and are propagated almost entirely by the division of old clumps.

Cicely is an old plant that is seldom used today. It grows easily from seeds.

Coriander is an annual propagated from seeds sown in the late fall or early spring.

Cumin is grown from seeds planted in the early spring.

Dill should be sown where the plants are to grow. Thin out early.

Fennel seed is sown in early April.

Horehound is a perennial herb that is easy to grow from seeds or cuttings or by division. Candy was once made at home from horehound before the job was taken over by the stick candy makers. Sticks of horehound candy sooth a simple cough or a sore throat.

Horehound Candy

Boil 2 ounces dried horehound in 1½ pints water for about ½ hour. Strain and add 3½ pounds brown sugar. Boil over a hot fire until the mixture is sufficiently hard. Pour out in flat, well-greased metal trays. As soon as the candy is cool enough to retain its shape, mark into sticks or small squares with a knife.

Horseradish is a root that is peeled and shredded or ground to make a pungent condiment. Before jars of prepared horseradish were available in grocery stores, it was grown and prepared at home.

Hyssop is a hardy perennial grown from seeds or by division. The leaves are used in soups and stews.

Lovage is seeded like caraway. The leaf stems are good when used like celery.

Marigold petals are used either fresh or dried in broths, soups, and stews.

Mint grows heartily in beds that last for years. When the plants eventually die, a neighbor is often able to provide a new start. Mint leaves in various flavors are favored in tea and other beverages.

Parsley is frequently grown in the home garden as well as in pots indoors.

Perilla has an odor resembling that of cinnamon.

Rosemary grows hardy from seeds if they are planted indoors.

Rue, next to wormwood, is the most bitter tasting of all herbs. The tiny, young, minced leaves give a delightful flavor to canapés, chicken salad, or broth.

Sage plants are highly prized for their leaves, which are dried and used to add a unique flavor to stuffing for poultry and also in making sausage.

Sesame is a tall gangly plant grown from seeds.

Sorrel is easily grown from seeds planted in March. The leaves have a sour taste but are good in salads.

Summer savory is an annual that is easily produced from seeds. The leaves, young shoots, and flowers are used in salads, meat and poultry dressings, croquettes, and stews, as well as cooked with beans and peas.

Sweet marjoram is an annual grown from seeds planted in early April.

Tarragon is a hardy perennial propagated by root division. Both tarragon and horseradish can be obtained from large seed companies. Cook the young tops with greens.

Thyme has hardy perennial shrubs that are propagated from seeds or cuttings or by division.

Woodruff is a perennial grown from seeds or by division. The Germans use it for flavoring wines.

• • • • •

NUTS

The nuts grown in North Carolina include pecans, black walnuts, hickory nuts, chinquapins, hazel nuts, butternuts, chufus or grass nuts, chestnuts, and peanuts.

A great abundance of pecans is grown in the east. Black walnut trees are scattered over the state, though a great many more walnut trees now stand in dining rooms as tables than in forests. Hickory nuts are enclosed in a hard wooden coating and the "goodies" are difficult to pick out, but once you get enough to put into a cake or cookies, you will be glad you made the effort.

At one time there were many American chestnuts in the western part of the state, but a blight killed every tree. In the days when chestnuts were plentiful, they were used in stuffing for poultry, cream of chestnut soup, and croquettes. They were also creamed.

PEANUTS

Peanuts, or "goobers," are widely grown in the eastern part of the state.

Roasted Green Peanuts

Cover the bottom of a shallow baking pan with peanuts. Place in a 300° oven for 35 to 40 minutes, stirring often. Remove from oven before the peanuts are lightly browned.

Peanut Brittle

This recipe makes good use of goobers.

½ cup light molasses or corn syrup
2 cups granulated sugar
½ cup brown sugar

½ cup water
¼ cup butter
⅛ teaspoon salt
⅛ teaspoon soda
1½ cups peanut meats

Combine molasses, sugars, water, and butter. The top of a double boiler makes a good container. Cook, stirring occasionally, to 270° on a candy thermometer. Continue cooking, stirring more frequently, to 300° (or when a small quantity dropped into cold water forms a very brittle ball). Cook over moderate heat to prevent burning.

Remove mixture from heat and quickly stir in salt, soda, and peanuts (the salted variety is satisfactory but if used, omit salt in recipe). Pour onto a buttered baking sheet. Stretch out thin. Cool and break into pieces. Makes about 1 pound.

• • • • •

GRAINS

BUCKWHEAT

A field of green buckwheat with its white flowers is as pretty as a bed of real flowers. Such fields were scattered in the upper Piedmont region but now are almost gone.

At one time, the real buckwheat flour for stacks of cakes was widely available. These cakes are even mentioned in the second verse of the song, "Dixie":

> Dars buckwheat cakes an' Ingen batter,
> Makes you fat, or a little fatter.

The old custom was to start a yeasty buckwheat batter the night before so there would be buckwheat cakes the next morning. It must have been a man reared in that era who once wrote me: "Why don't you stop writing about all these new fangled foods and do a real service to housewives and tell them how to make a sponge [raised dough] for buckwheat cakes with real buckwheat flour."

WATER-GROUND CORNMEAL

In the old days dried corn was taken to a water-powered gristmill, where the grains of corn were dumped into a chute that fed them in between two large rotating millstones. Anyone who has never seen one of these large millstones cannot fully appreciate the remark, "She's just a millstone around his neck." The meal produced in this manner makes a corn bread of distinctive texture. Some farmers did not take their corn to the mill for grinding but instead ran the grains through a hand-turned grain-crushing mill right "on the place."

The old gristmill, which used to be a gathering place, is a part of the passing parade. One such mill has been preserved in a poem by the late James Larkin Pearson, poet laureate of North Carolina. The poem is about Andy Gould's mill, located in Wilkes County near Moravian Falls before it was inundated by the waters of the Yadkin River many years ago. This is part of the poem:

> My Maw she said the meal was out—
>> Thar weren't another dust.
> She couldn't bake no supper bread
>> With brown an' crunchy crust
> My Paw he shelled a turn o'corn
>> An' poured it in a sack,
> An' off to Andy Gould's Mill
>> He lugged it on his back.
> I toted jist a little turn
>> Bekaze I was so small,
> An' brother John weren't big enough,
>> To tote no turn at all.
> But he jist went along with us
>> As little fellows will,
> To cross the river in the boat
>> At Andy Gould's Mill.*

The story goes that the passing of the gristmill made a ghost town of Parkwood, which was near Hallison, some eight miles from Carthage in Moore County. In 1896 Parkwood was a thriving town of 3,500 people, and its main enterprise was the manufacture of mill rock for gristmills. As the demand for mill rock decreased, the town gradually died.

*Reprinted by permission of James Larkin Pearson.

RICE

Brunswick once was North Carolina's leading rice-growing county and in 1860 produced 7 million pounds, with peak production in 1899. From March until the harvest in September, the fields had to be alternately flooded and grassed. Competition from the southwest, where ditching was unnecessary, doomed the rice crop in this section. The crop declined swiftly, and by 1909 only 248 acres were planted in rice; by 1932 not an acre was raised. Rice fields or paddies still stand at Orton Plantation near Wilmington but have not produced rice for years.

WILD RICE

Wild rice, which is not really a rice at all but rather the seed of a marsh grass, grows along the North Carolina coast. It is sometimes called wild oats. Some can be found at Orton Plantation. Mrs. Kenneth Sprunt, Jr., of the plantation said that if you had any idea how hard it is to gather, then you certainly would not be surprised at the cost in the stores.

•   •   •   •   •

SWEETENERS

SORGHUM

From early fall to late spring a cruet of sorghum, or molasses, was standard equipment on tables. The old-fashioned cruet is made of glass with a pewter top. Sorghum is lighter in color than commercial molasses and has a more delicate flavor, which is a little malty.

Sorghum is still made but the supply is limited. In late October or early November it appears in neighborhood grocery stores and at farmers' markets packed in fruit jars or jugs. Most of the sorghum will turn to sugar or ferment in the warm spring weather. But in a household that loves to "sop," the supply is gone long before warm weather arrives, and the family begins looking forward to a new batch in the fall.

Sopping sorghum is rather an art—one based on the individual. Some folks begin by slicing off a big hunk of soft butter. Sorghum is poured over the butter and the two are stirred together. Big flecks of yellow butter mingle with the golden syrup. A hot biscuit is pushed around and around in this mixture until it is coated. Those who are dainty push the biscuit with a fork but most often, the biscuit is pushed with the fingers.

There are those who stir some of the drippings from fried salt pork or red ham gravy into the sorghum for sopping.

The type of sugarcane used to make sorghum is slightly different from the kind grown to produce sugar. Sorghum cane has not proved to be a satisfactory source of sugar. The small brown seeds are planted with the corn planter using a handmade screen whose openings are smaller than those used for planting corn. Sorghum seeds grow on top of the plant in a tassel instead of on the side of the stalk in a shuck like corn.

Once the sorghum is planted, it grows like corn (though not as tall) and requires similar care. Excess rain near the end of the growing season will dissolve a portion of the juice in the stalk, which reduces the yield of syrup. The usual yield is about five gallons of sorghum from fifteen gallons of juice. After the cane has matured, the stalks are cut down with corn knives. The cutting is done before the first killing frost.

These days sorghum makers are scarce. The manufacture of granulated sugar in huge vats in large factories provides little to attract the attention of the casual observer. But this is not so in the traditional way of making sorghum—the process is fascinating to watch.

Sorghum makers usually rig up their own contraption to squeeze the juice from the cane. Sometimes the rig is nothing more than a pair of hand-operated rollers similar to those on a washing machine. Most often, the rollers or the press are nailed to a post and obtain power from a mule walking around and around in a circle while it pulls a long pole fastened to the rollers. As the mule walks, the rollers rotate. A man feeds the stalks of sorghum between the rollers, and the juice runs down a little spout into a bucket or tub. The juice is greenish brown and is about as appetizing looking as the water of a stagnant pond.

The second—and last—piece of equipment used is a large tin tray about eight feet long and three feet wide. The tray is built over an outdoor oven and has tin mazelike partitions. The freshly squeezed juice is poured into one end of the tray to cook. The sorghum is drained off the opposite end, which is lower, as the cooking is completed. The cooked syrup is pale brown in color with highlights of gold.

It takes about one and one-half hours to heat the first tray of syrup in order to turn it into sorghum. After the first batch, a small portion can be drawn off about every thirty minutes. One or two persons work continually with a perforated tin skimmer on a long stick to remove the scum from the top of the cooking syrup.

The sorghum is stored in a barrel or bottled in jars. The comparison, "as cold as molasses in January," comes from the experience of those who have tried on a cold morning to draw a cruet full of the liquid stored in a big barrel in the smokehouse.

Along with drummers (the traveling salesmen of the early part of this century), there were men who went from farm to farm to make sorghum. With a mule and a homemade press, the traveler squeezed out the juice and set up a frame for cooking the syrup. When money was short, his pay was often a portion of the sorghum, which he would exchange at a country store for other merchandise.

Had it not been for sorghum, or "long sweetnin'," there would have been no table sweetener except honey during the Civil War. For years after the war, coffee and many other substances were sweetened with sorghum. What little sugar there was was saved for special occasions. The child who took sugar in place of sorghum in the presence of guests could expect a parental reprimand in the privacy of the family.

SUGAR "TITS" AND SUGAR BREAD

When white sugar became more plentiful, many a fretful baby was soothed with a sugar "tit." A sugar tit was made by tying sugar tightly in a small square of clean white cloth. The baby sucked it the way a modern baby sucks a rubber pacifier. Sugar bread was a favorite of older children. It was prepared by spreading slices of light bread with butter and then coating them liberally with sugar.

HONEY

To a North Carolina honey lover, one honey outranks all others. It is sourwood honey, a speciality of North Carolina bees. The honey has a delicate, delightful flavor and, when pure, it is pale golden in color. Connoisseurs put two honeys at the top of the list: sourwood and orange blossom. So even if sourwood does have to share a little glory with orange blossom honey, the competition is strictly top bracket.

Another pale-colored honey produced here—locust honey—is also a top-quality product. For my taste, locust honey is as distinctive as sourwood. It is a great deal more scarce, too.

Quite a bit of honey is called sourwood when it really is not. Anyone who knows the taste of the real thing can tell the difference right away. The production of sourwood honey somewhat resembles the production of wine—some years are good, some are not. Experts calculate that there is only about one very good sourwood year out of seven. What makes a good sourwood year is a mystery. Every year sourwood trees are loaded with thousands of pretty white blossoms. When the blossoms are there but the nectar is not, it will be a slim year for sourwood honey.

Because sourwood is found primarily in the mountains, there are bee-keepers who have what they call migratory apiaries. Bees from the east are taken west when the sourwood is in bloom. Some bees go in the opposite direction. In the spring, western bees might be taken east when the maple trees and blueberries begin to bloom. When those blooms disappear, the bees continue their trip to catch the flowering blackgum, privet bush, briarberry, gallberry, apple, willow, basswood, vetch, black-berry, tulip poplar, buckwheat, clover, and, finally, goldenrod. Poplar and clover are perhaps the most common kinds of honey.

The bulk of the honey on the market is a mixture of several flavors. This type of honey is considerably darker in color than sourwood. The darker the color, the more marked the flavor.

Regardless of the origin of the nectar, a frame of honey freshly taken from the hive is a thing of beauty. The first filled frame that comes into the house in the new honey season is an event. The honeycomb is so full that it seems as if honey is just about ready to pop out of the little waxy pockets. The symmetry of these little pockets in the honeycomb has always amazed me. Cutting the honey out of the frame to fill the covered jar for the table makes a honey lover want a hot biscuit and a slab of butter right that minute. In the pre–chewing gum era, children chewed away on a wad of honeycomb.

Today, combless honey reaches the market. Without its comb, honey seems naked and possessed of little more character than a jar of table syrup. Pouring syruplike honey over a biscuit is nothing like the joy of covering the biscuit with honey still enclosed within the neat combs. There is just something about seeing honey dribble down over a hot biscuit from a cut cross section of comb.

"SUGARIN' OFF TIME"

There are not many still living who remember "sugarin' off time," but the late Zona Hughes, of Plumtree, did for an interview in the 1960s. Mrs. Hughes retired in 1953 after teaching for fifty-seven years.

At one time the mountains in the Spruce Pine area of western North

Carolina were covered with hardwood trees, which were virgin timber. Among these hardwoods were the sugar maples. About every mountain farm had a grove of sugar maple trees, called sugar orchards because the sap of the trees was sweet and mountaineers made syrup and sugar from the sap.

In the early spring, usually in March after a hard freeze followed by a warm spell, the sap would begin to rise. Men would bore holes in the trees two or three feet from the ground with an auger. Into these holes they would drive round spigots, or spouts, which were usually made from elder bushes cut eight or ten inches long. The elder bushes had large piths that could easily be pushed out with a sharp stick. Sometimes, the men would split the stick and lift out the pith with a knife. Some folks called these spouts spiles.

The water, or sap, of the tree would run out through the spouts and drip into a container placed on the ground at the root of the tree. People used different kinds of vessels to catch the sap. Some used troughs, two or three feet long, that were dug or scooped out of split logs of a soft-wood like poplar. Even the children helped empty the troughs so they would not run over.

The sweet water was carried to large kettles or pots. Some folks cooked the sap in a cane molasses boiler. Usually the furnace for boil-ing was in a shed built in the center of the orchard. It took gallons and gallons of sap and hours and hours of boiling to make the syrup, or tree molasses as the syrup was called, and even more gallons and hours to make it into sugar. This was "sugarin' off." When the boiled liquid was thick enough for syrup, it was poured into pitchers, crocks, and jars. The syrup kept indefinitely. To make it into sugar, the syrup was boiled until it granulated. Then it was poured into smaller vessels such as teacups and little dishes.

Sugar Eggs

For a childhood treat, a sugar egg was made by piercing a little hole in each end of an egg. The egg was blown out with a straw. The hole at one end was stopped up with beeswax, and the shell was filled with hot maple sugar syrup. When cold, the shell was peeled off, leaving a sugar egg.

DAIRY PRODUCTS

North Carolina is not a dairying state, but at one time all but the poorest rural families had at least one old "milch" cow. In the days before metal pails, it was the practice to milk in a piggin, an old pail with a raised stave for a handle. A *coffee cow* was a rather sorry cow—one that gave enough milk for the coffee but not enough for the family to drink.

CHURNING

For many years the only way many families had butter was by home churning. Clabber or cottage cheese, buttermilk, and whey were the by-products of churning. In fact, churning about every other day was as much a part of household activities as baking and dusting.

The first step was to collect the milk from one or more milkings, depending on the number of cows. Then the milk was stored in a crock in a cool place until the cream came to the top. The cook skimmed off the cream and placed it in another crock, repeating this step until all the cream had been removed.

Some churned from unsoured cream but most preferred soured cream. In summer the cream would sour before you could get the dinner dishes washed, but in winter in houses unblessed with central heating, as was most often the case, it took a long time for the cream to sour. A common way to make it sour was to place the covered crock on the hearth in front of the dying fire before going to bed. Other times it might be pushed to the back of the wood stove. That was risky, for the cream could get too hot, making the butter white and waxlike. One old churner told me: "Land sakes, getting the cream too hot makes the butter as white as clabber cheese."

The soured cream (which is far more sour in taste than the dairy sour cream of today) was poured into the churn. The dasher churn was shaped like a rounded drum, a little bigger at the bottom than at the top. The top had a hole in it—the plunger with a circle of wood on the bottom stuck out through the hole.

The churner grasped the plunger and pulled it up and down. It took a good forty-five minutes for the agitated cream to turn to golden fluffy mounds of butter. At this point, the semisoft substance was scooped out with the hands and washed several times. Then the salt was worked in and the butter was packed gently into the mold, producing a round half-pound cake. (Most of the molds were round, but some were square.) The fresh butter went to the springhouse to chill.

Many a housewife in the city had a regular "engagement" for country butter, which was delivered to her each week. In some communities it was easy to identify the butter maker by the print that the molds made on top of each cake.

BUTTERMILK

After the butter was removed from the churn, there remained the buttermilk dotted with tiny flecks of butter—the bits that did not cling to the fluffy mounds scooped out. That kind of buttermilk, chilled as cold as springwater, was always widely consumed. A glass with a noontime meal of turnip greens and hot corn bread dripping in butter was fare as fine as many a Tar Heel could dream of having.

Today's grocery stores stock buttermilk regularly, but sweet milk converted with lactic acid is a far cry from the old variety.

CLABBER

Clabber, or curdled milk, was common in the days before commercial ice and automatic refrigeration. Because clabber was readily available, cooks made good use of it. Present-day commercial cottage cheese is a wonderful product, but the tang and tender texture of grandmother's clabber cheese is a very happy memory.

To make it, the milk left after skimming off the cream was allowed to stand in a large container at room temperature until it soured. Then the soured milk was placed on the back of the stove to heat gently. When the milk became just a tad hotter than lukewarm, the whey divided from the curd and became clabber. The whole works was then poured into a cheesecloth bag or sugar bag (sugar came in cloth bags) and hung over the dishpan to drain. The bag held the cheese and the whey was fed to the hogs.

Clabber Cakes

1 cup sifted flour
1 teaspoon soda

½ teaspoon salt
1 cup clabber [soured milk or clabber cheese]

Sift together flour, soda, and salt. Add clabber and blend—the batter will be lumpy. Cook like pancakes on a hot griddle.

Bonney Clabber or Loppered Milk

Clabber was also served for dessert. Those whose modern tastes run to sour cream should appreciate this old recipe.

Cover a bowl of milk and keep it in a warm place until it turns into a smooth, firm, tender clabber. Chill. Spoon out of the bowl carefully into individual dessert dishes and serve with cream, sugar, and nutmeg or cinnamon.

CHEESE

Time was when just about every homemaker in the region of Sugar Grove and Crumpler made their own cheese. The reason was that there was insufficient outlet for their milk supply. A few continue to make their own cheese.

The cheese makers put the surplus milk on the back of the stove in a large container with a rennet tablet and let it heat gently to form curds. The drained curds went into homemade cheese presses to form a firm block. The block of cheese was then aged in the cellar or sometimes in mountain caves.

Now, with better methods of mountain transportation, the milk goes to market. A good portion of it is delivered to the Kraft Cheese Factory in West Jefferson.

Homemade Yellow Cheese

This is the way Mrs. M. E. Reeves of Laurel Springs made cheese.

Heat 1 gallon clabber milk, stirring occasionally until it is just comfortable to the finger. Strain through cloth, being sure to remove as much whey as possible.

Heat curd over boiling water with 1 egg, dash of salt, and ¼ teaspoon soda, stirring occasionally, until smooth. For softer cheese, add a little cream. For harder cheese, add egg yolk alone.

Be sure the cheese is thoroughly melted and blended before pouring into a mold. The cheese will not blend smoothly if there is too much whey left in the curd.

Cottage or Clabber Cheese

This recipe was contributed by Mrs. Roy Holder of Kernersville. She said: "This is an easy way to make cottage cheese. It is never tough and we like it very much."

1 gallon clabbered milk
1 gallon boiling water

Pour boiling water over the clabber, cover, and let stand for 10 minutes. Drain well, season with salt, and moisten with cream.

Keeping Food before Ice

It was a happy time when a commercially built icebox stocked with commercially frozen ice became standard equipment in the average home. Iceboxes could be found in most homes shortly after the turn of the century. Before that time there was no easy way of keeping food safely cold in hot weather. What prevented epidemics of food poisoning is a mystery.

In the middle of summer, the remains of the big meal prepared for dinner in the middle of the day were served for supper because the food would not keep overnight. One way of keeping food was to heat it boiling hot morning and night.

There were, of course, spring and well houses. A springhouse was a small house built over a spring that was piped so the cold water would fill a trough. Crocks of milk, butter, and other foods placed in the chilly springwater stayed cool. A well house was a similar structure built near the well. Cold well water was pulled up and put in troughs. Now and then a woman would fill a well bucket with freshly made butter and lower it into the well to cool.

Before commercial ice, most communities had icehouses that were filled with blocks cut from the ponds in winter. The icehouses were often like basements dug deep into the ground. Sawdust was sprinkled between the blocks of ice to keep them from freezing together. Icehouses were the source of ice for making ice cream and for cooling other foods.

Salting, curing, drying, pickling, brining, and canning were the methods used to preserve supplies of food for future use. (Ways of preserving food are also described in Chapters 5 and 9.)

· · · · ·

MEAT

SALTED PORK

Whereas hams traditionally were cured, other cuts of fresh pork were salted. After the meat like a pork loin "took" the salt, it was hung in the smokehouse. The salted meat was soaked and then cooked just like fresh pork.

Sausage in Lard

After the slaughtering was done, it was the practice to "fry down" sausage cakes or patties and keep them in lard in stone crocks or fruit jars through the winter. Pork tenderloin was cooked and preserved in the same way.

CURED OR DRIED BEEF

In the days before refrigeration and freezing, curing fresh beef was a way to preserve it. The late J. Coke Marion, a meat expert of Sparta, prepared the beef in the following manner.

In the winter, he took a quarter of good grade beef and salted it down just as he would a country ham. After the salt treatment, he hung up the beef for six months or so to cure. The meat was prepared so it would be ready to serve around April, for when the hot summer weather came, its flavor would be too strong.

Cut cured beef into slices and grill as you would a steak. It is not dry and compact like commercially dried beef but is juicy and has a flavor that is out of this world.

Jerky

Meat from deer and other animals was "jerked" from the bones to eliminate the sinews. After salting for twenty-four hours, it was hung to dry in the sun or over the fire.

• • • • •

FRUITS AND VEGETABLES

DRIED APPLES

In most homes, sun-dried apples were a standby in the winter diet. The late Ethelyn Richardson, of Laurel Springs, who dried about four hundred pounds of apples each fall, supplied the following information.

A bushel of apples will dry down to four pounds. Any way you calculate it, that is a mess of apples to peel, core, and dry. Mrs. Richardson dried hers in specially constructed three-foot-square wire trays that were stacked six inches apart in a frame built over an oil space heater in her dining room. The thinly sliced apples were completely dry in twenty-four hours, which prevented them from turning dark. For out-of-hand eating without cooking, she selected a mellow "fallow water" apple. These dry a bit darker than other varieties due to a larger sugar content.

Storing Dried Apples

To store dried apples, spread the fruit on trays or cookie sheets. Heat in a slow oven (about 200°) until hot through. Cool, put in fruit jars, and screw the lids on tightly.

Oven-Dried Apples

Use well-ripened sour or tart apples. Peel and cut into quarters; core. Slice quarters lengthwise as thin as possible. Place sliced apples on a baking sheet not over ½-inch deep and turn oven on to warm. Place apples in oven. Turn the apples over about every 2 hours until they begin to dry.

To dry 2 or more pans at a time, place a cup in the middle of the first pan and use it as a support for the second pan. This way 4 sheets can be dried at the same time. Depending on the oven, it takes about 12 hours.

When apples rattle when stirred, put all the apples into 1 pan; heat oven to 300° and bake for about 30 minutes. Store in an airtight container. The dried apples will keep for 2 years. If your oven tends to collect moisture, crack the door for a few minutes when the apples first start to dry.

Fumigated Apples

Some folks fumigated apples with sulfur fumes to preserve them for winter use. Fumigated apples are fresh looking and bright in color; they have an almost fresh flavor.

To prepare in a metal or wooden washtub, peel and core apples, cut into eighths, and drop into tub. Make a well in the center and place a pan in it. Lay a cloth folded to make several thicknesses in the pan and on it pour half a box of sulfur. Ignite the cloth and immediately cover the tub tightly with oilcloth and an old quilt—"Else the fumes will smother you." Leave covered for half a day or more. Store the apples in glass or stone jars.

Another way to prepare them is to place peeled and quartered apples in a basket. Slip the handle over a broom or stick to support it in a hanging position inside a barrel. Place the sulfur in a container in the bottom of the barrel. Ignite sulfur. Cover apples tightly so the fumes will penetrate the fruit.

A third method is to sprinkle sulfur over hot coals in a pan in the bottom of a box with a tight cover. Tie the apples in cloth bags and hang them over the sulfur.

Bleached Apples

It is said that bleached apples will keep all winter in jars or earthen pots like the old-fashioned churn. The flavor, according to some, is the nearest thing to the taste of a raw apple itself.

Peel and slice apples and put them on a screen in a tight room. Put about a teaspoon of sulfur on a hot iron to burn it. Get away from the iron, as you will not be able to stand the smell of the fumes.

DRIED PEACHES

Peaches were dried in the sun like apples.

CORN

Hominy

Soak corn overnight. Add 3 heaping teaspoons lye to 5 quarts shelled corn. Cover with water and cook until the hulls come off. Wash in cold water and rub between the palms of your hands until the rest of the hulls come off. Put in cold water and bring to a boil. Drain and place in a pressure cooker. Cover with water about 3 inches above the corn. Cook for 30 minutes on 15 pounds of pressure. Remove and let pressure come down.

Pack corn in quart jars. Add 1 teaspoon salt to each jar and cover with the water the corn was cooked in. Process for 3 to 5 minutes using 15 pounds of pressure.

When ready to serve, add 2 to 3 tablespoons ground cracklings and simmer on the stove for a few minutes.

Another Version of Hominy

Start with strong wood ashes. Put the ashes in a wooden container and pour water on them. The water will become lye when it goes through the ashes. Pour the corn in the lye and cook until the husks come loose. Take the corn out of the lye and rinse it in water several times. The hominy is now ready to use.

Note: If your lye is not strong enough, you can add soda to remove the husks.

Sour Corn

Corn cut from the cob was prepared in a barrel just like sauerkraut. In the winter, it was cooked and seasoned with meat drippings. Its flavor had a twang to it.

Whole ears of corn were also stuck into crocks of pickled green beans.

Dried Corn

The corn was blanched on the cob in a big container—like the black wash pot—full of hot water. Then it was cut from the cob in two cuttings, placed on a drying cloth, and put in the sun to dry. The drying cloths were kept just for the purpose of drying. Dried corn was cooked with salt pork just like dried beans.

DRIED SWEET POTATOES

Sweet potatoes were dried in two ways. One way was to boil the potatoes in their jackets until tender. They were peeled and sliced as for candied yams and then placed on a cloth over a rack in the hot sun. The sun dried the potatoes and shriveled them. Although they could be cooked, they were most often eaten dried. Many children regarded this sweet as their candy.

The other way of drying sweet potatoes was to cook and mash them. They were then dropped in little mounds on a cloth and dried in the hot sun.

DRIED BEANS AND PEAS

Shellie beans and black-eyed peas were common dried foods.

FIVE

Indian Cookery

A s in all of America, the Indians were in North Carolina before any-body. Though their methods of cooking were distinctive, few have been carried over into modern times. Nevertheless, as a result of the outdoor dramas, *The Lost Colony* in Manteo and *Unto These Hills* in Cherokee, there has been renewed interest in Indian lore. The Cherokee Historical Association, Inc., has re-created a Cherokee Indian village that is open to the public. Oconaluftee Village, in Cherokee, gives visitors a good impression of how Indians lived. A visit to the museum near the Lost Colony theater in Manteo is informative, too. There you will find a few old Indian cooking utensils.

The Indians' diet consisted largely of fish, wild game, and corn, to-gether with other edible plants that grew naturally or that they were able to cultivate. The early squaws used only clay pottery and clay ovens in their cooking. A little later these women acquired iron pots, which rested directly on the logs of the fire or were propped up by rocks. Or the pot might be suspended over the fire cauldron-fashion from a tripod made of sticks.

Of course, a good portion of the meat, game, and seafood was barbe-cued over the open fire. A whole animal might be held in place over the coals by a crude wooden rack. Small birds and fish were speared with sticks that were pointed on one end, with the other end stuck into the ground near the fire.

• • • • •
LYE HOMINY

Hardwood ashes were collected in a container with holes in the bottom. Water poured through the ashes became lye and was used to take off the skins of the corn. Once the skins were loosened, the corn was rinsed in a nearby stream. In place of today's metal or plastic colander, Indians used a handwoven basket as the sieve.

• • • • •
CORN BREAD

Corn bread was of the corn pone variety, made primarily with cornmeal and water. It was baked on hot coals or in pottery and later in an iron skillet over the open fire. Sometimes corn dodgers were wrapped in green corn leaves or dried fodder, tied with strong grass, and dropped into boiling water to cook like dumplings. The corn bread was made without salt, for the old Indian cooks claimed that salt made it crumble.

• • • • •
BEAN BREAD AND CHESTNUT BREAD

These two breads were quite distinctive. For the bean bread, cooked dried beans and some of the liquid they were cooked in were added to the cornmeal and shaped with the hands into dodgers or pones. These were wrapped in corn leaves, tied, and dropped in boiling water to cook.

Chestnut bread was made the same way but with the addition of chopped cooked chestnuts and the water in which they were cooked.

• • • • •
SWAMP POTATO MEAL

When there was not enough cornmeal, the Indians roasted swamp potatoes in ashes until they were done, then mashed them into a meal that was dried. Swamp potatoes likely are one of the tubers that grow wild in the state, probably the *Apios tuberosa* or a related species.

• • • • •
"GRITTED" BREAD

To the average tastes, most of the old Indian dishes seem a little strange. One of the exceptions is "gritted" bread, which is most tasty and quite acceptable in flavor.

Mary Cornwell, former home demonstration agent of Haywood County, recalled the days when she boarded in a home where the lady of the house made gritted bread all during the fresh corn season. The home-maker used fresh corn that was a little too old to serve fried, stewed, or boiled. The corn was not hard, but by being a little past the juicy stage, it contained more starch, which is desirable in making the bread. The woman grated the corn on an old washboard in which she had punched holes with a large nail. The rough edges tore the corn into tiny shreds.

Some make the grated corn into bread with the addition of salt, soda, buttermilk, a little flour, and eggs in a manner similar to that used in making spoon bread. The following recipe, however, is closer to the Indian method. It really is delicious.

Indian Gritted Bread

Grate 4 ears of corn, a little past their prime juicy state, on a coarse grater. Add ½ teaspoon salt and ¼ teaspoon soda and pour into a small and shallow greased baking dish.

Bake in a 375° oven for 1 hour, or until firm and browned. Cut into squares and serve hot with butter.

• • • • •
DRIED MEAT

That portion of fresh meat, game, or fish that was not used right away was cut into thin strips, stuck on sticks, and dried or cured before the fire for future meals. The smoky flavor that the meat absorbed must have made it quite tasty.

• • • • •
PEMMICAN

Pemmican was a pastelike mixture resembling loosely packed plug tobacco. It was made by pounding dried venison or bison with a hammer, then blending it with rendered kidney fat, pounded whole wheat and oats, and dried fruits such as prunes, raisins, or apricots.

The pemmican was formed into a loaf, wrapped in cloth, and dipped in melted wax. It was used when tribes traveled, and through the winter it supplied food when rations were skimpy.

• • • • •
FRIED GRASSHOPPERS

Some Indians fried grasshoppers in their own oil. Apparently grasshoppers, thus treated, have a nutty, appealing flavor.

• • • • •
ROASTED MUSHROOMS

Indians knew which toadstools were edible and which were poisonous. The edible ones were placed on hot coals, sprinkled with salt, and roasted. When the Indians had grease, they sometimes fried the mushrooms.

• • • • •
INDIAN LIMAS

Indian limas are large, flat beans covered with purple netting like an uncooked pinto bean. They are now available dried and canned in supermarkets.

• • • • •
DRIED CORN ON THE COB

The Indians dried shucked corn on the cob. Before cooking the corn, they shucked and soaked it. Then they boiled it just as you would dried beans.

• • • • •
BLOOD LOAF

To make blood loaf, the Indians drained the blood of a freshly killed animal into a container and added some salt, stirring to prevent clotting. Next, they poured the blood into a clean bladder, added black pepper, and tied up the bladder securely before dropping it into boiling water and cooking it until the loaf was done. After the bladder cooled, it was opened and sliced to serve.

• • • • •
LEATHER BRITCHES OR BREECHES

Leather britches or breeches were string beans that had been strung up with a darning needle, hung in a cool place to dry, and then soaked. They were cooked like fresh beans with salt pork.

Though Indians originated this procedure, white men and women in some counties prepared string beans in the same way.

Dried Cabbage Leaves

Remove the large outer leaves of heads of cabbage and string the leaves on a thin stick. Hang the stick in the sun or inside to dry.

To cook, cover with hot water and simmer until tender. Season with meat drippings.

Dried Pumpkin

Peel a pumpkin and cut into rings. Hang the rings on a stick and dry slowly in front of the fire. To cook, stew just as you would fresh pumpkin.

Peach Leather

The late Dr. Douglas Rights, who was president of the Wachovia Historical Society, found reference to peach leather in his study of American Indians in the central part of the state (Forsyth and nearby counties). This confection is now made commercially.

Cook 2½ cups mashed ripe peach pulp with ½ cup sugar in a heavy skillet over low heat until thickened.

Spread out a thin layer on oiled baking sheets. Cover with mosquito netting. Dry in the hot sun for 3 days. Bring inside at night. When the leather draws away from the sides of the pan, it is done.

Lay on a bread board sprinkled with granulated sugar. Sprinkle sugar over the top. Roll out thin—one old cookbook said, "thin as a knife blade." Cut into strips and roll up like small wafers. Dust again with sugar. Pack in a tin box. The peach leather will keep indefinitely.

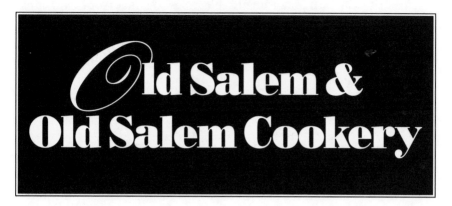

Old Salem & Old Salem Cookery

The first Moravian settlers arrived in what was to become Bethabara on November 17, 1753. The group gathered in an abandoned cabin there and "rejoiced heartily" for that shelter and for a safe trip from Bethlehem, Pennsylvania. The occasion was marked by their sharing of the first Carolina love feast.

After the founding of Bethabara, which is about three and one-half miles from Winston-Salem, the Moravians founded Bethania, about six miles from Winston-Salem. In 1766 a group of twelve men arrived in present-day Old Salem and began cutting logs to build the first home. That settlement grew into one of the most distinctive in America. The emphasis of the early settlers, who possessed a German heritage, was on the church, the home, and a man's trade or profession.

These settlers built sturdy buildings, as evidenced by the number that still stand. The first three homes erected in Old Salem no longer exist, but the Fourth House—restored to its original state—can be found on South Main Street. Fourth House was restored before Old Salem, Inc., began its restoration of the entire village. Old Salem is now one of the showplaces of America.

Unlike the structures in other colonial villages, most of the buildings in Old Salem could be returned to their original state through restoration rather than complete rebuilding. The rebuilding was vastly simplified because of the detailed records kept by the early settlers. A good portion of these records, which were translated from the German, were used in the restoration and contributed to its authenticity.

Old Salem's architecture is unique. Distinctive features include the hooded doorways, buildings flush with the street, cobblestone sidewalks, square brick floors in some of the buildings, distinctive brick, Dutch doors with a swinging upper half, and corner fireplaces.

Of the Dutch doors, the story is told of a girl who had come from the west to attend Salem College in Old Salem. The girl, unfamiliar with doors, started into one of the old buildings and gave the door a mighty push. When the upper portion swung open, she exclaimed, "My God, I've broken the door."

• • • • •

THE MORAVIAN CHURCH

The Southern Province of the Moravian church has its headquarters in Winston-Salem. In addition to those in Forsyth County, there are churches in Charlotte, Greensboro, King, Leaksville, Mayodan, and Raleigh, as well as in Florida and Wisconsin.

The creed of the Moravian church is simple—the church is a brotherhood or fellowship of God and man. The average Sunday morning worship service in a Moravian church is considerably like the one followed in a Presbyterian church, though Moravians include more litany or responsive readings.

In the Christian tradition, the Moravians place special emphasis on Christmas and Easter. Thousands attend the Moravian sunrise service on Easter morning in Old Salem, and many have described it as a deeply moving religious experience. Because of this service, Winston-Salem has become known as "The Easter City" and "The City of the Equal Dead." The name, City of the Equal Dead, comes from the fact that, in the Moravian graveyard, all tombstones for adults are flat and uniform in size; a smaller size is used on the graves of children. The flat tombstones stand out in sharp contrast to massive, towering stones in other cemeteries, which tend to be an expression of the greater wealth of the deceased.

Just before the sun comes up on Easter morning, the Moravian bishop steps out the front door of the ancient Home Moravian Church and, standing under the arched hood that covers the entrance, proclaims: "The Lord Is Risen." The bishop leads the procession to God's Acre, the graveyard in which all tombstones are uniformly flat. In the graveyard, the husbands and wives are separated—that is, the men are buried together in one area and the women in another.

Music has always played an important part in the Moravian church service. It is traditional for youngsters to study a wind instrument so that they can play in the Moravian band. During the Easter morning procession to the graveyard, the band is divided into groups. The groups play antiphonally as the procession moves toward the graveyard. It is also the custom for the band to be part of a Moravian funeral procession.

MORAVIAN BLESSINGS OR GRACES

Come Lord Jesus, our Guest to be,
And bless these gifts bestowed by Thee.
Amen.

This is the blessing most often said in Moravian homes. Children learn it soon after they are old enough to talk and continue to say it throughout their lives. Because eating together signifies a fellowship, it is customary in some homes for those gathered around the table to join hands, especially when guests are present, and repeat the blessing together.

The late Mrs. J. Kenneth Pfohl, wife of the late Bishop J. Kenneth Pfohl of the Southern Province, made a collection of other graces. These are the Moravian blessings that Mrs. Pfohl collected:

Be present at our table Lord,
Be here and everywhere adored,
From Thine all-bounteous hand our food
May we receive with gratitude.
Amen.

Jesus' mercies never fail,
This we prove at every meal.
Lord, we thank Thee for Thy Grace
Gladly join to speak Thy praise.
Amen.

Come, Lord Jesus,
Be Thou our guest,
And let this food
For us be blest.
Amen.

We humbly thank Thee Lord our God,
For all Thy gifts on us bestowed,
And pray Thee graciously to give
The food by which we daily live.
Amen.

Be present, Lord at this repast,
And bless what Thou provided hast.
Amen.

LOVE FEASTS

No church service is more distinctive than a Moravian love feast. Love feasts are held in connection with holidays such as Christmas, New Year's, and Easter and on days of special significance to the church such as church anniversaries and a day set aside to honor missionaries.

During the love feast, every person in the church receives a large flat yeast bun and a mug of coffee containing cream and sugar. The love feast is symbolic of the fellowship of the church. The idea behind the simple meal is that those who break bread together are united in the fellowship the way a family is.

Though coffee is now a part of the love feast, it was not always so. In 1789, the Congregation Council of the Moravian church took this stand: "Coffee shall be served at the Christmas love feast, instead of tea hitherto used. The coffee love feast shall be on Great Sabbath, on August 13th, on November 13th, at Christmas and at the close of the year. If the 13th of August comes in very hot weather, sangaree may be served." (Sangaree is a mixture of red wine or vinegar and water with sugar and spices.)

Tea was once the favorite love feast beverage. It is still served in some European churches. On a few occasions churches have tried substituting lemonade for coffee at hot weather feasts, but the substitution was not a popular one.

Love Feast Coffee

This is the old way of making the coffee.

Tie a pound of coffee in a bag and drop it into 3 gallons boiling water. Reduce heat and let stand without boiling for about 15 minutes. Stir bag through water with wooden paddle now and then.

Remove the coffee bag when the liquid is strong enough—this is where the experience of the coffee maker comes in to make the coffee taste the same each time. Stir in sugar and dissolve. Add milk and keep hot until ready to serve. Serve in love feast mugs.

In the early days, the coffee was made in copper and iron kettles and the hot beverage was poured into pottery urns to cool a little before serving. The man in the church who made the coffee held an important position. His uniform for the occasion was a long white apron. Now, with modernized church kitchens, the coffee is made in regular institutional urns.

At serving time, the coffee mugs are lined up in trays built for that purpose. Men of the church carry the heavy trays to each row of seats in the church.

The traditional accompaniment for the coffee is a sweet, flat yeast bun. At one time sugar cake was sometimes served. Women of the church called *dieners* (from the German word for servants), dressed in white with a little white doily over the head, pass the buns in large baskets, which go up and down the rows like a collection plate.

When Old Salem was quite young, the buns were prepared at the Brothers' House on South Main Street, which housed the bakery, the brewery, and the butchery. In 1774 a community bakery was established, as some of the Brethren felt that it was not proper for young women to go to the single brothers' house. Between 1800 and 1927 Winkler's Bakery made the buns. The tops of the Winkler buns were gashed with a knife before baking to make a *W*.

Modern-day buns are also gashed, but with *M* for Moravian. Most of the buns now served in the Winston-Salem area are baked at Dewey's Bakery in Winston-Salem. They are available on special order from the bakery.

Love Feast Buns

This is the recipe of an old-time bun maker—Ella Stewart of the Sedge Garden community.

Beat 4 eggs. Add 4 cups sugar, 1 cup soft butter and lard (mixed), 2 tablespoons salt, 1 cup warm mashed potatoes, 1½ pints liquid yeast or 3 cakes yeast, and 2 gallons flour. Add lukewarm water to make a soft dough. Turn out on a lightly floured board and knead until smooth. Put in a warm place until "light."

Make into buns about 4 inches in diameter. Place on greased sheets so they do not touch and let rise until light. Bake until golden brown. Just after removing from the stove, brush with cream or melted butter. Makes about 45 buns.

At love feasts, the buns are served cold. In Moravian households, it is customary for the mother to tuck some of her best tea napkins in her purse—enough for each member of the family with a couple of extras in case a visitor is seated nearby.

Love Feast Candles

On Christmas Eve, after the love feast has been served and the coffee cups have been collected, the lights in the church are turned off and ushers appear with trays full of lighted candles. They are distributed to everyone in the congregation. The lighted candles, together with the Moravian star, are a symbol of Christ as "the light of the world."

Homemade candles of beeswax and tallow, made using the formula of the early settlers of Old Salem, appear in most of the churches. The candlemaking begins in the summer. December sessions are devoted to trimming parties: a red crepe frill is put at the base of each candle to catch drippings so they will not fall on one's hands. Candle holders were used in the early days, but as attendance grew, they became impractical.

The late Dr. Adelaide Fries's translation from the Gamein Diarum (Unity Diary) for December 24, 1747, shows that candles were used on that date at a love feast in Marienborn, Germany. It was not until the following year that such a service was held by the Moravians in Herrnhut, Germany. On that occasion, the candles were tied with red ribbons "to symbolize the lighting of a blood-red flame in the hearts of worshipers."

It appears that the first time the Moravians used candles at a Christmas service in America was in 1756 in Bethlehem, Pennsylvania. Translations of diaries also show that candles appeared for the children's love feasts in 1762 in Bethabara and Bethania. In these services, according to the diaries, the light of the candles symbolized "the flame of love." An entry of December 24, 1770, gives this statement: "At 6:00 P.M. a love-feast was held for the children, appropriate hymns were sung and small lighted candles were distributed, which they joyfully carried home, still burning."

THE MORAVIAN STAR

The star has been a symbol of Christmas since that first Christmas thousands of years ago. It has been used in every sort of decoration since that time, but none has the impressive meaning of the stars used in Winston-Salem, the home of the Southern Province of the Moravian church. The Advent stars, also called Herrnhut or Moravian stars, are usually put up four Sundays before Christmas, the first Sunday in the Advent season.

In her book, *Customs and Practices of the Moravian Church*, Adelaide Fries stated that the inventor of the Moravian star was unknown. Her analysis of its origin was as follows. Undoubtedly, the star was developed during evening handicraft sessions held about 1850 in the Paedagogium in Niesky, Germany. The star factory was started in Herrnhut, Germany, in the late 1880s. When the factory was closed during World War II, a group of Moravians in Winston-Salem took up the business of making stars.

"The Morning Star"

> Morning Star, Oh cheering sight,
> Ere thou camest, how dark Earth's night . . .

The tradition of singing "The Morning Star" on Christmas Eve started in Old Salem, where its composer, the Reverend Francis Florentine Hagen, was born in 1815. He wrote the music in Bethania between 1844 and 1854, according to Donald McCorkle, a former director of the Moravian Music Foundation. The words to "Morning Star" were translated from the German by the Reverend Martin Houser. The carol is sung antiphonally by a soloist and the congregation. In some congregations, the choir sings the solo part. In other congregations, there is considerable competition for the privilege of being the soloist.

MORAVIAN SISTERS

Following the German custom, the women of the church formerly wore little white caps. It has not been determined whether the ladies wore these caps all day, but according to Mrs. Thomas Boyd, who was connected with the Wachovia Museum for years, it is likely that they did. They certainly wore them to church. Because they went to church four times a day in the early days, there would not seem to be a great deal of sense in removing the cap each time. It might be that the ladies took off the cap itself but left on the little scull cap or liner as they worked around the house.

A set of dolls wearing the early caps may be seen in the Wachovia Museum. The color of the ribbon on the cap indicated the marital status of the wearer. Little girls wore a beautiful cherry red. At about age eighteen, unwed sisters changed their ribbons to pink. If a woman remained a "single sister," she continued to wear a pink ribbon. After marriage, the ribbon was blue. Widows wore a white ribbon.

Because the church played such an important part in the lives of early settlers, the following story seems quite likely. A single sister claimed that she never had to time boiling eggs. She merely sang through a certain hymn and in that length of time, the eggs were cooked just right.

• • • • •

THE WACHOVIA MUSEUM

Unlike most museums, the Wachovia Museum has a fine collection of cooking equipment. There are dozens of handmade tin cookie cutters. Some are in the pattern of a tiny child's hand—undoubtedly, the man of the house used his child's hand as the pattern for making the cutter. There are springerle rolling pins with recessed designs.

The collection includes old coffee mugs from the days when love feast coffee was served in even larger portions than it is now. There are all sorts of coffee roasters to use on the hearth and coffee grinders—one fascinating one grinds only one bean at a time. There is a hand-operated mixer for making cakes, a sausage stuffer, wafer or waffle molds, and waffle irons and a toaster to be used over an open fire. The old tin roaster, which was designed to stand in front of the fire, shows how birds or chickens were roasted. The birds were placed on horizontal rods. The curved tin back prevented splattering and contained a door that opened from the back for basting. There is also a smaller version of this fireplace roaster.

The museum has a rivel board, which is the only one I have ever heard of. It seems that hops, mashed potatoes, and cornmeal were combined to form a thick paste; this was put on the corrugated wheel of the rivel board, which pressed out the water and broke it into tiny pieces ready for drying. (For more about rivels, see Chapter 11.) Also of interest are the molds for making pewter spoons and plates and the corn grinder.

· · · · ·

OLD SALEM KITCHENS

The kitchens of the old buildings are of special interest. In many, the Dutch oven is the outstanding feature. The kitchen of the Salem Tavern, where George Washington was a guest between May 31 and June 1, 1791, is on two levels. The portion that connects with the rest of the house is a raised platform floored with square bricks. Steps lead down into the kitchen, where an old fireplace is complete with cooking equipment.

The Dutch oven and firebox with buried pots are intact in the lower floor of the Brothers' House. In the subterranean basement of the same building, hooks are visible on the arched, white-washed ceiling. These hooks were used to support ropes to which planks were attached to provide a cool area for the storage of perishable foods.

FIREPLACE COOKERY

The open fireplace in the kitchen of the Salem Tavern is an example of how cooking was done in such a facility. The fireplace is completely furnished with the cookware of the period. That includes a spit and cranes that hold pots to swing in over the fire.

Naturally, printed cooking directions or recipes for the open fire are few, if any. According to an old newspaper clipping, the following instructions for stuffing and roasting a bird were written by a woman named Amelia Simmons in 1796: "One pound soft wheat bread, three eggs, a little sweet thyme, sweet marjoram, pepper and salt and add a gill of wine. Fill the bird therewith and sew up, hand down to a steady solid fire, basting frequently with salt and water, and roast until steam emits from the breast." (The clipping doesn't indicate where Amelia Simmons lived.)

For the celebration of Christmas in Old Salem in 1975, a traditional dinner cooked in a fireplace was re-created. The goose was roasted on a rotating spit over hot coals and served with a sauce as the first course, along with sippets and parsley, artichokes, broiled yams, and corn pudding. (Sippets are bits of fried bread used as a garnish.) After the goose and before the second course came the "snacks" of smoked meats, radishes, and cheeses. (In the old days, cooks preserved radishes by storing them in the root cellar.) The second course consisted of beef tongue with lemons and capers, winter salad, green peas, beets, French rolls, and blackberry wine.

• • • • •

WINKLER'S BAKERY

The residents of early Salem bought their bread from Winkler's Bakery, which for years was housed in the building that now stands on South Main Street. The yeasty aroma of freshly baked loaves of bread tingled the nostrils and sent housewives off to buy a supply.

In addition to the bread and Moravian sugar cake, the bakery made a wide variety of cookies. Little children wandered in and out of the shop, where they eyed the delicacies over the counter and exchanged their pennies for bagfuls. (Claudia Winkler of the bakery family was still living when this book was originally researched.)

• • • • •

THE COFFEE POT

The giant coffee pot that stands in Old Salem is a landmark of Winston-Salem. The pot was built as an advertisement in 1859 by Julius Mickey, who had a mercantile establishment on the corner and a tinsmith's shop in the upper portion of the building. The purpose of the coffee pot was to attract attention to his roofing, tin, and stove business.

According to tradition, a Yankee soldier hid in the pot during the Civil War. The pot is seven feet, three inches high. The diameter is twenty-seven inches at the top and sixty-four inches at the bottom. It has been estimated that if the pot were real, it could hold 740½ gallons of coffee.

CANDLE TEA

Each December, for a period of three to four days, the women of Home Moravian Church sponsor an event called the Candle Tea in the Brothers' House on South Main Street. For the event, the women wear the old costumes and caps.

During the tea, visitors are able to see the Christmas candles being made by hand. The aromatic melted beeswax is poured into old-fashioned molds and then unmolded. In addition to the candlemaking, there is a display of the traditional Moravian Putz in the subcellar. The Putz is an elaborate manger and village scene made up of hundreds of miniature figures collected over many years. It is the kind of thing that thrills children.

After touring the house, guests are served mugs of Moravian coffee and sugar cake in the old kitchen.

ASTROLOGICAL GARDENING GUIDE

In 1828 John Christian Blum began publishing his famous almanac. To this day, *Blum's Almanac* is the gardening guide for those who believe in the signs—of which there are many. There are those who plant their seeds "in the signs." Others disclaim any power of the signs and plant their seeds "in the ground."

The best time for planting is when the moon is ruled by Cancer. The next best signs are Scorpio and Pisces. If you cannot plant in one of those three signs, plant in Taurus, Libra, and Capricorn. Avoid planting in Aries, Gemini, Capricorn, Aquarius, Leo, Virgo, Libra, and Sagittarius.

The moon is also used as a guide for other activities. Cabbage should be made into sauerkraut on the waxing of the moon so that the brine will stay up. Unless a hog is killed in the right sign of the moon, slices of the ham, when laid in the pan, will curl up instead of remaining flat while frying.

SALT—A VITAL SUBSTANCE

The late Mary Wiley, a Winston-Salem historian, brought to light the following information about the role of the early Moravians in obtaining salt.

The success or failure of a pioneer settlement depended to a large degree on access to salt. This was especially true of the sparse settlements of northwestern North Carolina—the "back country," as the aristocratic colonists of eastern North Carolina designated it. The thrift and foresight of the Moravian settlers of Wachovia (now Forsyth County) in procuring salt and sharing it with their non-Moravian neighbors fostered the development of the rich northwestern section of the state; otherwise, the growth of this area would have been considerably slower.

Suggestive of the dependence of the backcountry settlers on the Moravians for salt is this entry in the Bethania Diary of December 28, 1775: "This week and last many people came from 100 and more miles away to buy salt; it gave out, so that we were not able to supply the later comers as we wished. Some went away weeping."

It was no easy matter for Moravians to obtain salt. They had to journey overland to the Cape Fear River; to Petersburg, Virginia; or to Charleston, South Carolina. For days they traveled in their clumsy wagons laden with skins and wheat, beeswax, and butter to barter for salt. Sometimes when they reached their destination, the stores had little salt for sale. The return trip was also hazardous. An old diary reports that every grain of salt was lost when a wagon tried to ford a swollen stream.

Once in the early days of Bethabara, the Brethren experimented in the making of salt; they boiled the brine obtained from the salted meat they had on hand. The Bethabara Diary states that "they found the salt thus made good and strong." On another occasion, when the pioneers of Wachovia were entirely out of salt, they tried using hickory ash in place of salt. But they found that this substitute was not good for their health—it made them hoarse, then speechless.

THE BACKGROUND OF MORAVIAN COOKERY

Moravian cooking has a German heritage, for it was that heritage that was brought to Old Salem by the early settlers who came to this country from Moravia. The type of cooking is considerably like that of the Pennsylvania Dutch. Slight differences come from the fact that the Moravians in Pennsylvania settled among the Germans, whereas the Moravians in North Carolina settled among the English.

Many of the old dishes possess German names. Certainly, the nomenclature of cakes and cookies is directly based on the German kuchen. According to the late Dr. Lucy Wenhold, cake as Americans know and make it is not European and certainly not German. In German *Kuchen* refers to (1) any sort of cookie and (2) sweetened yeast bread baked either in loaf form or as a flat cake an inch or two thick. For that reason, Moravian cookery includes sugar cake, coffee cake, loaf cake such as strietz, and the brown Christmas cookies that are called Christmas cakes.

CAKES AND COOKIES

THE TRADITIONAL CHRISTMAS CAKES

These crisp, paper-thin ginger cakes have become world famous. There is no longer an abundance of cooks who will tackle the job of making them, but at Christmastime, it is possible to get them by mail.

Making the dough is not so much of a task; it is the rolling and baking that is tedious. The custom is to make the dough at least the night before baking. Some cooks continue to store the dough on the back porch or in the refrigerator and "bake off it" for four to six weeks. They claim that the spices have a chance to get through the dough better that way.

The first step in making the dough is getting black Puerto Rican molasses. Storekeepers used to stock it by the barrel and drain it off in containers brought by their customers. I have found that the regular black cooking molasses works beautifully, but, according to veteran bakers, "it just isn't the same."

Once the dough has ripened overnight or longer, it is ready to roll. If you have ever encountered a back-breaking job in the kitchen, rolling Moravian Christmas cakes is it. The best way to roll them extra thin is on a cloth-covered board with a rolling pin tightly covered with a child's white sock. It is best to try to roll the dough without adding flour, for extra flour makes the cakes tough and decreases the spicy taste.

Rolling and baking is really a two-person operation, as the thin cakes bake so quickly that you can burn up many a panful if you get busy rolling and forget to watch the oven. I remember, as a child, standing by the wood stove to watch pans of the cakes baking in the oven. I had to take them out just at the right minute and put in another pan. We filled two big lard cans with a day's baking, which is some turnout of Moravian cakes. They should be stored in a tightly covered metal container to stay crisp.

The old recipes are essentially the same—black molasses, lard and butter (mixed), sugar (generally brown), flour, a little soda, and spices. Some cooks would add brandy. Those who like the cakes to have a bite add cloves with a heavy hand. There are those who think ginger makes the bite, but it is really the cloves.

Moravian Christmas Cakes

This recipe turns out a fine batch of cookies. The blend of spices is very good. The flour is usually just about the right amount, but, of course, the texture of the dough will depend on the temperature.

¾ *cup butter and lard or shortening, mixed*
¾ *cup brown sugar*
1 pint black molasses
7½ cups sifted flour
4 tablespoons ground cloves
4 tablespoons ground cinnamon
4 tablespoons ground ginger
1 teaspoon salt
1 tablespoon soda
¼ *cup boiling water*

Cream butter and lard with sugar. Add molasses. Sift flour with spices and salt. Add soda to boiling water. Add flour mixture and soda water to creamed mixture. Work well with the hands—call in the man of the house and let him work the dough if your hands are weak. That is what Grandma used to do.

Cover and store the dough in a cold place overnight, preferably longer.

Roll to infinite thinness on a board. Bake on greased cookie sheets in a moderate oven (about 375°) for a very few minutes, or just until the cakes begin to brown.

A pastry brush and melted shortening is the best way to grease a cookie sheet today, but many is the time I have seen the sheet greased with a cloth tied to one end of a small stick cut from a tree. The cloth portion was mopped into melted lard.

White Christmas Cakes

Cream ½ cup butter with 1 cup sugar (either white or brown). Add 2 eggs and beat well. Stir ¾ teaspoon soda into 1½ tablespoons buttermilk. Add to creamed mixture with 1 teaspoon vanilla. Mix.

Add enough flour to make a soft dough. Chill. Roll out, cut, place on a baking sheet, sprinkle with white sugar, and bake in a moderate oven.

Palmetto Cake

In the quaint old Moravian town of Bethania in Forsyth County, a Palmetto cake is a *must* for Christmas.

½ pound butter
1 pound sugar
6 eggs
1 pound seeded raisins
1 pound flour
2 teaspoons baking powder
1 pound English walnuts
1 coconut, grated
¼ pound candied pineapple (optional)

Cream butter and sugar. Add eggs. Dredge raisins in ½ cup of the flour. Add remaining flour to creamed mixture and mix thoroughly. Add remaining ingredients and bake in a 275° oven for about 3 hours. Store in a tight container with a quartered apple in a cool place for 2 weeks. Makes about 5 pounds.

Springerles

This recipe, which came from Mrs. John Johansen of Winston-Salem, the wife of a Moravian minister, is unique in that the cookies are soft as compared with the traditionally hard ones.

4 eggs
1 pound powdered sugar
A lump of soft butter about the size of a large egg
½ teaspoon anise oil (optional)
3 tablespoons anise seed
3⅓ cups sifted flour

Beat eggs until blended; gradually add sugar and continue beating. If using an electric mixer, beat at moderate speed for about 10 minutes. For hand beating, increase the time to 20 minutes. During the beating, add the butter so it will be well blended. The butter will keep the cookies soft.

At the end of the beating time, add the anise oil if used and anise seed, then, gradually, the flour, and mix the batter well. Roll out the dough, which will be rather soft, on a well-floured board. Keep the thickness at least ⅛ inch so the cookies will be plump. Use a well-floured springerle board or rolling pin to press the designs on the dough, cut apart with a sharp knife, and gently place cookies on a large tray to dry.

Allow them to remain overnight or for about 10 to 12 hours. Bake on greased and floured cookie sheets in a 350° oven for 10 to 12 minutes. Do not allow them to brown—they should be pale yellow in color. The cookies will stay soft for about 2 weeks. They freeze very well.

Shrewsbury Cookies

This cookie was a favorite in the family of the Reverend Mr. Hagen, composer of the "Morning Star." Mrs. Oscar E. Mills, his granddaughter, contributed the recipe. Who knows but that the composer munched Shrewsbury cookies as he wrote the music. According to Mrs. Mills, "They are a small spice cookie with no special eye appeal and are especially good dunked in morning coffee."

Put 1¼ pounds (5 cups) flour in a large bowl and add 1 pound brown sugar and 1 teaspoon of a mixture of cloves, allspice, cinnamon, and nutmeg. With the hands, rub 6 ounces (¾ cup) butter into flour mixture thoroughly until fine and mealy. Beat 4 eggs and pour over flour. Dissolve 1 teaspoon soda in a little vinegar and add. Mix thoroughly with a wooden spoon.

Pat the dough together and round up to make a ball. Chill overnight in the refrigerator. Roll ⅛-inch thick and cut with a 2-inch biscuit cutter. Bake in a 375° oven until light brown.

Note: For easy handling of the dough, use a pastry cloth with a cover on the rolling pin. Use a minimum of extra flour on the cloth. If desired, prick the design of a Christmas tree on each cookie.

Winkler's Ginger Cakes

Stir 1 quart molasses into 6 ounces lard and blend well. Add 1 ounce soda to 1 cup sour milk. Mix with molasses and lard. Sift ¼ ounce each of cinnamon, cloves, and ginger with flour. Add enough flour to make a dough that will roll.

Roll out about ½-inch thick. Cut into strips 2 × 5 inches and place on a greased baking sheet. Bake. Brush with brown sugar water.

Love Drops

This is a Winkler's Bakery recipe.

Beat 6 egg whites until foamy. Gradually add ¾ pound white sugar and continue beating until stiff. Fold in ¾ pound flour. Flavor with lemon rind and extract. Drop by the teaspoon on a greased sheet. Bake.

Ginger Nuts

Mix 2 teaspoons soda, 3 cups sugar, 4 tablespoons ginger, and 2 teaspoons cloves. Add 6 beaten eggs. Add 1 teaspoon salt to 4 cups flour and blend with egg mixture. Add more flour to make a dough that can be rolled. Roll out and place on a greased baking sheet.

Bake in a hot oven (about 425°) for about 5 minutes. Take out when the cakes puff way up. They will fall.

Note: There was no fat listed in this recipe.

Pepper Nuts

This recipe must have originated with the German *Pfeffernusse*.

Cream 1 cup butter and lard (mixed) with 2 cups white sugar. Add 3 eggs and blend. Mix 4 heaping cups flour with 1 teaspoon cream of tartar and grated nutmeg. Stir into creamed mixture alternately with 1 teaspoon soda stirred into about ¼ cup milk. Flavor as you like and drop on baking sheets not too close together. Add a few raisins, currants, or chopped citron if desired.

Tea Cakes

Beat 4 eggs. Add 3 cups brown sugar and 1 teaspoon nutmeg. Add ½ pound melted butter and 1 cup buttermilk. Sift ½ teaspoon salt, 2 heaping teaspoons soda, and 1 heaping teaspoon baking powder with about 8 cups flour and add to egg mixture. Add enough additional flour to make a soft dough. Roll ¼-inch thick. Bake in a moderate oven (about 350°) until light brown.

Jackson Cakes

This is a Winkler's Bakery recipe.

Cream ½ pound butter with 1 pound white sugar. Beat in 6 eggs. Add 1 teaspoon soda sifted with flour. Add enough flour to make a dough that will roll. Flavor with lemon. Roll out and cut with a round cutter.

Shrewsbury Cakes

Rub together ⅜ pound butter and 1 pound flour. Add ¾ pound sugar, the yolks of 4 eggs, and beaten whites to which a little soda has been added. Let stand overnight and in the morning roll out, cut with a cookie cutter, and bake.

Seed Cakes

Mix 1 whole egg, 1 egg white, ½ pound butter, ¾ pound sugar, and 1 pound flour. When ready to roll out, sprinkle dough with caraway seeds and roll seed into dough. Cut and bake.

THE COFFEE CAKE WITH PUDDLES ON TOP

No coffee cake in the world—and there are hundreds of kinds—is better than Moravian sugar cake. Moravian cooks make it throughout the year but especially at Eastertime, when there are a great many visitors on hand. It is made from a rich yeast dough topped with "puddles" of brown sugar and butter with a dusting of cinnamon and baked in sheets in shallow baking pans. The dough is made with mashed potatoes, which produces a moist, tender product.

Julia Ross's Moravian Sugar Cake
(Tested)

1 package active dry yeast
½ teaspoon granulated sugar
1 cup warm (105° to 110°) water
3 cups unbleached all-purpose flour (spooned into cup and leveled)
2 tablespoons dry skim milk powder
3 or 6 tablespoons dehydrated potatoes (3 if using
finely ground variety, 6 if using flakes)
⅓ cup granulated sugar
¾ teaspoon salt
2 large eggs, room temperature
½ cup butter or margarine, softened
Topping

Sprinkle yeast and ½ teaspoon sugar onto water in a large mixing bowl. When dissolved and beginning to show signs of life, add all other ingredients except 1 cup of the floor. Beat on medium speed of a mixer for 5 minutes. With a spoon add the other cup of flour to make a soft dough. Cover and place in a warm spot to rise until doubled in bulk (about 1½ hours). Beat down and let rise again if you have time (about 45 minutes). Now turn dough into a greased baking pan 17 × 11 × 1 inches and use hands to spread evenly over entire surface. Cover and let rise until light (about 1 hour).

TOPPING

1 tablespoon light cream or milk
⅔ cup brown sugar, packed

1 teaspoon ground cinnamon
½ cup butter or margarine, melted and cooled

When the dough is light, brush with cream. Combine the sugar and cinnamon and sprinkle evenly over entire surface of the dough. With fingertips make shallow indentions in dough 1 inch apart. Sprinkle butter over all. Bake for 15 minutes in a 375° oven. Makes 20 generous servings.

ALTERNATE METHOD FOR OVERNIGHT RISING

This method was first devised so that the dough could rise in the refrigerator overnight, be put into the pan just before going to the Moravian Easter sunrise service, and baked on returning home. Put on the coffee and everything will finish at the same time.

Late in the day on the day before you need the sugar cake, make dough as above except use 2 packages of yeast. After it rises in the bowl once (about 1 hour), stir down, cover with foil, and place in the refrigerator. A half hour later, punch down because it will have risen again before the dough became sufficiently cool to retard yeast growth. Next morning, place in a pan and let rise until light (about 1½ hours).

Hot Roll Moravian Sugar Cake

A Moravian sugar cake made with a package of hot roll mix won a $15,000 prize in the 29th Pillsbury Bake-Off held in Miami in 1980. Since that time, the formula for the hot roll mix has been changed slightly to accommodate a change in the original winning recipe. The following recipe, which was adjusted in 1991 to use the new roll mix, was provided by Marlene Johnson of Pillsbury.

1 package hot roll mix
1¾ cups warm (120° to 130°) water
⅓ cup sugar
⅓ cup instant potato flakes
⅓ cup instant nonfat dry milk powder
Margarine or butter
2 eggs
⅔ cup firmly packed brown sugar

1 teaspoon cinnamon
½ cup chopped nuts

Grease a 13- × 9-inch baking pan. In a large bowl dissolve yeast from the hot roll mix in warm water. Stir in half of the flour from hot roll mix, sugar, potato flakes, dry milk powder, ⅓ cup melted margarine, and eggs; beat for 2 minutes at medium speed. Stir in remaining flour from hot roll mix; beat well.

Cover dough loosely with plastic wrap and a cloth towel. Let rise in a warm place (88° to 85°) until light and doubled in size (about 45 minutes). Stir down dough; spread evenly in prepared pan. Cover; let rise in a warm place until light and doubled in size (about 45 minutes).

Heat oven to 375°. Make small pockets in dough by pressing lightly with a floured fingertip. Sprinkle with mixture of brown sugar and cinnamon. Drizzle with ½ cup margarine and sprinkle with nuts. Bake for 15 to 20 minutes, or until golden brown. Makes 15 servings.

German Streussel Cake

One of the ways in which little Moravian girls began their cooking experiences was to make the streussel topping for streussel cake.

To prepare the cake, make a batch of Moravian sugar cake dough and spread it thin in a baking pan. Let rise. When the dough is light, cover the top with crumbs made of 6 tablespoons butter, ½ cup flour, and ½ cup brown sugar. Bake.

German Apple Cake

Make a batch of Moravian sugar cake dough and spread it thin in a baking pan. Let rise. When the dough is light, cover the top with apple slices. Add brown sugar, melted butter, and cinnamon. Bake.

Crumb Cake

This cake is good with coffee.

Mix 1½ cups sugar, 3½ cups flour, a little cinnamon, and 2 teaspoons baking powder. Work in ½ cup shortening. Take out ½ cup of this mixture and reserve for topping.

Beat 2 eggs and add enough milk to make 1 cup of liquid. Add to flour mixture. Pour into prepared pans and top with reserved crumbs. Bake.

German Puffs

Boil 2 ounces butter in ½ pint cream. Stir until cold. Then beat 2 eggs, strain them into the cream, and mix that by degrees into 2 tablespoons flour.

Butter custard cups and into each put 3 spoonfuls of batter. Bake puffs for ½ hour and serve the moment they are done with a sauce of melted butter and sugar or with lemon juice.

German Peach Cake

Beat 2 eggs. Add 1 cup peach juice, 1½ cups sifted flour, 1 tablespoon butter, and 1 heaping teaspoon baking powder. Pour into a well-greased baking dish. Cover the top with peach halves, round side up. Sprinkle the peaches with powdered sugar and nutmeg. Bake in a hot oven for 20 minutes. Serve hot with hard sauce.

Thick Ginger Cake, "Mustercake," or Trainer's Gingerbread

This was the kind of cake made for soldiers in training after the American Revolution or the kind packed in soldiers' knapsacks when they were called to duty.

Pour ½ pint melted lard into a mixture of 1 quart molasses and 1 cup brown sugar. Stir 1 ounce or 8 scant teaspoons soda into 1 cup sour milk and add to molasses mixture. Thicken with enough flour to roll on tins [whatever that might mean] and mark in squares with a knife. Bake in a moderate oven (about 400°).

German Strietz

The old cooks made strietz at Christmastime and continued to eat it for many months. This recipe was brought to America by a Danish woman, who gave it to Lucy Wenhold's mother, Mrs. H. A. Leinbach. Dr. Wenhold updated the recipe.

Make the sponge by sprinkling 1½ packages granulated yeast into ½ cup lukewarm water and let stand without stirring for 5 to 10 minutes. Add 1 pint milk and 1 pint sifted flour and mix well. Place in a bowl and allow to rise in a warm place until light.

Add ½ cup butter, 1¼ cups sugar, 2 eggs, 1 teaspoon salt, ½ pint warm milk, ¼ teaspoon cinnamon, ¼ teaspoon nutmeg, 4½ pints sifted flour, 2 cups raisins, 1 cup chopped citron, 1 cup currants, and 1 cup slivered almonds.

Let rise in a warm place until double in bulk. Knead down and put into 4 greased loaf pans. Allow to double in bulk in a warm place. Bake in a moderate oven (about 350°) for 30 minutes, or until done.

Yeast Loaf Cake

There were those who prepared a mixture quite similar to strietz but called it a yeast loaf cake.

Butter Semmels

At suppertime, dissolve 1 yeast cake in ¼ cup lukewarm water. Add ½ cup sugar and ½ cup mashed potatoes. Cover and let stand in a warm place.

Just before going to bed, add 1 pint sweet milk, 2 beaten eggs, 3 pints flour, 1 teaspoon salt, and ½ cup butter and lard (mixed). Knead until the dough blisters and drops clean from the hands. Set in a warm place to rise until morning.

Roll out ¼-inch thick and cut into 2-inch squares, fold over, and set in a pan 1 inch apart. Let rise and bake in a hot oven. Brush with melted butter and dust with powdered sugar.

Rolled Gingerbread

Sometimes called hard ginger bread, this is really a rolled cookie. It was called rolled gingerbread when sold by Winkler's Bakery. This recipe came from Mrs. Kathleen Adkins Blackwell.

1 cup butter
1 cup sugar
1 pint molasses

1 teaspoon soda
1 teaspoon each of ginger, cinnamon, and cloves
Flour

Mix together butter, sugar, molasses, soda, and spices and add flour to make a very stiff dough. Roll out thin on a lightly floured board and cut with a cutter. Place on greased baking sheets and bake in a 375° oven until done.

Potato Puffs

Dissolve 1 yeast cake in 1 cup warm water before going to bed. Add 1 cup warm mashed potatoes and 1 cup sugar. Beat in 3 eggs and 1 cup melted lard. Add flour and 1 teaspoon salt to make a soft dough. Let rise in a warm place overnight.

Turn out on a floured board. Knead and roll out about 1-inch thick. Cut into strips about 1 inch wide and 8 inches long. Tie into a knot and place on a greased baking sheet. Let rise until light. Bake in a hot oven until brown. While hot, brush with sugar water and sprinkle with powdered sugar.

Sugar Biscuits

To 2 cups sugar add ¼ cup butter, 4 well-beaten eggs, and 1 teaspoon soda dissolved in 1 cup milk. Beat until smooth and then stir in flour until the dough becomes stiff enough to roll out.

Apple Johnny Cake

Mix 1 cup cornmeal, 1 cup flour, ½ cup sugar, and ½ teaspoon soda. Add 1 cup sour milk and 1 egg. Beat well and add 2 cups coarsely cut apples. Bake in a hot oven.

Deceptions

Mix sufficient flour with 1 egg to make a dough stiff enough to roll. Add a little sugar and salt. Roll very thin, cut into squares, and fry in fat.

Comforts

Mix 2½ cups flour, 1 cup sweet milk, pinch of salt, 3 tablespoons baking powder, and 2 eggs. Fry in deep fat like crullers.

Crullers

Mix 3 eggs, butter the size of an egg, 1 cup mashed potatoes, 1 cup white sugar, 4 teaspoons baking powder, nutmeg to flavor, pinch of salt, 1 cup milk, and flour to make a dough stiff enough to handle.

Roll out ½-inch thick, cut into strips 3 inches long, slash in center, and tangle.* Fry in deep hot fat. Roll in powdered sugar.

Strumbundles, Strumbendles, or Tanglebritches**

Cream 1 cup butter with 2½ cups sugar (brown or white). Add 4 eggs and mix well. Sift 2 teaspoons baking powder and a pinch of soda with 1 cup flour and add to creamed mixture alternately with 1 cup sweet milk. Add a little nutmeg if desired.

Add additional flour to make a dough that can be rolled. Roll out ¼-inch thick, cut with a jagging iron, and fry in deep hot fat. [A jagging iron is a cutter with jagged edges like those on fabric cut with pinking shears.]

Note: Some cooks cut a small slit in the middle of each strip and put one end of the dough through the slit before frying.

Strumpfbenled

This recipe came from an old Moravian cookbook written by hand.

Combine 9 eggs, 1 pound sugar, ¾ pound butter, 1 or 2 spoons of cream, a little pearl ash [apparently the ash from a special kind of wood], and enough flour to make the dough stiff enough to roll out. Bake in fat.

Wonders, such cakes, and fried cakes are all quite a bit like strumbundles.

Tangle means to stick one end of the dough through a slit.
**These spellings and others differ because (1) the words were translated from old German and (2) the early settlers were not good at spelling.

Wonders

½ pound butter
1 pound sugar
12 eggs
3 pounds flour
1 glass rose water
A little cinnamon

Beat butter and sugar together. Beat eggs until light and add to butter mixture; add remaining ingredients. Roll out, cut, and fry in lard.

Such Cakes

Combine 4 eggs, 1 cup sour milk, ¾ cup butter and lard (mixed), 1 small teaspoon soda, spices to taste, and flour to make a soft dough. Roll, cut, and fry in hot lard.

Fried Cakes

Combine 1 cup milk, ½ pound butter, 6 eggs, 2 pounds sugar, 1 pound raisins, 1 teaspoon saleratus [soda], and flour to make a stiff batter. Beat well and fry in boiling lard.

HEIFTA CAKELS

There is considerable variation in this spelling. One old cookbook called them heiferpeckels. The German spelling was probably *hoefekuechel*.

Evidently, these fried cakes were about the same thing as tangle-britches. Many cooks made them from Moravian sugar cake dough, rolled out thin and then cut into strips and fried. Some cut a slit down the center of each strip and put one end of the dough through the strip. The cakes were often dipped in sugar water after frying.

Ginger Pound Cake
(Tested)

This is a Winkler's Bakery recipe.

Cream ½ pound butter. Add 1¼ cups brown sugar (packed). Beat in 6 eggs.

Sift together 2 teaspoons cinnamon, 2 tablespoons ginger, 1 teaspoon nutmeg, and 5 cups flour. Add ½ tablespoon soda to 2 cups dark molasses and add to creamed mixture alternately with flour mixture and ½ cup sweet milk.

Pour into a tube pan that has been greased and floured, with the bottom lined with greased and floured brown paper. Bake at 300° until done.

• • • • •

THE TRUTH ABOUT CITRON TARTS

One certain way to find out the truth about something is to publish an incorrect statement about it in the newspaper. I did that once with citron tarts, pointing out that they were made like chess pies only flavored with lemon instead of vanilla. The next day's mail brought a letter from the late Mrs. Howard Rondthaler, wife of the president of Salem College, who wrote that a chess pie and citron tarts are not the same. The flavor of citron tarts is more delicate and the filling must never be stirred; rather, the ingredients must be "chopped" together.

When a number of old German people still lived in Salem, citron tarts, which are distinctively Salem tarts, were so called because they were always flavored with lemon and the German word for lemons is *citronen*.

Citron or Salem Tarts

Many years ago there lived in Old Salem two renowned caterers who went from house to house—wherever there was to be a big dinner or a wedding reception. They were Permela (Miss Melie) Church and Isabel Crim. Sometimes they took possession of the kitchen for several days before the special event. To this day, some folks still recall the taste-tingling delight of the food these two ladies served. This is their recipe.

6 egg yolks
Butter the size of an egg

1 cup light brown sugar
Lemon flavoring or a little grated lemon rind
and about 1 teaspoon lemon juice
Unbaked pastry

Do not stir filling. Cut the butter into the egg yolks and chop in the sugar and lemon flavorings.

Line small fluted tart shell pans with pastry and pour three-fourths full with the filling. Bake in a moderately hot oven (about 375°) until the filling is set and the fluted crust is touched with brown.

• • • • •

OTHER MORAVIAN DELICACIES

Brine for Meat

This is fine for tongues, beef, or a shoulder.

To 1 ordinary bucket of water add 3 pounds salt, 1 pound brown sugar, 2 ounces saltpeter, 1 ounce soda, and 1 ounce black pepper. Boil, skim, and set aside to cool.

The meat ought to stand in salt for 1 night and the water should be poured from it before it is put into the brine. The brine must be perfectly cool. Tie cloth over the top. In about 2 weeks the meat will be good, but it will keep for weeks in cool weather. Store in a cool place.

PON-HAWS AND SCRAPPLE

In the Pennsylvania Dutch country, natives call scrapple pon-haws. The Dutch make scrapple from the hog's head, the broth in which it was cooked, and cornmeal to thicken. Sometimes pork scraps are added. They also make what is called buckwheat scrapple, which is thickened with part buckwheat flour and part cornmeal.

There is probably a difference between pon-haws and scrapple, for the proportions used would differ from person to person. Old Salem Moravians prepared pon-haws from cooked ground pork liver, the broth in which it was cooked, and cornmeal for thickening. Their pon-haws was like a liver mush.

Liver Dumplings

This dish, which was often prepared by Mrs. Katherine Winkler Johnson of Old Salem, certainly shows the German influence.

Grind 3 pounds calf liver with 2 to 3 onions. Add 7 eggs and enough flour to make the mixture stick together when shaped into balls and cooked in beef broth. Make test balls to determine the proper amount of flour. Drop the balls into rich beef stock and cook until done. Serve in soup bowls with the broth.

Fried Cheese

Lucy Wenhold recalled making fried cheese dozens of times. She said that this cheese somewhat resembles Camembert or Brie and that it should be made from old-fashioned clabber cheese, which is made from unpasteurized milk. Because pasteurization halts the growth of bacteria, insufficient bacterial action remains to produce the cheese after pasteurization.

The clabber cheese, probably in a stone crock, stands in a warm place until it is ripe. "You know when it is ripe," according to Dr. Wenhold, because it smells to "high Heaven."

This is Grace Siewer's recipe.

Take ½ pound clabber or cottage cheese. Crumble with a fork, spread on a flat dish, and sprinkle with salt. Cover with another dish and put in a warm place. Stir with a fork every day until the consistency becomes gummy and the color changes to dark cream.

Melt 1 teaspoon butter in a saucepan, pour in cheese, and stir constantly until smooth. Pour into a bowl or cup. When done, the cheese is not very hard, but rather gummy and it can be served with a spoon.

Baked Cheese

Place a layer of cheese cut into small cubes in the bottom of a greased baking dish. Cover with bread crumbs. Sprinkle lightly with sugar. Continue with layers until the dish is filled, ending with bread crumbs. Cover with milk. Bake in a slow oven (about 300°) until the cheese is melted and the top is lightly browned.

Potato Pancakes

Mix 5 Irish potatoes that have been boiled and mashed with 3 eggs, 1 quart sweet milk, salt, and flour to make a batter. Fry on a hot griddle and serve at once.

Dumplings for Soup

Mix 2 eggs, 1½ cups flour, 1½ cups milk, and ¾ cup butter and place in a pan. Stir over heat until the mixture thickens and loosens from the pan. Let cool and stir in 2 more eggs. Drop into soup with a spoon. Boil in the soup for 10 minutes.

Schnitz and Dumplings

Boil schnitz [dried apples] until tender, seasoning them with bacon. Make dumplings by mixing 1 cup buttermilk, 1 teaspoon soda, 2 teaspoons baking powder, pinch of salt, and flour to make a stiff batter. Drop from a spoon on top of the schnitz and cook for 30 minutes.

Noodles

Beat 1 egg. Stir in flour until stiff. Add salt. Knead with hands until no more flour can be absorbed. Roll out as thin as paper, fold into a large roll, and slice very thin with a sharp knife. Scatter the noodles and allow to dry, rescattering them at intervals.

Potato Noodles

Mix 1 dozen boiled potatoes, salt, 2 eggs, ½ cup milk, and flour to make a stiff dough. Roll thin, cut into small pieces, and fry in plenty of lard.

Fried Cucumbers

These are nice to serve with fish.

Pare cucumbers and dice lengthwise, not too thin. Let stand in cold, slightly salted water for a few minutes and then dry with a cloth. Dip in eggs, then in bread crumbs. Fry in deep fat.

Rice Fish

Grind rice, then boil it in milk until soft and pour into cups to cool. Turn out on a flat dish when cold. Eat with cream, sugar, and cinnamon.

Suet Pudding

Mix 1 cup finely shredded suet [beef fat] with 1 cup sugar and 2 egg yolks. Add 1 cup milk and 3 cups flour and blend until smooth. Add 1 teaspoon cinnamon, ½ teaspoon salt, ½ teaspoon nutmeg, 1 teaspoon baking powder, and 2 beaten egg whites. Add 1 cup raisins and 1 cup currants that have been floured. Turn into a greased mold and boil for 3 hours.

Hog-Killing Pie

Because this was an economical dessert, it was used to feed the hands during hog-killing time.

Cook 1 pound dried peaches and remove skins. Mash until smooth and add 1 cup brown sugar. Place in piecrust and dot with butter. Then put on the top crust and bake in a medium-hot oven.

Cabbage Salad
(Tested)

The day I copied this recipe from an old, handwritten Moravian cookbook, I made it. Never has my cabbage been better dressed.

Beat 3 eggs until very light. Add 6 tablespoons vinegar, ⅛ teaspoon ground mustard, and butter the size of an egg (3 tablespoons). Cook over boiling water, stirring, until it begins to thicken. Cool. If too thick, thin with vinegar or water. When cold, pour over a finely chopped or shredded head of cabbage.

Moravian Slaw

This slaw, also called Dutch slaw, is served routinely at Moravian church suppers in Winston-Salem as well as in Moravian homes.

Add sugar to vinegar to make "that sweet-sour taste" and heat along with a few celery seeds, stirring to dissolve sugar. Do not dilute the vinegar. Remove from heat and cool.

Add chopped green pepper and pimento as desired to chopped or shredded cabbage in a glass jar. Cover with vinegar solution. Put on the lid and let stand. The slaw may be eaten right away but it is better after a day or so.

Cucumber Catsup

Finely chop 3 dozen large cucumbers and 8 onions. Add 1 cup salt and let stand for a short time. Press out the water and add ½ cup mustard seed, 2 tablespoons black pepper, and celery seed, with some strong vinegar to thin it. Put into bottles or jars, leaving some room at the top. Fill up bottles with vinegar and seal.

Moravian Spiced Apples

8 ripe apples (2½ to 3 inches)
1 pint boiling water
3 to 4 tablespoons sugar
Red coloring (about 1 teaspoon)
1 stick cinnamon
2 whole cloves

Wash and peel apples. Put apple peelings in a small kettle with boiling water. Cook until done. Remove peelings. Add sugar, red coloring, cinnamon, and cloves. Add apples, 3 or 4 at a time, simmer, and turn until done. Remove apples and cook those remaining. When all apples are cooked, place in a container and pour syrup over them. Let stand overnight, turning to color and flavor evenly. Drain and serve.

"Dinner's Ready"

MENU PATTERN

Once cooks traded the open fire for a wood range in the early 1900s, just what did the typical North Carolina family eat during normal periods—that is, when the crops were fairly good and folks were not in or recovering from a war or in the midst of a depression?

The seasons had a marked influence on the menu. Whatever was in season always appeared on the table in abundance—often a meal included the same food prepared in different ways. The food was served until it went out of season or everyone "got a bait of it." ("Getting a bait of" means eating all you can hold plus a little more.) In her book, *A Flower for My Mother* (1958), the late and great food writer, Clementine Paddleford, recalled:

When sweet corn was ready, the very first pick was made a meal all by itself, nothing but roasted ears and bowls of melted butter. We had no fancy corn holders. We just took the ear in hand. It seems to me we are losing much these days when we no longer make a touch contact with the good things of the earth.

By supper's end we were a well-buttered lot, greased from ear to ear. Sweet-corn kernels on clothes and hair, skin in our teeth. A splendid party.

The first strawberries of the season were guests of honor at a strawberry-shortcake supper. This fruit was seasonal then, no eating of berries around the calendar.

When the berries were full and red ripe, dropping to the ground under the leaves, my job was to pick half a milk-pail full for the first shortcake.

The shortcake was baked in a dripping pan, no mangy single biscuit business of "one for you" and "one for me." A rich biscuit dough was used, baked to flaky perfection, then turned to a turkey platter, split in two, the bottom half lavishly buttered. Over this went the crushed berries. On with the top half. More crushed berries over this; whole berries for decoration. The juice ran in rivulets, making a crimson lake in the plate. Hurry this to the table along with a water pitcher of cream. Little more was needed to make a meal. Enough shortcake was made for second and third helpings.

In an effort to learn more about the food habits of North Carolinians, I asked several prominent people for information. One of these individuals was Frank Crane, the state's commissioner of labor, who gave me an excellent account of his food preferences. In 1960 he wrote:

> . . . I should warn you that I hardly qualify as an epicure or gourmet.
>
> None of the fancy salads, frilly foods or soufflé stuff for me. Being a person with a hearty appetite, I go for just plain good eating. More of our food came from the land on the Union County farm where I grew up, and we worked hard for it. My liking for plenty of good plain food probably was formed by my boyhood experiences of getting up before light and following the furrow behind a mule all day.*
>
> By the time night came, after twelve or fourteen hours behind a plow, I just naturally felt a hankering for three or four plates full of blackeyed peas, six or seven pieces of cornbread and a half gallon of buttermilk. I certainly would not leave out ham and grits. You just can't beat a breakfast of buttermilk biscuits, country ham, red-eye gravy, hominy grits and eggs and coffee. . . .
>
> In the midst of a hot afternoon of picking cotton and pulling fodder, it was wonderful to sit down and tear into a big watermelon that had been cooled in the spring box for several hours. I am very fond of watermelon and still eat them.
>
> As a youth I became acquainted with poke salad, collards, [and]

*"Before light" means before daylight and "following the furrow" means plowing.

creasy greens along with apple cider, sassafras tea and persimmon and locust beer. On several occasions I enjoyed bear steak and venison, and I like chitlins for an occasional change. I have also been known to partake of possum and taters.

In households on the lower economic level, breakfast was (and still is) likely to consist of hot biscuits, ham gravy or cream gravy made from drippings of salt pork, and coffee. Sometimes there was also corn mush or grits. In the winter, both dinner and supper in poor homes might have been limited to a plate of pinto beans cooked with salt pork and perhaps hog meat of some type, biscuits, and sorghum. Greens, such as turnip tops, mustard greens, cabbage, and watercress, were added whenever available. In the summer, with the addition of fresh garden produce, the fare was better.

It is difficult to visualize the quantities of dried beans that were cooked in this state. Many rural families bought them by the 100-pound bag, and rarely a day of the year passed when a pot of beans was not cooked. The winter diet of low-income families, described above, was notably lacking in fresh fruit, fresh vegetables, and milk and often failed to provide a sufficient quantity of protein. This type of diet led to the label "Pellagra-ridden South," and to the idea that Tar Heels lived off "meat, meal, molasses, and moonshine."

According to Dr. Bertlyn Bosley, formerly of the Nutrition Division of the State Department of Health, turnip greens, collards, and mustard and other greens saved the day for us nutritionally. Were it not for the widespread consumption of these vitamin-rich foods, the nutritional state of natives would have been sad indeed. Foods were added as a household's economic status improved, but even if money were no object, many foods were still limited by the season.

● ● ● ● ●

BREAKFAST

Breakfast, in its simplest form, consisted of bread (usually hot biscuits), redeye gravy, sausage gravy, cream gravy, butter, preserves, jam, jelly, honey, and sorghum. A more lavish menu offered some of the following: eggs, country ham, sausage, fried streaked cured side meat, fresh or salted fish, corned mullet, applesauce, fried apples, fried tomatoes, fried corn mush, hominy grits, buckwheat cakes or griddle cakes, and waffles.

Eggs prepared in various ways were often served by the large platter. The most distinguished service of eggs I have ever seen was in the Shore Hotel in Rural Hall. The Shore Hotel, now demolished, was a railway hotel in that the train stopped at the nearby station and passengers got off for a meal at the hotel. The kitchen, presided over by a skilled black woman, was in the basement, and food went to the dining room on the first floor by way of a dumb waiter. Every morning there were three big platters of eggs—one fried sunnyside, one easy over, and the third scrambled.

Bacon, called breakfast bacon, of the kind we have in abundance today, was rarely served, as it had to be bought and was expensive. But strips of crisp salt pork with cream gravy were common. Frequently, our school lunch consisted of sausage cakes or patties that were left over from breakfast and put into biscuits. (We also ate cold baked sweet potatoes for lunch at school.)

Quite often we had griddle cakes, which sometimes were made from the overnight kind of batter with buckwheat flour (for recipe see index). A treat was Log Cabin syrup poured from a can in the shape of a log cabin. Other times, our syrup was sorghum or molasses. The first commercial mixes were for pancakes and buckwheat cakes—wonderful additions and our introduction to convenience foods.

In the spring and summer there would be fresh strawberries, raspberries, and peaches with pitchers of thick cream. Occasionally, as a child I had a serving of clabber cheese sprinkled with brown sugar. In season, there were also slices of cantaloupe or mushmelon. In winter, we had stewed prunes. There was orange juice only for a sick child.

When the first nip of autumn came, children were made to put on their long and dreaded winter underwear. This is when a double boiler of oatmeal appeared on the back of the stove. Both continued until the spring thaw. About the only ready-to-eat cereal we had in warm weather was cornflakes, priced at five cents per box, which was often served with sliced bananas.

Before the electric toaster, toast was not served routinely, as it had to be baked in the oven of the wood stove. Slices of bread were also browned on both sides in butter and topped with a fried egg, with the browned butter spooned on top. Not only was sliced bread unavailable before the electric slicer, but also loaves of white bread had to be bought at the grocery store.

The coffee pot stood on the wood stove all day long.

DINNER

Dinner was usually served in the middle of the day. This consisted of a tableful of food, with considerably more variety in summer than in winter.

A column written in May 1984 by Lewis Grizzard of the Register and Tribune Syndicate gives us an idea of what filled the more affluent table. Under the headline "Gastronomic Naivete," Mr. Grizzard wrote that when he dropped in on his mother for a meal, she would say, "We don't have much of anything to eat," in the pattern of the South. Grizzard called it an effort to point up being humble; he also called it "po-mouth." He noted that people who live in rural areas where they have gardens and home-canned foods really do not know what it is like to eat in the city. His mother's not-so-much-to-eat table offered eight different kinds of fresh vegetables, vine-ripened tomatoes, "those wonderful little garden onions," creamed potatoes, country-fried steak smothered in delicious brown gravy, buttered corn bread, homemade yeast rolls, iced tea, pies, and cake.

In most homes it was the custom to fill the noonday table with selections from the following when in season: potatoes—mashed, boiled, salad, scalloped, fried, cooked with green peas; green peas, peas with dumplings; fried okra, okra stewed with tomatoes; green beans, green beans with potatoes or corn; squash, applesauce, fried or stewed apples; creamed carrots, turnips, or lima beans; lima beans with corn; black-eyed peas; cabbage—boiled, fried, or in slaw; corn on the cob, fried corn, stewed corn, corn pudding; greens; pickled beets; sliced tomatoes; sliced cucumbers; green onions; and chopped onions in vinegar. There were always breads, especially corn muffins or sticks. Among the desserts were pies and cobblers.

In winter, dinner was likely to include macaroni and cheese, pinto or other dried beans, chopped onions in vinegar, scalloped tomatoes or home-canned tomatoes served in individual bowls with a sprinkling of vinegar and sugar, relishes, and pickles.

Dinner might offer a main dish, most often chicken prepared in some way, but during the week the meal was mostly vegetarian. There might be a platter of fried pork chops or pork tenderloin available after hog killing, spareribs, fried country ham, or meat loaf.

Seafood was abundant on the coast but not inland; some fresh fish came from fish ponds and streams. Grocery stores had wooden buckets of salted fish. Salted fish, after soaking overnight in cold water, was sautéed in butter and served for breakfast.

Quail on toast, rabbit, and frog legs were often on the menu.

SUNDAY DINNER: THE WEEK'S MAJOR MEAL

A week, from Monday morning until Sunday noon, worked up to a mighty crescendo in the same way as a symphony, the culmination being Sunday dinner, a culinary event that was like a party. Not only was the food superb and more than plentiful but also the meal included an element of surprise in that it was never certain who was coming. The custom was to prepare for all who might be there.

Adults filled the dining table for the first sitting, more adults and older children for the second sitting, and mostly children for the third sitting. I was in college before I ever sat at the second or first sitting. For the first crossing of the Atlantic in that old and majestic ship of the Cunard line, the *Queen Mary*, the one thing I thoroughly understood upon boarding was signing up for the first or second sitting for dinner. And it was only when I was in graduate school in Philadelphia that I learned—much to my surprise—that everybody did not have Sunday dinner. When we visited relatives, they had Sunday dinner. When I went home with college friends for a visit, their families also had Sunday dinner. In Philadelphia, people ate a main meal on Sunday and often invited guests but they never served a tableful of food.

Sunday Dinner Menu

At the time of the 1986 North Carolina Barbecue Championship Cook Off, where the guest list included a number of members of the national news media, the North Carolina commissioner of agriculture, James A. Graham, looked for a place to entertain the group and highlight his Goodness Grows in North Carolina promotional campaign. The home of Danny Rambeaut in Raleigh was selected as the setting for the Flavors of North Carolina menu. Rambeaut is a florist with a full-scale catering business. This was his Sunday dinner menu: fried chicken with cream gravy, country ham with city redeye gravy, crispy fatback, candied sweet potatoes,* black-eyed peas,* butter beans,* green beans,* collard greens,* cucumbers and tomatoes, buttermilk biscuits and corn bread, banana pudding and sweet potato pie, and sweetened iced tea.

As for fresh vegetables, a short time ago Phyllis C. Richman, who writes about food for the *Washington Post*, reviewed Ben Barker's Magnolia Grill in Durham. She noted: "Many of his vegetables appear on the table the same day they are picked. One summertime special is a vegetable plate—'That's what my grandmother used to find for lunch'—of succotash, green beans with bacon fat, tomatoes sliced with cucumbers and red onions and corn pudding."

Other dinner highlights were, of course, at Thanksgiving and Christmas. A turkey rarely if ever appeared at any time other than Thanksgiving. That initial appearance was a moment of glory. For days afterward, leftover turkey was served in every conceivable form—indeed, we were glad to see the end of the bird until another year.

Commercially canned green or English peas were also on the Thanksgiving menu. They were such a treat—the only other green peas we had came from the garden when in season—that to this day I never open a can of peas without some feeling of awe.

•   •   •   •   •

SUPPER

Supper was often a "set-out" or warmed-over meal. In the summer, the foods left over from dinner were left sitting out or were "set out." In the winter, they would be warmed before they were served. A new pan of hot biscuits and a platter of country ham might be added, as well as— in winter—soup or oyster stew. We made wonderful cream of tomato soup from home-canned tomatoes; the secret was to keep the soup from curdling. A special treat was canned alphabet soup, a can or two diluted with enough water to feed half a dozen people.

At best, a bowl of oyster stew contained two or three oysters; oyster crackers dumped into the hot soup acquired some of the taste of the oysters. The memory of that oyster stew prompts me now to put a half pint of oysters into each bowl of stew.

*For recipe see index.

Another dish on the supper menu was creamed dried beef, made from slices of dried beef cut from a cured round of beef that hung in the grocery store. Fried frog legs and braised rabbit with a superb flavor were other treats. Men often went frog gigging (spearing) in the dark of night. They seemed to know where to go and almost never came back without a catch. Braised rabbit were also common. A favorite and a luxury were salmon cakes made from a can of salmon costing five cents per can.

EIGHT

The two leading main dishes in North Carolina are fried chicken with cream gravy and fried country ham with redeye gravy. If it were possible to tabulate the total number of servings of each down through the years in areas where the two have been abundantly available, I doubt if the difference would be much more than a ham or a chicken on either side.

In addition to ham, all kinds of fresh and cured pork are popular. Pork chops are coated in seasoned flour and fried. Pork shoulder and fresh pork ham are baked or fried. Sausage, often hot with red pepper, is a breakfast favorite.

A few years ago, mutton was quite common throughout the state. However, the smell of elderly sheep cooking has turned more than one individual against lamb forever. Brunswick stew is another top favorite.

About the only way to tenderize the type of beef available before the days of the aged western variety was to boil it for half a day. Even then the finished product was as stringy as a piece of raveled hemp rope. Many of the sliced pieces of this beef became fried beefsteak. The beefsteak was prepared in the same way as country-style steak. Flour, salt, and pepper were beaten into the meat with a mallet or the handle of a knife (the practice continues in many homes). This beating was so vigorous that one often heard the sound of a neighbor beating her steak.

The steak was then browned on both sides in hot fat in a black skillet, then covered with water and simmered over low heat until tender. It was only after World War I that more than a few people knew what it was to have a juicy slab of roasted prime ribs of beef or tender broiled steaks placed before them.

• • • • •

COOKING METHODS

FRYING

The black iron skillet was the most used piece of cooking equipment in the kitchen. Some kitchens had several because of the large percentage of foods that were fried—meats, poultry, fish, vegetables, breads, and pies.

At restaurants, especially those along the coast, all the fish was fried until at least several years after World War II, when broiling became popular. A plate of fried fish, fried hushpuppies or other fried corn bread, and fried potatoes was not unusual.

PARBOILING

A modern cookbook defines *parboil* this way: To cook briefly in boiling water or seasoned liquid. But parboiling has deeper meanings. Basically, parboiling means to precook. Different foods are precooked for different reasons. Some meat, fowl, and game are precooked to tenderize them and remove the wild taste.

The kind of beef generally available before World War II was not dry roasted as beef is today, because it was tough and needed simmering to tenderize. The cooked beef was browned in a hot oven. The broth from cooking the beef added flavor to the potatoes, carrots, and onions placed around the beef during browning.

Some fowl will never get tender by dry roasting. An example is a large goose I had in the oven for some three hours; nothing happened during that time except that the goose's skin became somewhat more taut, with no signs of ever becoming tender. I removed the goose from the oven and put it into a pot with water. After a couple of hours, it seemed tender. Browning in the oven finished the cooking process.

A hen or a turkey might be parboiled—but more for the abundance of broth for dressing and gravy than for a more tender bird. The cooked, drained bird (stuffed or unstuffed) is placed in a baking pan on the stuffing desired and browned in a hot oven as the stuffing cooks. Rubbing the breast with a stick of butter aids browning.

Greens such as turnip, mustard, and collard greens are parboiled in salted water to remove their characteristically dank taste and to tenderize.

. . . . .

CHICKEN

Fried Chicken

There are dozens of ways to fry a chicken but I do not believe that you can improve on this method.

Cut the chicken into pieces and coat in a paper bag that contains flour, salt, pepper, and paprika (the paprika gives the chicken a prettier color). In a heavy black skillet, have about ½ inch of hot fat—that may be lard or shortening. Many of the older cooks use part butter, which they claim makes the chicken brown better. Brown pieces slowly on all sides over moderate heat. Drain and serve, or steam first, if desired.

To steam, add a little cold water to the chicken. Cover tightly and allow to cook over low heat for about 15 minutes. Remove cover and continue cooking until the water has evaporated and the chicken recrisps. Serve with cream gravy.

Chicken Cream Gravy

Cream gravy is nothing more than a medium white sauce flavored with the chicken drippings. Use 1 tablespoon fat and 2 tablespoons flour to each cup of liquid. Strain off the fat in which the chicken was fried and use the brown portions in the gravy.

There are two ways to add the flour to the fat. It can be either stirred into the drippings in the pan or made into a paste with a portion of the cold liquid. The liquid may be either milk or water. Do not add the flour or the flour-liquid mixture to a hot pan. Have the pan moderately warm and stir constantly to blend well. Season to taste with salt and pepper. Thin a little, if desired.

Giblet Gravy

Follow the recipe for chicken cream gravy. Cook giblets in a separate pan. The liver takes less time than the others, so drop it in near the end. Chop giblets and add to gravy.

Baked Hen

The modern way of roasting a chicken is to put the prepared bird (stuffed or unstuffed) in an open pan and then roast it at 325° until done. That way sometimes you have tender meat, sometimes you do not. Using the old-fashioned method, you need never worry about tenderness. This is the way to do it.

Place the prepared bird in a pot and cover with cold water. Add salt and seasonings as desired. Bring to a boil and simmer (not boil) until there are indications of tenderness. Remove from broth, drain, and place in a roasting pan. Stuff with sage-rich dressing, using some of the dressing to cover the bottom of the pan. Brush hen with melted butter and bake in a slow oven (about 325°) for 1 hour or until bird is browned and dressing is done.

Skim off fat; boil down broth and thicken with flour paste to make gravy. Diced cooked giblets and chopped cooked eggs are often added to the gravy.

Corn Bread Dressing

8 cups corn bread crumbs mixed with biscuit
or light bread crumbs
1 onion, chopped
1 to 2 teaspoons salt
½ teaspoon pepper
Sage to taste
⅔ cup melted butter
Hot water or broth to moisten

Stir ingredients until well mixed and stuff fowl, or turn into a greased pan and bake.

Mrs. Alma Miller's Dressing for Baked Chicken

Collect leftover bread—including corn bread—and toast until dry. Run the dry bread through the meat grinder.

To about 2 gallons of dry bread crumbs, add about 1½ cups celery and 1 cup onions, both minced finely. Add about 1 cup pure chicken fat skimmed from the top of the broth. Here is the secret: Knead and work the fat into the crumbs until a small ball held in the hand breaks and falls apart when touched with the finger.

Season mixture with salt and pepper and add cold water to moisten. Pat down to make a layer about an inch thick in a baking pan. Bake and cut into squares to serve.

HARD-TIMES DRESSING

In the 1952 presidential election Senator Russell Long of Louisiana said that if the Republicans won, the American people would go back on a diet of "fried rabbit and peckerwood dressing." Senator Long had several requests for the dressing recipe but was unable to supply one. Mrs. Thad M. Reese of Boonville offered the following information to Senator Long:

> During the days of the Hoover administration, times were so bad that even the animals didn't get enough to eat so the meat didn't have much flavor.
>
> Folks didn't have enough money to buy light bread to make dressing so they made it out of cornmeal. Things were so bad in some cases that cooks had to resort to using sawdust to stretch the cornmeal.
>
> There weren't any good rich meat drippings to make gravy so they made what was called saw mill gravy from fatback, flour and water.

The recipe follows.

Fried Rabbit and Peckerwood Dressing

Catch a rabbit and skin it. Throw it in the pot and stew. Drain, coat with flour, and fry in lard.

Take some corn, nubbins and all, to the mill and have it ground or pound it on a stone to make meal. Pour off some of the water in which the rabbit was stewed and bring it to a boil. Add cornmeal to make a mush. If you do not have enough cornmeal, finish with nice clean white sawdust.

Run out in the backyard and grab a twig or two off the sage bush. Rub it to pulverize and add to the mush together with a chopped onion, salt, and pepper. Throw in a handful of peeled, chopped chestnuts. Turn into a greased iron skillet or bread pan and bake in a hot oven.

George Kempton's Brunswick Stew
(Tested)

Was there ever a better dish than Brunswick stew served with cole slaw and crisp corn sticks? The late George Kempton, Sr., was in real estate in Winston-Salem. His Brunswick stew, made with this recipe, was the best.

1 large stewing or baking hen (5 pounds or more)
1 pound lean veal or beef
1 rabbit or squirrel, if available
Water to cover
2 large potatoes, peeled and diced
1 large onion, diced
4 cups whole-kernel fresh white corn
4 cups small fresh lima beans
2 cans (8 ounces each) tomato sauce
3 teaspoons salt or to taste
½ teaspoon black pepper
½ teaspoon hot pepper sauce or to taste
1 tablespoon Worcestershire sauce
⅓ cup butter

Stew chicken and meat together in salted water to cover until the meat falls from the bones. Cool; shred with the fingers, discarding skin, bones, and fat. Put meat back into strained broth and continue to simmer.

In another pot, cook potatoes with onion, corn, lima beans, and tomato sauce in water to cover for about 20 minutes or until the potatoes are done. Combine with meat. The mixture will be thin like soup. Simmer for several hours, stirring occasionally, until thickened. Watch to prevent burning. Season with salt, pepper, hot pepper sauce, and Worcestershire. Add butter. Makes 4 quarts.

Baked Chicken Hash

Make up your favorite dressing and add coarse slivers of leftover chicken to it. Bake in a greased pan at about 400° until brown and crusty on top. Serve with chicken gravy.

North Carolina Chicken Pie

This is truly the old-fashioned way to make chicken pie. Some years ago the *Woman's Home Companion* awarded Mrs. Zeb Conley of Macon County a prize for this recipe.

Dress and singe a fowl. Put in a saucepan with boiling water to cover and add 1 sliced carrot, 1 stalk celery, 1 sprig parsley, and 1 sliced onion. Bring to a boil, cover, and simmer until the fowl is tender, allowing about 30 minutes per pound. When half done, season with salt and pepper.

Line a shallow baking dish with pastry, then a layer of cut-up boned chicken, then a layer of pastry. Boil chicken stock down to 3 cups, strain, and skim off most of the fat. Mix 4 tablespoons flour to a smooth paste with cold water and add to the stock. Bring to a boil, stirring constantly, and add to the chicken in the baking dish. Put in the oven and bake until the bottom crust is nearly done. Add remainder of stock, if any, cover with pastry, and cook slowly until the top crust is brown.

Chicken Layer Pot Pie

Cut a young chicken into pieces and cook. Cut corn from 8 roasting ears. Make regular pastry.

Put a layer of chicken in a pot. Cover with a layer of pastry. Dot with butter (use a lot of butter). Add a layer of corn and sprinkle with salt and pepper. Continue with layers.

Pour in enough broth or water to cover. Cover pot and boil for ½ hour.

Chicken and Dumplings
(Tested)

1 stewing chicken (5 pounds)
7 cups water
4 celery leaves
2 onion slices

2 bay leaves
Salt
Flour
2 cups milk
Dumplings (recipe follows)

Cut chicken into pieces. To water in pot, add chicken, celery, onion, bay leaves, and 1 teaspoon salt; bring to a boil. Reduce to simmer and cook for 2 to 3 hours, or until chicken is tender. Remove from heat; chill. Skim off fat; reserve.

Bring broth to a boil; strain. Reserve chicken pieces. Measure 2 cups strained broth into a kettle. Blend ⅓ cup chicken fat and ½ cup flour. Gradually add some of the broth, blending, then pour in the remaining broth. Add milk. Cook, stirring, until smooth and thickened. Season with about 1 teaspoon salt or to taste.

Make dumplings. Add chicken to kettle and bring to a boil. Then dip a tablespoon into the gravy in the kettle and then into the dumpling batter; do not make dumplings too large. Drop dumplings into kettle, trying to place them where the chicken pieces protrude from the gravy. Between each dumpling, dip spoon into gravy.

When dumplings are all in the pot, cover and steam chicken, dumplings, and gravy for 20 minutes without lifting the lid.

Dumplings or "Slickums"

Many prefer these flat, rolled dumplings to the puffy, rounded dropped ones.

2 cups sifted self-rising flour
⅓ cup lard or shortening
¼ to ½ cup milk

Cut lard and shortening into flour until the mixture is crumbly. Add milk to make a stiff dough. Use either sweet milk or buttermilk as you prefer—buttermilk makes a more tender dumpling.

Turn out dough on a lightly floured board and roll ⅛-inch thick. Cut into strips about 4 inches long and ½-inch wide. Drop dumplings into the buttery rich broth of stewed chicken. Cover tightly and simmer gently for 15 to 20 minutes. Makes 6 servings.

Hot Broth Dumplings

To 3 cups sifted self-rising flour, add 1 cup boiled chicken broth. Let stand until cold. Stir in 1 beaten egg. If dough is too soft to roll, add more flour; if too stiff, thin with milk. Roll out, cut, and drop into hot broth. Cover tightly and cook for 15 minutes.

Oven-Barbecued Chicken

In fat in a heavy skillet brown pieces of chicken that have been coated in seasoned flour. Remove chicken and arrange in one layer in a shallow baking pan. Cover with sauce for barbecued spareribs (for recipe see index) and bake at 325° for 45 minutes or until the chicken is tender.

Chicken Bod (Chicken and Rice Cooked in a Pot)

Completely cover a hen or a fryer with water and stew until done. When the chicken is done, season with salt and pepper. Add butter and 3 cups washed raw rice. Bring to a boil and stir only once as it begins to boil. Continue cooking over low heat until the rice is done.

• • • • •

PORK

Fried Country Ham

The aroma of frying country ham surrounds the house and goes out into the street, attracting the attention of passersby. It is an arresting aroma—one that lingers and is hard to ignore. The experience of walking by a house from which emanates the smell of frying ham is enough to make one dissatisfied with anything else that might appear on the dinner table at home.

To fry the ham, lay the slices in a cold heavy black skillet. Cook over moderate heat, turning, until ham is done and fat is crisp. Serve with redeye gravy, grits, and hot biscuits.

To make red gravy, drain off a portion of any excess fat. To the remaining portion add a little water. Bring to a boil and serve.

Note: Some old folks add about 1 tablespoon of strong coffee to the gravy.

Country Ham with City Redeye Gravy

4 slices (¼-inch thick) country ham
2 tablespoons butter
1 teaspoon sugar
½ cup water

Place ham slices in a cold skillet. Set heat at medium. Cook ham on one side for 2 to 4 minutes, or until lightly browned. (Do not overcook or ham will become hard.) Add butter to skillet, turn ham, and cook on second side for 2 to 4 minutes, or until lightly browned. Remove ham from skillet. Without loosening particles from pan, pour drippings into a gravy boat. Add sugar to pan and when it begins to brown, rapidly stir in water, loosening particles as you stir. Bring to a boil. Return drippings to pan, stir with sugar-water mixture, and serve. Makes 4 servings.

Note: Redeye gravy traditionally is served over ham slices, grits, or hot buttermilk biscuits.

Baked Country Ham

To bake a country ham, boil first.

Scrape off mold and pepper. Wash with soap and hot water. Rinse well. Put in a pot, skin side down, and cover with cold water. Bring to a boil, reduce heat, and simmer for 18 to 20 minutes per pound. Let ham cool in the liquid in which it was cooked.

Remove the skin. Score fat and rub with a mixture of 1 part fine bread crumbs to 2 parts brown sugar. Stick with whole cloves. Bake in a slow oven (about 325°) until well heated and browned.

Another Way of Boiling Country Ham

Soak ham in cold water overnight. Drain and place in a container. Cover with water to which 1 cup brown sugar and 1 cup vinegar have been added. Bring to a boil. Reduce heat and simmer for about 12 minutes per pound. Allow to stand in liquid until cool. Store in refrigerator overnight before slicing.

Barbecued Spareribs
(Tested)

I guess this is one of the best dishes ever to be carried to the table. Because the ribs are usually fatty, it is a good idea to put them in a shallow pan in a 425° oven for 15 to 20 minutes, or until a good portion of the fat runs off, before adding the sauce. Drain off fat.

1 onion, chopped
1 green pepper, chopped
2 tablespoons bacon drippings
2 tablespoons vinegar
2 tablespoons lemon juice
2 tablespoons brown sugar
2 cups tomato sauce
2 teaspoons salt
1 cup catsup
1 tablespoon Worcestershire sauce
Pinch of ginger and cloves
Black pepper
Tabasco sauce
½ cup diced celery
4 pounds spareribs

Lightly brown onion and green pepper in fat. Add all remaining ingredients except ribs and simmer until blended (about 10 minutes). Pour sauce over the top of ribs in a baking dish. Bake in a moderate oven (about 350°) for 2 to 3 hours, or until ribs are tender, basting occasionally. Serves 4 hungry people and 5 who are moderately hungry.

BACKBONES

Backbones are quite meaty. They are usually stewed until tender, sometimes along with a few spareribs. They may be served stewed, or drained and browned in the oven before serving.

FRIED FATBACK WITH CREAM GRAVY

Crispy fried slices of fatback or salt pork served with cream gravy and boiled new potatoes may not be eating "high off the hog," but it is a mighty tasty dish. The pure fatback or fat meat, streaked with a little lean, is cut into thin strips and fried slowly until crisp. The fat is used for seasoning vegetables, and the crisp slices are served with cream gravy made from the drippings.

Sausage and Sweets

This is the best combination of sausage and sweets you ever tasted— one with a truly old-time flavor.

For each serving, peel a medium sweet potato and slice into thirds lengthwise. Shape good pork sausage to make 2 flat patties about ½-inch thick or the size of the sweet potato slices. Place 2 patties, sandwich fashion, between 3 slices of potato, with potato slices on the outside.

Wrap in foil and squeeze openings together tightly. Place on a baking sheet and bake in a 350° oven for 1 hour, turning once during baking.

Nahunta Pork Center's Sausage

This is the recipe used when Alma Pierce, mother of Mack Pierce of the Nahunta Pork Center in Nahunta, carried sausage to the curb market in Goldsboro over thirty years ago.

16 pounds pork meat
5 tablespoons salt
3 tablespoons sage
2 tablespoons red pepper
1 tablespoon black pepper

Grind all ingredients together. Makes 16 pounds.

Sausage Gravy

1 pound pork sausage meat
¼ cup flour
2 cups milk
Salt and pepper (optional)

Cook pork sausage in a skillet, stirring until browned. Remove from heat. Pour off all but ¼ cup drippings. Blend in flour and gradually stir in milk. Return to heat and cook, stirring constantly, until mixture thickens. If needed, add salt and pepper. Makes about 2½ cups.

Ruth P. Casa-Emellos's Scrapple

After a career as a home economist for the *New York Times*, Ruth Parrish Casa-Emellos, a Moravian from Winston-Salem, retired to her native city.

4 large pig's knuckles
½ pound lean pork
3 quarts water
1 tablespoon salt
1 hot red pepper (optional)
½ teaspoon freshly ground black pepper
½ to 1 teaspoon sage
2¾ cups cornmeal

Simmer the knuckles and pork in water with the salt and red pepper until the meat almost falls from the bones—about 2½ hours.

Remove the meat from the broth, discard the bones, and grind the meat. Strain the broth and skim off the fat, if desired. Measure 2 quarts of broth into a large, heavy kettle. Reserve the remaining broth. Return the meat to the 2 quarts of broth and add black pepper and sage. Bring to a rapid boil.

Mix the cornmeal with 1 quart of the remaining cool broth, add to the boiling broth and meat, and cook, stirring, until thickened. Place on an asbestos pad over the lowest heat, cover, and cook, stirring often, for about 30 minutes longer. Adjust the seasonings. Turn into 2 large bread pans; cool. Cover and chill overnight.

To serve, cut into ½-inch slices, coat with flour, and brown over moderately high heat in butter or other fat. Makes about 12 servings.

Brains Scrambled with Eggs
(Tested)

1 pound brains
1 quart water
1 tablespoon vinegar
Salt
6 eggs
½ cup milk
¼ teaspoon pepper
3 tablespoons bacon drippings

Wash brains and simmer for 20 minutes in water to which vinegar and 1 teaspoon salt have been added. Drain, remove membrane, and separate into small pieces.

Beat eggs and add milk, ¾ teaspoon salt or to taste, and pepper. Cook brains in bacon drippings until lightly browned. Add egg mixture and cook slowly, stirring occasionally, until eggs are done. Makes 6 to 8 servings.

Note: After precooking, brains may also be served in a rich cream sauce, dipped in eggs and bread crumbs and fried in a small amount of fat, or dipped in melted butter and broiled.

Corned Ham

12 to 14 pounds fresh ham
1 to ½ pounds iodized salt

At both ends of the ham, take a sharp knife and carve around the bone, forming a cavity approximately 6 to 8 inches deep. Pack cavities with salt and place ham in a roaster, skin side down, on a layer of salt. Cover thoroughly with a thick layer of the remaining salt. Place a lid on the roaster and refrigerate for 10 to 14 days.

Remove the ham from the roaster and wash off the salt. Boil in clear water until tender.

CHITTERLINGS

For the preservation of the practice of eating "chittlin's and 'possums," there was an organization called the Surry County 'Possum and Chitterlin' Club. This club had regular dinner meetings at which these foods, plus any number of others, were served.

Sautéed Chitterlings

Cut prepared chitterlings into small pieces. Turn into a black skillet that contains a little hot lard. Fry until brown. Season with salt and pepper. Serve with vinegar, if desired.

Batter-Fried Chitterlings

Prepare the chitterlings for cooking. Cover with water and parboil until tender. Cool.

Make a batter of buckwheat flour, salt, soda, black pepper, and 1 egg. Dip chitterlings into batter and fry in an inch or more of hot fat in a heavy skillet until golden brown.

HOG MAW

Hog maw is the stomach of the animal. It is prepared in the same way as chitterlings. And also like chitterlings, the smell lingers on.

Haslet Stew

Haslet is the edible portion of the viscera of a hog including the liver, heart, and lights (lungs).

To prepare the stew, cut the best part of the liver and heart into small pieces, using only a small portion of the lights. Wash well and place in a heavy pot. Cover with water. Bring to a boil and boil for 5 minutes. Pour off the water and cover with fresh water.

Add 2 to 3 pounds backbones and spareribs cut into small pieces. Season with salt, black pepper, red pepper, and sage, and cook until tender. About 30 minutes before serving, add small cornmeal dumplings and cook in a tightly covered pot until done.

Hog Head Mush

Cook a hog's head in boiling salted water until very tender. Cool. Remove all bones and skin. Pull meat into fine shreds with the fingers. Add red pepper, salt, pepper, and sage, just as in making sausage.

Place meat and about 1 quart of the strained broth in a kettle. Bring to a boil. Stir in cornmeal to make a stiff mush. Stir well and pour into a pan. Chill. Slice and cook in drippings until brown on both sides.

Boiled Pig's Feet

Place clean pig's feet in a pot and cover with cold water. Bring to a rapid boil. Reduce heat and simmer for 4 to 6 hours, or until tender. Near the end of the cooking time, add salt to taste to the water.

Fried Pig's Feet

Cool boiled pig's feet slightly in stock. Drain well and dry. Coat in seasoned flour and brown on all sides in a small amount of fat in a heavy skillet.

Pickled Pig's Feet

Drain boiled pig's feet and cover with hot vinegar (plain or spiced). Cover and store in the refrigerator for 2 days or longer.

Pigtail Stew

2 pounds midlin' meat [fat cut from the middle of a hog],
salt pork, or streak of lean
5 pounds pig's tails, pig's feet, pig's ears, hog
liver, and spareribs, mixed
Salt and black pepper
2 to 3 pods hot red pepper
Bunch of fresh collards
6 sweet potatoes
Meat skins and bacon grease
Corn dodgers with cracklings

Cold buttermilk
Butter

Start with 2 large pots. Put the midlin' meat in a pot with water to cover. Bring to a boil; reduce to simmer and cook.

Meanwhile, clean pig's tails, feet, and ears, being careful to remove hair bristles on the ear tips and tails. Put all the meat in a second pot with water to cover. Add salt and pepper to taste. Clip in hot red pepper pods. Bring to a boil. Reduce to simmer and cook until all the meat is done.

Wash and cook collard greens, removing and discarding the stems. Clip leaves into the pot with the midlin' meat. Add salt to taste and clip in a little red pepper from a pod. Cover and cook collards slowly until done.

Grease the outside of washed sweet potatoes with meat skins, the skins remaining after salt pork has been cut away, or bacon grease. Roast potatoes slowly "to bring out the candy in them." (Candy is the sweetness.)

When other food is almost done, make corn dodgers. Put cornmeal in a bowl. Add a handful of cracklings and salt to taste. Add water to make a stiff dough. Shape into dodgers or patties by hand. In a little bacon grease in a hot, heavy black iron skillet, sauté the dodgers until brown on both sides.

To serve, put 2 or 3 big spoonfuls of collards on each plate. Add a sweet potato and 2 or 3 big spoonfuls of stew. Pass the corn dodgers. Have a cake of butter on the table and a glass of buttermilk at each plate.

NORTH CAROLINA BOILED DINNER

This dish consists of boiled fresh pork (ribs, backbone, or loin), greens, and potatoes topped with cornmeal dumplings.

Boiled Pot

This dish is a North Carolina version of the New England boiled dinner.

1 ham hock (2 if small)
2 medium heads of cabbage
4 white potatoes

4 ears of corn
4 carrots
Cornmeal dumplings

Boil ham hock until tender. Cut cabbage in quarters or eighths. Add vegetables to pot. When boiling, drop cornmeal dumplings around the edge of the boiling pot. Reduce heat and cook until vegetables are done.

CORNMEAL DUMPLINGS

Combine 1 cup cornmeal and 1 teaspoon salt with enough water to make dough that can be shaped with the hands. Shape dumplings larger than biscuits.

• • • • •

BEEF

Country-Style Steak

Because of the tough variety of beef that once was available, this dish was popular, as was any meat served with gravy. The best cut for this recipe is round steak.

Pound flour that has been seasoned with salt and pepper into the meat. Brown on both sides in a small amount of fat over moderate heat— a heavy skillet is ideal for this job.

To make a rich gravy, add water gradually and simmer until the meat is fork tender. For an even richer gravy, add a beef bouillon cube dissolved in hot water. Thicken gravy with a paste made of flour and cold water, if needed.

Skillet Hash

In most sections of the state, roast beef often ended up in hash.

4 tablespoons butter or meat drippings
2 cups chopped cooked meat
2 cups chopped cooked potatoes
½ cup finely chopped onion
¼ cup light cream
Salt (optional)

Pepper
Chopped parsley

Melt fat in a heavy skillet. Mix remaining ingredients except parsley. Dump mixture into the skillet and spread out evenly. Cook over low heat, shaking pan occasionally.

When hash is browned on bottom, fold like an omelet and turn out on a platter. Sprinkle with chopped parsley. Makes 6 servings.

Corned Beef

For 25 pounds of beef, use 1 ounce saltpeter, 1 pound brown sugar, and 1 quart salt. Rub the mixture into beef. Place meat in a crock or bowls. Turn every day. Use no water. The juice from the beef makes the liquid.

The corn beef will be ready to use in about 1 week. It will keep for some time if stored in a cool place.

Spiced Beef

This recipe was a favorite of Marcia Albertson, Pasquotank County's first home economics agent. It is still enjoyed for special occasions like Thanksgiving and Christmas.

25 pounds top round of beef
2 ounces saltpeter
1 quart salt
1 quart black molasses
2 ounces ground cloves
2 ounces ground allspice
1 ounce nutmeg

Rub beef with saltpeter and salt. Cover with remaining mixture and allow to stand for 21 days in a crock. Turn each day. Tie up meat in cheesecloth and put in cold water to cover, using part of the remaining marinade. Boil for 20 minutes to the pound. Cool in the liquid in which it was cooked.

· · · · ·

GAME

Few old-time cooks would ever think of cooking game without parboiling it first. With some game, that is the only way in the world to obtain a tender product.

The game is parboiled in salted water until there are indications of tenderness. It is then drained and placed, stuffed or unstuffed, uncovered, in a roasting pan. The cooking process is finished and the game browned by baking in an oven set at 325° or hotter. Some cooks finish off the cooking in a 400° oven.

Wild Ducks or Geese

Soak dressed birds in soda water (1 heaping tablespoon soda to 1 dishpan of water) for ½ hour. Wash and season with salt and pepper. Place on a rack in a roaster. Lay 3 strips of salt pork across the breast.

Add a couple of peeled onions and 1 to 2 cups boiling water. Cover and cook in a slow oven (about 325°) until tender. Pour off liquid. Stuff and bake, uncovered, for another hour.

Wild Pheasant

Chop 1 small onion, ½ medium peeled apple, and the pheasant liver and place in the cavity of each bird. Rub the outside with seasoned flour and brown lightly in hot butter in a heavy skillet. Remove to a deep pan with a tight cover.

Mix 1 cup chicken broth with 2 cups dry white wine and pour in pan. Cover and bake at 325° for 2 hours, or until the pheasant is tender. Remove pheasant. Just before serving, stir 1 cup heavy cream into pan and heat but do not boil. Thicken with a little flour paste, if desired.

Possums

Scald a possum with lye, scrape off the hair, and dress whole, leaving on the head and tail. Rub well with salt and set in a cool place over night.

Place in a large pan and add 2 pints of water. When about half baked, fill with a dressing of bread. After returning to the pan, place sweet potatoes, pared, around the possum. Bake all a light brown, basting frequently with the gravy. When served, place either a sweet potato or an apple in its mouth.

Meat Pie

This recipe is from a Blowing Rocker (a native of Blowing Rock).

Parboil any kind of game and pour into a pastry shell. Season with butter, salt, pepper, and grated onion. Add the top crust and pour ½ pint of thick cream over it. Bake until brown.

VENISON

Venison should be allowed to hang and age for a week or two before cooking. It is also a good idea to marinate it for 24 hours before cooking. For the marinade, add a couple of bay leaves and a couple of sliced onions to vinegar.

Broil the loins, roast the hams, and braise or stew the other parts just as you would beef.

Roast Venison

Place strips of salt pork on the meat. Roast, uncovered, in a 300° to 325° oven for about 35 to 45 minutes per pound.

Broiled Venison Steaks

Dot the steaks with butter and broil to the desired degree of doneness. Season with salt and pepper and serve. Most people prefer venison a little underdone.

Venison Steaks

Wash and sprinkle the steaks with salt. Wrap them tightly with a cut onion in oiled foil. Chill overnight. Heat pan and sear meat, add 1 cup hot water, and cook slowly until well done.

Cover with a sauce made with 1 medium onion, 1 stalk celery, ½ cup chili sauce, and the juice of half a lemon.

Fried Quail

Coat quail in seasoned flour and place in a skillet about half full of hot fat. When quail begins to brown, reduce heat and continue cooking until brown and tender.

Smothered Quail on Toast

Coat quail in seasoned flour. Fry in a small amount of fat in a heavy skillet until browned. Add a little water. Cover and continue cooking until tender. Thicken liquid and serve over quail on toast.

Broiled Quail

Season small quail with salt and pepper and rub the insides with soft butter. Wrap a strip of bacon around each and fasten with a toothpick. Broil under low heat, turning, for 20 minutes, or until done. Serve on toast.

RABBIT AND SQUIRREL

Rabbit and squirrel are prepared in ways similar to those used for chicken. A rabbit is often parboiled and then coated with seasoned flour and fried, or fried and then braised. It is also made into stews and pies.

Squirrel stew is probably the most popular squirrel dish. It is made like chicken stew but with an abundance of butter.

Chestnuts for Poultry and Game

Peel and skin chestnuts and put in a covered baking dish. Sprinkle with salt, pepper, minced celery, and minced carrots. Cover with rich chicken broth. Cover and bake at 325° for 1 hour.

Wine Sauce for Game

Mix ½ cup currant jelly, 2 tablespoons butter, 2 tablespoons lemon juice, rind of 1 orange, and 2 tablespoons orange juice. Cook in the top of a double boiler until jelly is melted. Remove from heat and add ½ cup port wine.

OTHER MAIN DISHES

Whole Egg Pie

This old recipe came to me from Prudie Fulton of Belews Creek. Mrs. Fulton said you will think you are eating chicken pie.

Roll out ordinary piecrust and lay in a pie pan, letting it come out over the edges of the pan. Break in 4 whole eggs and divide them around. Then pour in ⅔ cup warm water. It will float the eggs but that is all right. Salt and pepper to taste and put in chips of butter—the more the better.

Cover with a top crust that has been slit and mash edges together. Put more butter on top. Bake at 325° to 350°.

Chicken Corn Soup

Once a year in Newton, the Women's Guild of the Grace Evangelical and Reformed Church put on a special supper featuring a chicken corn soup that was famous in that part of the state. The soup, somewhat like Brunswick stew, is an old Pennsylvania Dutch favorite. It is made with chicken, veal, corn, rice, gravy, milk, and butter. The recipe of the Women's Guild is a secret, but you will find that this one makes a most acceptable chicken corn soup.

Cut a 4- to 5-pound hen into pieces and place in a pot. Cover with cold water. Add a couple of ribs of celery, 2 bay leaves, and 3 or 4 whole peppercorns and bring to a boil. Cover and simmer until tender.

Allow chicken to stand in broth until cooled. Skim off excess fat and reserve for some other purpose. Pull meat from bones and use breast and legs in chicken pie. Shred meat finely and add to strained broth. Season with butter, chopped parsley, salt, and black pepper. Add 2 cups whole-kernel corn. Thicken with a paste of butter and flour. Just before serving, stir in 2 chopped hard-cooked eggs.

Note: For chicken corn stew, add meat from breast and legs.

Peanut Soup

1 tablespoon butter
2 tablespoons flour
1 quart milk
1 cup peanut butter
Salt

Over low heat make a sauce of butter, flour, and milk. Blend in peanut butter. Season to taste with salt.

Irish Potato Soup

Boil potatoes until they are done. Mash through a strainer. Season with butter, salt, and pepper. Add milk and heat.

Bread Soup

Cut slices of bread into cubes and brown in butter in an iron skillet. Mix a beaten egg with milk and heat. When ready to serve, stir in diced bread.

Seafood & Fish

No state tops North Carolina when it comes to seafood and fish. That is because of its extensive coastline and its sounds, rivers, lakes, and streams. Dare County claims to have the greatest variety of fish of any county in the United States. Shrimp, oysters, clams, crabs, and fresh fish have always been popular on the coast where they are available. Both fresh fish and salted fish are popular inland.

The kinds of fish, especially those along the coast, change from time to time depending on the weather and the currents. At one time, for instance, there were whales and scallops off our coast. In recent years, there has been a gradual movement of tropical seafood from the South.

A fish is a fish but, from that point on, great variations in nomenclature appear in various parts of the country. This often makes identification difficult. The following are found in North Carolina's waters.

· · · · ·

SALTWATER FISH

ALEWIVES

Also called herring, an alewife is a small fish that is most often salted and occasionally smoked. The roe is sometimes canned. Dried herring was the favorite dish of the missionary Parson Earl, who arrived in eastern North Carolina from Bandon, Ireland, in 1754. He later became rector of St. Paul's Episcopal Church at Edenton and built a home on the Chowan

River called Bandon, once the home of the late John Fletcher and his wife, Inglis, the author.

Dried Herring

To dry herring, place it in brine strong enough to float an egg and leave for 3 days. Hang up to dry.

BLUEFISH

This is a lean fish, averaging two to three pounds. It is best broiled.

BUTTERFISH

A small fat fish, averaging one-fourth to one pound, the butterfish is fine for pan frying in butter or coating in meal and frying. It may also be grilled.

CHANNEL BASS OR DRUM

This is one of the state's most famous fish, weighing between three and ten pounds. Some are much larger. The whole fish may be baked or boiled. Steaks may be broiled or fried.

Old-timers salted drum and stacked it in the pantry. Salted drum should be soaked before cooking.

Hatteras-Style Drum

The way the natives on Hatteras Island eat drum is a lot like the way North Carolinians sop molasses.

Boil drum in water seasoned with salt and pepper until done. Lift the fish on a platter. Assemble bowls of mashed potatoes, crisp cubes of fried salt pork, salt pork drippings, and chopped onions.

Place a serving of mashed potatoes on a plate. Top with fish, salt pork, and onions. Pour drippings over the top and stir all together. Fork into the mélange and feast.

Ocracoke Dinner

This meal is native to Ocracoke Island.

Fish suitable for poaching (drum, snapper, or mackerel)
Salt, whole peppercorns, bay leaves, and lemon juice
½ pound bacon, streaked lean, or salt pork
½ pound butter
Boiled potatoes
Hard-cooked eggs, peeled
Chopped onions

Poach fish in salted water with whole peppercorns, bay leaves, and lemon juice only until the fish flakes easily. Fry bacon until crisp, drain, and crumble. Melt butter in bacon drippings.

Place a serving of fish, boiled potatoes, and whole boiled egg on a plate. Sprinkle with onions. Over all pour hot bacon drippings and butter. Sprinkle with crumbled bacon.

Dare County Fish Cakes

12 medium potatoes
4 tablespoons butter
2 teaspoons sweet basil, chopped fine
Salt and pepper
1 pound channel bass, boiled and flaked finely
4 eggs

Peel and dice potatoes. Boil, drain, and mash. Add butter, basil, and salt and pepper to taste. Add fish and eggs and beat vigorously until very light and fluffy. Drop by the spoonful into a small amount of fat and brown.

SPANISH MACKEREL

Another favorite, the Spanish mackerel is fat and averages from one to four pounds. Bake whole, or broil or fry split fish or steaks.

SPOT

This is a lean fish, averaging one-fourth to one and one-half pounds. Fry.

TUNA

Tuna of an edible variety turns up occasionally on the coast. It takes a skillful eye to identify the variety but little skill to cook it. Simply cut into chunks and simmer in boiling salted water until tender. Drain, cool, and use as you would canned tuna.

• • • • •

FRESHWATER FISH

BASS

Smallmouth and largemouth bass are lean, averaging one to four pounds.

BREAM

Some regard bream (pronounced brim) as the finest fish in the world. Averaging one-fourth to one pound, they are excellent for frying, broiling, or baking.

Fried Bream

According to one fisherman, the fish should be hooked leisurely and playfully so that its nerves will not become taut. Nervous conditions affect the digestive system of both the fish and, subsequently, the consumer. After landing, the fish should be kept content and active until cleaning. Cook immediately after cleaning.

Coat in cornmeal and fry in hot peanut oil in a heavy skillet.

CARP

This fish is lean and weighs between two and eight pounds. A European fish, carp was introduced to North Carolina in 1879. Natives have a rather low regard for its flavor. Around the Currituck area, carp is caught, fattened up on cornmeal (it feeds by sucking), and sent up North, where it enjoys considerable popularity with certain groups.

CATFISH

In a good part of North Carolina a cat refers neither to the hep or tom variety. A cat is short for catfish, not a fish widely used—except for the farm-raised catfish, which are fairly popular—but one greatly favored by some.

A catfish is so named because it has whiskers like a cat and is a nocturnal creature—that means it prefers to prowl at night, which makes night the best time for catching catfish. The cat is round and has a big head, which is the reason it is sometimes called a bullhead. The head of a three-pound catfish will weigh close to a pound. This fish has no scales—to prepare for cooking, skin it. The cat has three sharp fin bones—two on the gills and a dorsal fin down the middle of the back. When riled up, it can painfully bury a fin into a person.

The cat is caught strictly with bait. Raw liver is a favorite. A cat may weigh up to twenty pounds but the average is about two to three pounds. These fish are cooked most often by frying.

CROAKER OR HARDHEAD

This lean, fine-flavored fish is rather common. Averaging from one-half to two and one-half pounds, it is a great favorite for frying.

FLOUNDER

The flounder is a lean fish averaging from one-fourth to five pounds. Often filleted, it is broiled, fried, or baked.

GROUPER

This is a lean fish weighing between five and fifteen pounds.

HOGFISH

Hogfish are fat and range from one-fourth to one pound.

KING MACKEREL

This top favorite has an average weight of six to eight pounds. It is cut into steaks and broiled or fried. Also bake or broil whole.

LAKE TROUT
(RAINBOW, GERMAN BROWN, AND BROOK)

Lake trout are fat and come in a wide variety of sizes, with an average from about one and one-half to three pounds. They are fine sautéed in butter, fried, baked, broiled, or grilled over coals.

MULLET

Called the sea mullet, it is really whiting. A top favorite, especially in eastern North Carolina, and popular for fish roasts, it is served fried. It is also corned and salted. This lean fish averages from one-half to three pounds.

RED SNAPPER

Fat and weighing between two and ten pounds, this wonderful fish is found around rocks or wrecks several miles off the North Carolina coast. It is wonderful baked.

Morehead-Style Snapper

This is one way Morehead natives prepare red snapper.

Place prepared red snapper in a greased baking pan. Gash top and over it lay thin slices of salt pork. Place thinly sliced peeled potatoes and onion slices around the fish. Sprinkle all with salt and pepper. Bake in a 325° oven for 1 hour, or until the potatoes are done.

ROCKFISH

A rockfish is really a striped bass. Lean, it averages from two to five pounds. It is superb for baking plain or stuffed; it is also used in stews or muddles, boiled, and fried.

SEA BASS

This fish is lean, averaging from one to four pounds. Bake whole, or broil or fry fillets or steaks.

SEA TROUT (WEAKFISH)

Lean, the sea trout averages from one to four pounds. Either bake whole, split fish and fry, or make into fillets to broil or fry.

SHAD

Fat and averaging from one and one-half to five pounds, the shad is one of the world's fine fish in season from February until May. Its abundance of feathery bones make it annoying to eat unless baked in such a way as to soften the bones.

Baked Shad
(Tested)

Using this recipe, you can put a baked shad on the table with bones as unnoticeable as those in a can of salmon.

Wipe cleaned shad with a damp cloth. Sprinkle inside and outside with salt, pepper, and lemon juice. Fold in greased aluminum foil, using the heavy-duty variety or three thicknesses of the regular foil. Place on a baking sheet and bake at 250°.

Bake a 1½- to 2-pound shad for 5 to 5½ hours. Bake a 2½- to 5-pound fish for 5½ to 6½ hours.

SHEEPSHEAD

This is a fat fish averaging from one to six pounds.

WALLEYE PIKE

A member of the perch family, this fish averages from one and one-half to four pounds. Bake, broil, or fry.

• • • • •

GENERAL DIRECTIONS FOR COOKING FISH

Fried Fish

Coat fish in seasoned flour or a mixture of seasoned flour and cornmeal, cornmeal, or cracker meal and fry in hot, shallow fat in a heavy skillet, turning only once. Or fry in deep fat. For a crisper coating, dip fish in egg beaten with a tablespoon of water before dipping in flour.

Baked Fish

Place fish in a greased shallow baking pan. Brush with melted butter or margarine. Sprinkle with salt and pepper. Bake in a 350° oven until fish flakes easily. A large fish takes 12 to 20 minutes per pound, a smaller fish about 2 minutes per ounce.

Fish may also be wrapped in greased foil for baking.

Broiled Fish

Place fish on a greased broiler rack 3 to 5 inches from the heat source. Brush with melted butter. Sprinkle with salt and pepper. Broil for 5 to 10 minutes, or until fish flakes easily. Thin fish or fillets do not require turning. Turn thicker ones once.

• • • • •

SEAFOOD

CLAMS

Clams of the cherrystone variety are common along the coast. They are served raw on the half shell with the customary sauces or in the following ways.

Fried Clams

Coat clams in crumbs and fry just like oysters.

Steamed Clams

Place a small amount of water in a pot. Add clams. Cover and steam for about 10 minutes, or until clams open. Serve hot in the shell with melted butter.

Roast Clams

Wash clams and place in a baking pan. Roast in a 450° oven for 15 minutes, or until clams open. Serve hot in the shell with melted butter.

Baked Clam Hash

1 quart clams
3 slices bacon
1 chopped onion
1 quart diced cooked potatoes
¼ cup chopped parsley
2 eggs, beaten
Salt, pepper, and paprika

Drain and chop clams. Fry bacon until crisp; remove bacon from pan and drain. Cook onion in drippings until golden. Add remaining ingredients and bacon. Turn into a greased baking pan and bake in a 350° oven for 30 to 35 minutes. Makes 6 servings.

Mamie Piner, Clam Fritter Queen

The late Mamie Piner was a native of Swansboro, a picture-book little fishing village in the eastern part of the state on the highway between Jacksonville and Morehead City, where she owned and operated Mamie Piner's Seafood Restaurant. The fritter queen was a jolly woman with curly auburn hair and twinkling eyes and had a robust love of cooking. She had cooked all her life but began preparing food in quantity during World War II: "Those soldiers went fishin' and brought in everything under the sun for me to cook. They seemed to like the way I did it so much I decided to open a restaurant."

The specialty of the house was, of course, clam fritters, the like of which I have never tasted. They were flat like pancakes. The secret of the flavor, she pointed out, was black pepper. She put one-half teaspoon into each serving, which consisted of six or seven fritters. Her recipe follows.

Mamie Piner's Clam Fritters

To 1 mixing spoon [3 tablespoons] of chopped clams, add 1½ tablespoons chopped onion, 1 egg, ½ teaspoon black pepper, 1 mixing spoon flour, and water to make a pourable batter. Add salt to taste.

Drop batter by the spoonful into a small amount of hot fat on a heavy griddle. Cook until lightly browned on both sides. Serve at once.

Mamie Piner's Shrimp and Crab Combination or Stuffed Shrimp

This concoction was another specialty at Mamie Piner's Seafood Restaurant. The tomato sauce for this dish was her secret.

Split fresh shrimp open butterfly fashion and place in a thin layer of tomato sauce on a sizzling steak platter. Top with crabmeat mixed with bread crumbs, more sauce, and seasonings. Broil the whole works and serve piping hot.

CRABS

Blue crabs are abundant along the North Carolina coast. A considerable amount of the fresh meat is packed and sent to metropolitan markets. Natives do the usual things with crabmeat. It is superb simply sautéed in butter. Cooks also devil the meat in a variety of ways.

Soft-shell crabs sautéed in butter or coated in batter and fried in deep fat are a great favorite. These crabs are rather rare because they are soft shelled for only a matter of hours. A special setup is required to provide them. For example, the natives of the fablelike village of Salter Path near Morehead City have crab pounds that yield soft-shell crabs.

Lena Ritter's Baked Crab Cakes

This culinary discovery was made at the Carolina Coastal Celebration held at the North Carolina State Fairgrounds in Raleigh in 1989. Ms. Ritter, who is following seven generations of her family as a fisherwoman in the Stump Sound, was president of the North Carolina Coastal Federation.

1 pound backfin crabmeat
3 heaping tablespoons chopped fresh parsley
¼ cup mayonnaise
1 egg, beaten
1 teaspoon Old Bay seasoning
Juice of ½ lemon
½ teaspoon hot pepper sauce or to taste
½ teaspoon Worcestershire sauce
2 slices fresh white bread, crusts removed, rubbed by hand
to make fine crumbs

Carefully pick over the crabmeat to remove any shells, while leaving lumps intact. Add parsley.

Combine mayonnaise, egg, Old Bay seasoning, lemon juice, hot sauce, Worcestershire; add to crabmeat and gently fold together. Add bread crumbs and fold together again.

Shape into cakes of desired size. Place in a shallow baking pan generously coated with soft butter. Bake in a 375° oven for 10 to 12 minutes. Serve bottom side up (bottoms brown better).

Crabmeat Dressing
(Tested)

This recipe is the result of combining three that I picked up on the coast of North Carolina. It is the best crabmeat dressing that I have ever tasted. It is delicious stuffed in a fish and baked or simply baked separately in a shallow pan and then cut into squares to serve with baked fish.

1 can (6½ ounces) crabmeat
2 eggs, beaten
2 tablespoons melted butter
½ small onion, finely diced
¼ medium green pepper, finely diced
½ cup diced celery
¼ cup chopped parsley
¾ cup fine corn bread crumbs

1 slice white bread, rubbed into crumbs
¼ teaspoon Worcestershire sauce
Salt and pepper
¼ teaspoon dry mustard

Open crabmeat and pick out any pieces of cartilage or shell that are present. Mix with remaining ingredients and stuff a fish, or spread out in a greased shallow pan and bake with the fish. If cooked separately, bake at 400° for about 25 minutes.

OYSTERS

Oyster territory extends all the way from Roanoke Island south to the South Carolina line. Hyde County has large beds of oysters in the water near Swan Quarter. Onslow County is distinguished for its excellent beds of New River oysters.

In quality, North Carolina oysters rate with the best produced in America. Most of the industry is located in Pamlico Sound. Dredges are used to harvest oysters from deep water. Oyster tongs or iron bars or rakes are used in shallow water. The six-foot fall of the tide in the Shallotte and Lockwood Folly areas of Brunswick County leaves the oyster beds high and dry at low tide. It is possible to drive in with wagons or jeeps to harvest the oysters.

North Carolina is well suited for oyster production. First, there is an abundance of seed oysters. The geographic location is ideal, for the winters are not severe and the summers are not tropically hot. In this state it is possible to produce an oyster large enough to market in two years or less. The process takes five years in the Delaware Bay area and about seven years in Long Island Sound.

In North Carolina waters, natural enemies such as starfish, small snails called oyster drills, and various worms that harm oysters or compete with them for food are relatively small in number. Restrictions on oyster acreage, pollution, and the beds' lack of protection from destructive forces such as hurricanes have kept the state's oyster industry from developing to a greater extent than it has.

Fried Oysters

Drain oysters thoroughly on paper towels. Dip in seasoned flour, then in egg beaten with 1 tablespoon water, and finally in fine dry bread crumbs. Fry in deep hot fat until golden brown.

Oven-Fried Oysters

Drain large oysters thoroughly on paper towels. Add seasoning salt to flour in a paper bag and shake the oysters in the bag to coat.

Dip in beaten egg. Lift from egg and roll in fine dry bread or cracker crumbs. Place in a well-greased shallow baking dish. Dribble a little melted butter over the top of each oyster. Bake in a 400° oven for 10 minutes, or until lightly browned. Serve with chili sauce or tartar sauce.

Pan-Roasted Oysters

Drain 1 pint oysters and place in a shallow buttered baking dish. Melt 2 tablespoons butter; add ½ teaspoon salt, ½ teaspoon Worcestershire sauce, and ⅛ teaspoon pepper and pour over oysters. Bake in a 400° oven for about 10 minutes, or until edges begin to curl. Serve on buttered toast. If you like, spread anchovy paste lightly over buttered toast under oysters. Makes 4 servings.

Oven-Steamed or Broiled Oysters

Place drained oysters in 1 layer in a shallow buttered baking dish. Dot with butter. Place in a 375° oven or under the broiler for a few minutes, or until edges begin to curl. Serve with melted butter and lemon juice or other sauce as desired.

Minced Oysters

This recipe was contributed by Mrs. Gordon Blackwell to *Carolina Cooking*, published by the Junior Service League of Chapel Hill.

Chop 1 pint oysters very finely and place in a saucepan. Add ⅛ pound butter, ¼ teaspoon black pepper, and ¼ teaspoon mustard, with grated nutmeg, red pepper, celery, celery seed or celery salt, and salt to taste. Into this mixture break 2 eggs.

Place over medium heat and stir until heated. Thicken with browned bread crumbs. Put in shells with bread crumbs on top and a small piece of butter on each. Place in a moderate oven to brown lightly. Serve very hot.

Ocracoke-Style Oysters

Drain 1 quart oysters. Cook in butter in a saucepan until the edges curl. Add 2 slices crisp crumbled bacon. Heat together and serve.

Pickled Oysters

Heat a quart of oysters gently for a few minutes. Lift oysters from the liquor. Add to the liquor 6 whole cloves, 6 whole peppercorns, 6 bay leaves broken into bits, 1 small red pepper, 1 cup vinegar, and 1 teaspoon celery salt. Bring to a boil and pour at once over oysters. Store in the refrigerator.

Sauce for Oysters or Shrimp

Combine ½ bottle chili sauce, ½ cup vinegar, and ½ stick butter and heat. Use for dunking roasted oysters or boiled shrimp.

SHRIMP

For years shrimp from North Carolina rivers have claimed a top price in metropolitan markets. In addition to the usual ways of preparing shrimp for cocktail, frying, and Creole are the following.

Shrimp Pie

In a greased casserole, put a layer of cooked shrimp, a layer of chopped green pepper, and a layer of chopped celery. Sprinkle with salt and pepper and dust with cayenne. Repeat layers.

Make a rich medium-thick cream sauce. Pour over casserole. Cover with a layer of crumbled Ritz crackers. Sprinkle with grated cheese. Bake in a 350° oven until bubbly.

Shrimp Cosmopolitan

This recipe was contributed by Carolyn Evans to the *Bonnie Fare Cook Book*, published by the Junior Service League of Laurinburg.

2 pounds raw shrimp
Seasoned flour
Butter
3 slices bacon
¼ cup green pepper, chopped
1 onion, chopped
2 cans (10½ ounces each) mushroom soup
1 teaspoon Worcestershire sauce
Hot pepper sauce
Toasted English walnuts

Clean shrimp. Coat in flour and fry in butter until lightly browned. In another pan, cook bacon until crisp. Remove from pan and drain. In bacon drippings, cook green pepper and onion until soft.

In a saucepan combine shrimp, crumbled bacon, green pepper, onion, soup plus 1 soup can of water, Worcestershire, and hot pepper sauce. Heat and serve over rice. Sprinkle with walnuts. Makes 8 servings.

Pickled Shrimp

Cook 2 pounds shrimp, a handful of celery tops, and ¼ cup mixed pickling spices (tied in a bag) in boiling salted water until the shrimp is done. Drain and cool in running cold water. Shell and remove veins.

Mix 1 cup salad oil, ¾ cup white vinegar, ¼ teaspoon black pepper, 2 teaspoons celery seed, 1 teaspoon salt, and a few drops of Tabasco sauce. Pour over shrimp, which has been arranged in layers with 1 large chopped onion. Cover and chill thoroughly. The shrimp will keep for a week in the refrigerator.

• • • • •

SEAFOOD MUDDLES, SOUPS, AND STEWS

North Carolina's fascinating concoctions from denizens of the deep include its famous muddles, chowders, bisques, and stews.

Rockfish Muddle

This recipe came from Jacqueline Williams, former home demonstration agent for Hertford County. The muddle is much better cooked in an open pot outdoors.

14 to 15 pounds rockfish
3½ pounds salt pork
2½ pounds onions
2½ quarts canned tomatoes
Salt, black pepper, and red pepper
6 dozen eggs
1½ to 2 pounds crackers
2 pounds butter

Boil rockfish in water to cover until done enough to remove bones. Take out the fish and remove all bones; save the fish broth. Chop meat and fry until golden brown or browner. Fry salt pork; remove from drippings. Chop onions and fry in drippings until partly brown. Pour off excess fat.

Return fish, salt pork, drippings, and onions to broth. Add tomatoes and cook for about ½ hour or more. Season with salt and peppers to taste. Beat eggs well and add to mixture, then crumble crackers and add. Cook for a few minutes. Add butter and cook for about 2 minutes. Be sure and stir. Add more water if desired.

Murfreesboro Rock Muddle

Muddle parties are famous in some sections. Here is the recipe used for a party in Murfreesboro.

For 50 pounds of dressed rockfish, cook 10 pounds bacon. Drop the fish, cut into large chunks, in the hot fat. Add 15 cans (1 pound each) tomatoes, 25 pounds chopped onions, and about 2 pounds crackers to make muddle the desired consistency. Cook all together. Add the cooked, crumbled bacon.

PINE BARK STEW

It is an old Tar Heel custom to prepare stews of the muddle type in black iron wash pots over an outdoor fire. In the old days this fire was often made from pine bark, and that is how the name of this stew came to be.

CONCH STEW

Conch meat is not available in markets but an occasional mess of it can be obtained from coastal fishermen. The meat is something like the abalone of the West Coast. It is pounded, stewed, minced, and put into a stew with onions, potatoes, and tomatoes. According to some, the flavor is out of this world.

Oyster Stew
(Tested)

A little flour in oyster stew does worlds for the flavor—not enough flour to thicken but enough to abolish the "water" consistency of hot milk and to carry the oyster flavor throughout.

For 2 servings, cook ½ pint oysters gently over low heat in 4 tablespoons butter. Season with salt, pepper, paprika, and a squirt of Worcestershire sauce. Blend in 2 tablespoons flour. Add 2 cups milk and heat but do not boil.

Core Sound Oyster Stew

Cut ¼ pound salt pork into small cubes and fry until crisp and lightly browned. Add 2 quarts oysters, 1 cup water, ½ teaspoon black pepper, and salt to taste.

Heat and serve, or add cornmeal dumplings, cover, and steam for 15 minutes or until done. (Cornmeal dumplings are likely to appear on the top of any seafood stew made in the east.)

CLAM CHOWDER

Those favored with a supply of fresh clams have definite opinions about the proper way of making clam chowder—an opinion about clam chowder seems to be almost universal. One elderly man on the coast asked a woman with a pail of clams: "You ain't gonna put 'maters or milk in it, are you?" In regard to milk in clam chowder, another old-timer said: "It'll piesin ye."

There are those who do put milk in clam chowder, some who put tomatoes, and many who put neither.

Carteret County Clam Chowder

¼ pound salt pork, cut into small cubes
2 medium potatoes, cubed
1 medium onion, chopped
1 quart clams, chopped
1 quart water
Salt and pepper
Cornmeal dumplings

Fry pork until crisp and brown. Add potatoes, onion, clams, and water. Simmer until potatoes are done, adding water to keep mixture from becoming too dry. Season to taste with salt and pepper. Drop cornmeal dumplings on top of the chowder. Cover tightly and simmer for 15 minutes.

New Bern Clam Chowder

Chop 3 medium potatoes and add to 1 quart boiling water. Boil for 10 minutes. Chop 1 quart clams and add to potato mixture along with a No. 2 can of tomatoes; simmer for 10 minutes longer.

Fry 3 or 4 slices of salt pork until crisp. Dice and add to chowder. Chop 2 onions and fry in pork drippings until golden; add to chowder. Season with 1 to 2 tablespoons Worcestershire sauce and salt and pepper to taste.

Crab Stew

This interesting recipe for crab stew came from New Bern.

4 dozen hard crabs
1 pound salt pork, cubed
2 pounds onions, peeled and sliced
Salt and pepper
½ cup vinegar
Worcestershire sauce, tomato catsup, and hot pepper
Cornmeal

Prepare crabs for stew, washing well. Fry salt pork until brown and put in a deep pot. Add alternating layers of crabs and onions with hot water to cover. Add salt and pepper to taste and vinegar. Bring to a boil and boil for 15 minutes.

Add Worcestershire, catsup, and hot pepper to taste. Cook for 15 minutes longer. Sprinkle in a little cornmeal. Let cook until thickened. If not as thick as desired, add more cornmeal. Makes 8 servings.

Crabmeat Stew

1 small onion, chopped
2 tablespoons butter
2 tablespoons flour
1 cup milk
1 cup cream
2 cups crabmeat
1 teaspoon Worcestershire sauce
½ cup cooked fresh corn
½ cup cooked fresh butter beans
Salt and pepper

Cook onion in butter until golden. Blend in flour. Add milk and cream and cook over low heat until smooth and thick. Add remaining ingredients and heat. Add more milk for a thinner stew.

Note: Some coastal cooks make crab stew without flour. To thicken the cooked stew, they gradually add cornmeal until it reaches the desired consistency.

Sea Crab Bisque

This bisque is a specialty in Kitty Hawk.

½ pound butter
2 tablespoons flour
2 cups milk
1 teaspoon salt
¼ teaspoon red pepper
¼ teaspoon mace
¼ teaspoon nutmeg
1 pound fresh back fin crabmeat
3 cups thin coffee cream
Sherry

Melt butter in the top of a double boiler. Add flour and blend. Add milk and cook, stirring, until thickened. Add seasonings and crabmeat. When ready to serve, add cream and heat. Place one bouillon spoon of sherry in a bouillon cup, add bisque, and serve.

Shrimp Stew

Shrimp is also sufficiently plentiful along the coast to use for a stew like this one.

1½ pounds green shrimp
1 large onion, minced
¼ cup butter
¼ cup flour
Dry mustard to taste
Paprika
½ teaspoon sugar
1 teaspoon salt
⅛ teaspoon pepper
3 cups rich milk

Boil shrimp; peel, devein, and chop coarsely. Cook onion in butter until golden. Blend in flour, mustard, paprika, sugar, salt, and pepper. Add milk and cook over low heat until thickened. Add shrimp. Heat and serve.

Catfish Stew

This recipe was contributed by Paige Underwood, former home economics agent for Perquimans County.

3 medium potatoes, peeled and diced
3 tablespoons bacon fat drippings
1 large onion, chopped
Water
1 pound dressed catfish with backbone removed,
cut into small pieces
3 tablespoons flour
Salt and pepper

Brown potatoes in bacon drippings. Add onion, 1 cup water, and fish. Cook slowly for about 15 to 20 minutes.

Blend flour with 1 cup cold water and add to fish mixture. Simmer until thickened. Season to taste with salt and pepper.

Note: The fish can also be prepared by browning in bacon drippings and removing backbone as it becomes tender.

Tomato Catfish Stew

Catfish stew is often made with cream of tomato soup, as in this recipe.

½ pound bacon
1½ pounds onions
2 cans condensed cream of tomato soup
1½ pints water
2 pounds catfish
Salt and pepper
⅔ bottle tomato catsup

Fry bacon until crisp. Drain. Chop onions and cook in bacon fat until light brown. Add soup and water and bring to a boil. Add catfish and simmer for 15 to 20 minutes. Season with salt and pepper to taste. Add catsup and stir lightly. Serve with rice, crackers, or light bread. Makes 6 servings.

Scrambled Catfish Stew

This stew is thickened with beaten eggs.

4 catfish, dressed
Flour
½ cup bacon drippings
2 Irish potatoes, peeled and diced
1½ cups water
1 onion, chopped
3 eggs
½ cup milk
½ cup light cream
Salt and pepper

Coat fish in flour seasoned with salt and pepper. Brown on both sides in hot bacon drippings. Add potatoes, water, and onion and cook until potatoes are tender. Stir often to prevent burning. Beat eggs; add milk and cream with salt and pepper to taste. Pour this into fish mixture and stir until all is well blended.

Catfish Stew with Boiled Eggs

4 pounds dressed catfish
1½ pounds chopped onions
1½ pounds smoked side meat, cut in ½-inch cubes
6 hard-cooked eggs, chopped
⅛ pound (¼ cup) butter
1 cup evaporated milk
Salt and pepper

Boil fish and onions together with just enough water to cover until fish leaves the bones. Fry side meat until crisp. Pour grease into fish mixture. Heat. Add eggs and butter and simmer briefly. Remove fish from heat and add milk. Heat gently and serve.

Layered Catfish Stew

This stew is somewhat like a casserole.

Fry ½ pound bacon until crisp. Remove bacon and drain. Arrange the following in layers in the drippings—4 pounds dressed catfish, 4 pounds diced potatoes, and 2 pounds diced onions. Add 1 cup hot water. Cover and simmer over low heat for 1½ hours, without stirring. Pour in 1 can condensed tomato soup, ¼ cup butter, hot pepper sauce, and salt and pepper to taste. Heat and serve.

• • • • •

FISH ROE

Shad roe is, of course, the prize package of the roe family. It is enough of a delicacy to make those who like it bow with low salaams in its presence.

Occasionally shad roe is sautéed and served with bacon as a main dish, but most often it is served with baked shad. When serving sautéed roe to accompany shad, cut into small pieces and distribute with servings of shad.

Sautéed Roe

Cook gently in a little butter in a heavy skillet until done. Try to turn only once to prevent breaking the membrane. Season with salt and pepper. Serve with lemon wedges.

Creamed Roe

Creamed roe is served as a sauce for shad. To prepare, sprinkle roe that has been sautéed or parboiled with lemon juice. Chop coarsely and add to a rich medium-thick cream sauce.

MULLET ROE

According to some, the roe of the large mullet rivals the flavor of shad roe. The fresh or "green" roe is sold in coastal markets.

MENHADEN ROE

Along about Thanksgiving, when the big menhaden fleets start coming in along the coast, you hear natives saying that "the pogy boats are in." That is the signal to grab a bucket and head for the dock to get a mess of menhaden eggs, often referred to locally as "Carteret County caviar."

Menhaden is North Carolina's most valuable commercial fish. Menhaden oils are used in the manufacture of perfume, soap, paint, insect sprays, and so forth. The fish scrap is utilized primarily in fish meal, while the solubles are used chiefly as vitamin additives in animal feeds.

The fishermen who go out with the menhaden fleets do not bother with the roe, but some of the helpers on the boats take it out as the boats head back to shore. The helpers get the money for the roe. Even if the pogy boats come in at 3:00 A.M., there will be rows of people with buckets waiting for roe.

This roe peculiarly belongs to North Carolina because menhaden, like the birds, moves from cold weather to warm, and as it moves south the roe develops. A roe is "ripe" or ready for eating just about the time the fish reach Cape Hatteras. So the roe is available for only about two months in the fall. When the fish get past North Carolina, the roe is too near hatching time to be good.

Many believe that the flavor of menhaden roe is just as good as that of shad roe. Some call it mammy shad roe. It is smaller in size than shad roe and yellow in color. The fresh roe is sautéed like shad roe. It is also dried.

DRIED ROE

Morehead natives have a distinctive way of preserving mullet and menhaden roe. This is an old-time practice. After soaking in salt water, the roe is pressed between two boards to squeeze out as much moisture as possible.

The roe is then placed in the sun to dry. The dried roe is dipped in melted wax. It keeps indefinitely in its waxy covering.

Canned Fish Roe Cakes

This is a delicious way of serving canned roe, which was once widely available. The cakes are wonderful with crisp bacon and scrambled eggs.

Beat an egg and add a scant cup of bread crumbs and the drained contents of a 9-ounce can of fish roe. Mix well and shape into 6 oblong patties. Place patties in a heavy skillet containing a small amount of hot fat. Brown on both sides, turning only once. Serve with lemon wedges.

Herring Roe and Scrambled Eggs

Served with cornmeal griddle cakes, this was a popular breakfast dish at The Carolinian in Nags Head.

Use a good brand of herring roe. For each serving, take 2 tablespoons herring roe from the can and brown it lightly in bacon fat. Add 2 beaten eggs, scrambling them to taste either medium or soft.

Cornmeal Griddlecakes

These cakes are popular with corned spots and other salted fish.

Combine 1½ cups cornmeal, 6 tablespoons shortening, and 3 cups boiling water. Let stand for 5 minutes. Add 2½ cups milk. When cool, add 6 beaten eggs and 3 tablespoons molasses.

Sift together 3 cups flour, 3 teaspoons salt, and 3 tablespoons baking powder and add to cornmeal mixture. Add more milk if consistency is not proper for griddle cakes. Cook on a hot, greased griddle. Serve with honey or syrup and butter.

• • • • •

TURTLES

Mud turtles, which are also called snapping turtles, are quite common in this part of the country. Their shell, which is about 8 to 10 inches long, is rather flat compared to the more rounded shell of the terrapin, which is not eaten. Terrapins are the ones seen traveling across highways now and then.

Mud turtles are cooked by parboiling. The meat is then removed, coated in flour, and fried. It is served plain or with gravy. The meat may also be made into stew. Many consider the meat of the mud turtle to be sweet and succulent.

The sea turtle, which is often huge, is a relative of the mud turtle. It is also cooked, though some claim that the meat has little flavor.

Sea Turtle Hash

This recipe has been in the family of Odessa Wasili of Currituck County for generations of Cape Hatteras fishermen. Her mother prepared the hash in an iron pot over a wood fire in the fireplace. Mrs. Wasili now makes it in the pressure cooker.

Scald sea turtle's legs with boiling water. Remove the outside layer of skin and nails. Rinse. Place whole legs in a pressure cooker with 1 quart water and 1 teaspoon soda. Cook at 15 pounds pressure for 30 minutes. Remove legs and cool. Dice meat.

Dice ¼ pound salt pork and fry in a heavy pot. Remove pork and cook 4 chopped onions in drippings. Add 1 cup water, 4 pounds diced white potatoes, diced turtle, salt pork, and 1 cup water, with salt and pepper to taste. Cover and simmer until the potatoes are tender and the gravy has cooked down to a minimum.

Vegetables & Fruits

VEGETABLES, SALAT, AND SALADS

Salat (pronounced *sa*-lat) is one thing and salad is another. Salat means greens, most often cooked turnip greens but also kale, collards, cress, and mustard greens.

Salads, as the tossed salad is served today, did not exist before World War II. There were no bottled salad dressings on the market. Mayonnaise and boiled salad dressing were homemade. When the garden offered lettuce, it usually was served with only sugar and vinegar or a hot bacon dressing. When tomatoes, cucumbers, and green onions were in season, sliced tomatoes were on the table three times a day. Sliced tomatoes might be combined with sliced cucumbers in vinegar, or the cucumbers in vinegar were in a separate dish. Radishes and green onions were also popular.

In winter, chopped onions in vinegar and relishes such as chowchow were served as accompaniments. These relishes were so good that we did not miss green salads.

Cole slaw and hot slaw were common, as was potato salad, which appeared at every outing. Chicken salad, including mayonnaise chicken and pressed chicken, were popular main dishes.

When Jell-O and Knox unflavored gelatin reached the market, congealed salads became extremely popular, especially for luncheons. For years homemakers put a congealed salad in the refrigerator on Saturday to serve on Sunday.

Creamed Artichokes

Boil young whole Jerusalem artichokes in salted water until tender. Drain, peel, slice, and serve in cream sauce.

DRIED BEANS

Pinto Beans

Tons of pinto beans go into North Carolina pots every year. Before cooking, a dried pinto bean is about the size of a regular canned baked bean, as in a can of pork and beans. Its mottled skin is white and brown. When cooked, it is almost the color of kidney beans, though not quite as red.

The standard way to cook pintos is to place a hunk of salt pork, cut into slices almost down to the rind, in a pot of water. Bring the water to a boil and boil the pork for about an hour. This process begins right after breakfast. Meanwhile, pick over and wash the dried beans. Add the beans to a liberal quantity of the water in which the pork has boiled, bring to a boil, and simmer for 2 to 5 hours. Near the end of the cooking time, add water in small quantities at a time—just enough to prevent the beans from sticking. The old folks have a secret for cooking dried beans without having the skin pop. It is to cook the beans at a simmer and never allow them to come to a riproaring boil.

Most of the time the pintos are served plain, but in the winter it is the custom to have a big bowl of onions cut up in vinegar on the table. A spoonful of the chopped onions is placed on top of the beans and the two are stirred together. In the spring, young green onions are often served with the beans—a fine combination.

These days folks who do not have the time or the inclination to boil their own beans are using canned ones cooked the old way with pork, including Luck's from Seagrove.

Other Dried Beans and Peas

The Great Northern dried bean is also popular. About the size of a navy bean, it is white before cooking but turns a blush pink when cooked.

As soon as green black-eyed peas are gone in the fall, people start cooking the dried ones. The dried peas are good, but they have a different flavor and texture.

Hopping John

Cover 1 ham bone, hog jowl, or hunk of salt pork with water and cook for 2 hours. Add 1 cup dried black-eyed peas that have been washed and soaked overnight. Cook until almost tender. Remove meat and add 1 cup washed raw rice with salt and pepper. Boil until the rice is tender and the liquid has evaporated.

GREEN BEANS

"Snaps"—string beans or green beans—are cooked the same way as pintos and for about the same amount of time. They are most often served plain, but in the spring tiny new potatoes are cooked with the beans. (Later in the season corn is added to make succotash.) The tiny new potatoes are laid on top of the beans near the end of the cooking time and allowed to steam until done.

Ears of corn and slices of summer squash are cooked in the same way. When the squash is done, it is lifted from the beans and mashed with butter, salt, and pepper.

Green Beans and New Potatoes

Drop the shank end (about 4 inches of it) of a country ham into a pot of boiling water. Have enough water to cover the beans you plan to add. Simmer meat for about 45 minutes. Add prepared green beans (about 2 to 3 pounds). Bring to a boil, reduce heat, and simmer for a couple of hours.

An hour before the beans are done, place 12 to 18 small new scraped potatoes on top of the beans. Cover and continue cooking until the potatoes are done. Chances are, with a country ham bone, additional salt will not be required, but taste and see.

BUTTER BEANS

Butter beans to Tar Heels are what lima beans are to others. The fresh young beans are shelled from their pods (and what a job!) and cooked in boiling salted water until tender. The seasoning for them is salt, pepper, and a king-size lump of butter (or better yet, make it two lumps of butter).

Butter beans are, of course, cooked with corn to make succotash, which is best seasoned with butter, too.

Danny's Butter Beans

2 cups shelled fresh butter beans
2 cups water
2 tablespoons butter
1 tablespoon bacon drippings
½ teaspoon salt

In a saucepan, stir all ingredients together. Cover and cook over medium heat until the beans are tender—about 45 minutes. Makes 2 to 3 servings.

CABBAGE

Cabbage is a standby throughout the year. It is popular both raw in various kinds of cole slaw and cooked. The old cooks boil it, like greens, until it turns pink, using pork drippings for seasoning. Others cook the cabbage in a minimum of boiling salted water only until it is barely tender and then season it with butter.

Creamed Cabbage

Make a paste of flour and cold water and stir into boiled cabbage.

Hot Cole Slaw
(Tested)

This is a luscious favorite.

4 to 5 cups cabbage, cut coarsely
Water
⅓ cup vinegar
3 tablespoons flour
1 tablespoon sugar
3 tablespoons meat drippings or butter
Salt and pepper

Cook cabbage in a small amount of boiling salted water for 5 to 8 minutes. Drain and save liquid. Add water to liquid to make 1 cup. Combine liquid, vinegar, flour, sugar, and drippings as for white sauce. Heat until slightly thickened. Add cabbage and heat. Makes 6 servings.

Fried Cabbage
(Tested)

This method of preparing cabbage may destroy a vitamin or two but it produces a wonderful dish—wonderful to those with southern tastes.

Chop cabbage coarsely. Cook in boiling salted water just enough to wilt—about 3 minutes. Pour into a sieve or colander and drain well.

Dump cabbage into a heavy skillet that contains hot bacon drippings. Cook, turning frequently, until well browned. Add additional bacon drippings as needed. Season with salt and a liberal sprinkling of black pepper.

CARROTS

The way to cook carrots is in boiling salted water to cover. If desired, add a teaspoon of honey or sugar. When the carrots are done, all the water should be gone. Add a lump of butter and shake pan to coat the carrots well.

Creamed carrots are another favorite. Even for creaming, a little touch of sugar or honey helps the flavor.

Creamed Carrots
(Tested)

1½ tablespoons butter
3 tablespoons flour
½ teaspoon salt or to taste
Pinch of sugar
⅛ teaspoon pepper
1½ cups milk
3 cups diced cooked carrots, drained

Melt butter in saucepan; blend in flour, salt, sugar, and pepper. Add milk, stirring until smooth and thickened. Add carrots. Heat. Makes 6 servings.

Baked Cauliflower

This is a favorite recipe of Ainsle Alexander, former home demonstration agent of Lincoln County.

1 medium head of cauliflower
2 tablespoons butter
½ cup finely chopped onions
2 tablespoons flour
1½ cups canned tomatoes, well drained
1 teaspoon salt
⅛ teaspoon pepper
¾ cup grated cheese
¾ cup fine cracker crumbs

Break cauliflower into flowerets and cook in boiling salted water until tender. Drain well and place in a casserole.

Meanwhile, cook onions in butter until golden. Blend in flour. Add tomatoes and bring to a simmer. Add seasonings and pour over cauliflower. Mix cheese and crumbs and sprinkle over the top. Bake in a 400° oven for 20 minutes. Makes 6 servings.

CORN

When fresh corn or "rosen" ears are in season, it is likely to appear on the table as creamed corn, stewed corn, fried corn, corn on the cob, and maybe corn pudding or succotash. Almost every cook has her or his own way of preparing each dish. The ingredients used—butter, bacon drippings, milk, cream, salt, pepper, and sugar—are the same but the amounts and methods vary. The corn in the finished product tastes very much the same with each method.

Creamed Corn
(Tested)

To prepare creamed corn, use white corn. As my chemistry professor, the late Charles Higgins, said, yellow corn is for horses.

3 cups tender white corn kernels
Water
½ teaspoon salt or to taste

2 tablespoons flour
1 cup heavy whipping cream
Freshly ground black pepper

Put corn in a saucepan; add water to barely cover and salt. Bring to a boil, reduce heat, and simmer for 5 to 8 minutes.

Meanwhile, make a smooth paste of flour and a small amount of the heavy cream; add remaining heavy cream and pour over corn. Cook, stirring, until thickened. Sprinkle with pepper. Makes 3 cups.

Stewed Corn

Melt a good chunk of butter in a heavy pan. Add corn and stir to coat each grain. Add water to almost cover. Bring to a boil and cook until tender. Season with sugar, salt, and pepper.

Fried Corn

The old-fashioned way of cutting corn for frying is to run a sharp knife down the length of each row of kernels, cutting the grains in half. If the kernels are large, they are cut off with two cuttings down the cob rather than one. The back of the knife blade is then run down the cob to squeeze out the milk.

Fry salt pork slices in a heavy black skillet. Remove pork and dump corn into hot drippings. Cook for a few minutes. Season with salt and pepper.

Fried Pepper and Corn

Chop 1 green pepper and 1 onion. Fry in a little butter in a heavy skillet. Add corn cut from 4 ears of corn. Fry for 10 minutes or until done, stirring. Season with salt and pepper.

Corn Custard
(Tested)

This custard is in the corn pudding department and is one of the best corn dishes I have ever tasted. It is perfect served with fried chicken.

The original recipe as I found it in an old cookbook called for 2 cups of heavy cream. I cut the recipe in half, and that is the way it appears here. Bake in a shallow baking dish so the top will brown prettily.

1 cup finely cut fresh corn
2 eggs
1 cup heavy cream
½ to 1 teaspoon salt
⅛ teaspoon pepper

Run a sharp knife down the length of each row of corn, cutting each grain through the center. Cut kernels from cob in two cuttings rather than just one. Scrape cob with the back of the knife.

Beat eggs and add remaining ingredients. Pour into a buttered shallow baking dish and place in a pan of hot water. Bake at 325° for 1 hour or until a knife, when inserted, emerges clean. Makes 4 to 5 servings.

Corn Pudding
(Tested)

2 cups thin cream
2 cups cream-style corn
2 tablespoons melted butter or margarine
1 tablespoon sugar
1 teaspoon salt
⅛ teaspoon pepper
3 eggs, well beaten

Add milk, corn, butter, sugar, and seasonings to eggs. Turn into a greased casserole. Place casserole in a pan of hot water and bake in a moderate oven (about 325°) for about 1 hour. Makes 6 servings.

Green Corn Pudding

1 quart fresh corn (cut from cob and scrape cob)
1 teaspoon salt
⅛ teaspoon pepper
3 eggs, beaten
2 cups milk
4 tablespoons melted butter
2 tablespoons sugar

Mix all ingredients together and pour into a buttered baking dish. Place dish in a pan of hot water and bake at 325° for 1 hour, or until firm. Makes 8 servings.

Grilled Corn

This is a luscious variation of corn on the cob. Corn prepared in this manner tastes like old-fashioned roasted ears.

Cook corn on the cob in boiling salted water for about 5 minutes. Drain ears and place on a broiling pan. Brush with melted butter and broil under hot broiler until partially browned. Keep brushing with melted butter as corn broils.

GREENS

Greens of all sorts are popular. Probably most popular of all are turnip greens or tops. Tar Heels also enjoy mustard greens, kale (curly and leafy), collards (in the fall and winter), rape and poke greens, and "cressies." The cressies may be land cress or watercress, which grows in bottomland without cultivation.

Each of these greens has its own taste—the taste of turnip greens and cress is most distinctive. No kitchen odor is more marked than that of a pot of turnip greens as they come to a boil—it is a dark, dank green odor.

The washed and "looked" leaves (examined for insects, etc.) are parboiled in water. Most often the drippings from salt pork are poured over the drained, parboiled greens. In the eastern portion of the state, there are cooks who drop fluffy cornmeal dumplings on top of the cooked greens, cover the pot tightly, and simmer until the dumplings are done. Sometimes two or three kinds of greens are cooked together.

Tip for Washing Greens

Use water that is slightly warm. Put a little vinegar in the first water. Use three waters.

POT LIQUOR

Pot liquor (or "likker") is a great deal more than the liquid in which turnip greens, cabbage, collards, and pintos or green beans are cooked. To be called pot liquor, the liquid must be super-concentrated. Only careful cooking concentrates the liquid properly. When the food is cooked, there is very little liquid left—it is full of every soluble, non-volatile vitamin to be found in the food. The flavor is distinctive and delicious (if you were reared on it).

In the years when mothers knew no more about vitamins than videos, unweaned children were fed pot liquor by the teaspoonful right at the table. The children thrived on it because vitamins were present in their natural state rather than in the form found in modern synthetic preparations. The way adults eat pot liquor is to spoon a little over corn bread or a hot biscuit.

LETTUCE

It was always a great day when the first tender shoots of garden lettuce were ready to be gathered. So the leaves would be their freshest, they were gathered almost at the last minute—before dinner was ready to "take up." The leaves wilt fast. Once the early spring supply was gone, there was no more lettuce until the next season.

The old folks like great bowls of the cut-up lettuce sprinkled with sugar and then doused with vinegar. When served with hot bacon dressing, it is sometimes called scalded lettuce.

Smothered Lettuce or Mountain Spring Salad

This recipe came from the Nu-Wray Inn in Burnsville.

Select fresh spring lettuce before it heads. Chop enough lettuce to fill a bowl. Add 3 young onions and onion tops chopped finely, 1 teaspoon sugar, and salt to taste. Pour 2 tablespoons vinegar over mixture. Fry 5 slices of cured country bacon crisply and place strips on lettuce. Pour hot bacon grease over all. Serve immediately.

OKRA

Fresh, tender okra is stewed or fried. It is added to canned soup mixtures for winter use.

Fried Okra

Cut the ends from tender okra pods and slice in 1-inch pieces. Drop in a brown bag that contains seasoned flour together with a little cornmeal. Shake to coat.

Remove from bag and shake off excess flour. Fry in a heavy skillet that contains a shallow layer of bacon drippings or other fat. Turn frequently until browned on all sides.

Sunset Farms Okra

6 strips bacon
2 medium onions
2 green peppers
6 cups okra slices, cut in about ½-inch lengths
4 medium fresh tomatoes
Salt and pepper
1 tablespoon minced parsley

Cook bacon until crisp. Drain and crumble. Chop onions and peppers and cook in the bacon drippings until golden. Drain off excess fat. Add okra and cook until golden. Add tomatoes that have been peeled and chopped. Season with salt and pepper. Cover and simmer for 20 minutes. Just before removing from the heat, add crumbled bacon and parsley. Makes 6 to 8 servings.

Okra and Onions

2 tablespoons meat drippings
12 tender pods okra
1 medium onion
Salt and pepper

Place meat drippings in a heavy skillet. Slice okra thinly and chop onion. Add to hot fat and simmer until tender. Season with salt and pepper.

Fried Green Onions

This recipe came from the Nu-Wray Inn.

Chop green onions and tops coarsely. Pour 1 tablespoon of grease into a hot skillet. Heat and then place in enough onions to fill the pan. Add ½ cup hot water. Cook slowly for about 30 minutes. Do not stir while cooking. Just before done, sprinkle 1 tablespoon of sugar and salt to taste over onions. Serve hot.

ENGLISH PEAS

I do not know what connection the English ever had with peas, but to a Tar Heel a green pea is an English pea. Peas are one of the first garden vegetables to mature in the spring. The first mess is ready in May. Now that those ghastly bright green, hard-centered, slightly flavored frozen peas are the only kind of fresh peas some folks will ever know, the memory of freshly gathered garden peas becomes even more precious. The tiny frozen peas currently on the market resemble tender fresh ones.

Even the picking is fun. The process may be a little hard on aching backs, but going up and down the rows of vines, still damp with dew, to fill a basket with fresh pods is a rewarding activity. The pods of freshly picked peas are slick and tight, the way a rubber football is, not flabby like the ones that have ridden the rails for miles and days.

Shelling peas is not the most pleasant experience in the world, but each pod does hold a kind of fascination—you wonder if it will be full of mature peas or half-mature fakers. No one has ever shelled a mess of peas without having a handful of them go scooting out over the floor, but that is part of the job.

Once the peas are ready for the pot, on the fire they go in the barest minimum of salted water. Some cooks add a little sugar. Peas cook in just a little while if tender. If they are not tender, as only fresh peas are, cooking will never make them so. As they cook, their tender little skins shrivel and then they shrivel some more. When the peas are done, all the water should be gone and in goes a big hunk of butter. Once the tiny pellets are coated with butter, they are ready for the table.

Sometimes a little thickener is stirred into the peas. Other times, they are cooked with new potatoes or dumplings.

Peas and New Potatoes

Scrape, never peel, small new potatoes and cook until tender in boiling salted water. In another pot, cook new peas. Season both with butter and then combine them in a medium-thick cream or white sauce. Sprinkle the top liberally with black pepper and serve.

New Peas and Dumplings

Many an individual can make a meal from this dish.

Cook the peas in boiling salted water—have some water remaining after they are cooked. Season with a lot of butter.

Roll out biscuit dough to a thickness of about ¼ inch and cut into strips about 1-inch wide. Lay the strips on top of the cooked peas. Cover the pot tightly and simmer without peeking for 12 minutes. Sprinkle black pepper over the top before serving.

GREEN BLACK-EYED PEAS

There is only one dish better than green black-eyed peas that have been simmered to sweet tenderness with a hunk of salt pork, and that is a pot of black-eyed peas mixed with young kernels of fresh white corn.

Danny's Black-Eyed Peas

¼ pound ham hocks
1 teaspoon lemon pepper
1 quart water
2 cups shelled fresh black-eyed peas
Salt (optional)

Wash ham hocks. Place in a Dutch oven or heavy-bottom saucepan with lemon pepper and water. Bring to a boil, reduce heat, and simmer, uncovered, for 1 hour. Add peas, cover, and cook over medium heat until the peas are tender—about 1½ hours. Taste and add salt if needed. Makes 4 servings.

Fried Black-Eyed Peas and Onions

Fry a cut-up onion in a little meat drippings. Add a bowl of leftover black-eyed peas and cook.

Scalloped Green Peppers

Cut green peppers in half and remove seeds and membrane. Cut into strips about ½-inch wide. Drop peppers into boiling salted water and cook for 5 minutes or so. Drain well and place in a casserole.

Make a cream sauce of 2 tablespoons butter and 2 tablespoons flour to each cup of milk. Season with salt and pepper and pour over peppers. Cover with a liberal coating of grated sharp cheese and buttered bread crumbs. Heat in a moderate oven (about 350°) to brown crumbs.

Poke Stalks

Cut the young stalks when they are about as big as your little finger and show only a little ruffle of leaves around the top. They should be only a few inches above the ground.

Scrape stalks, leaving leaves on. Soak in salted water before cooking. Tie in little bundles like asparagus and cook in boiling salted water. Add butter and season with salt and pepper.

IRISH POTATOES

I guess the potato favorites are boiled potatoes, "creamed potatoes," and potato salad.

Boiled potatoes are seasoned with pork drippings or butter and are cooked to the point that when they reach the plate, the touch of a fork is all it takes to mash them. Young new potatoes are often served with crisp slices of salt pork and milk gravy made from pork drippings.

In North Carolina creamed potatoes mean mashed or whipped potatoes. The leftover mashed potatoes usually turn up as potato cakes the next day. Potato cakes are made by shaping leftover seasoned mashed potatoes into cakes, coating them with flour, and browning them on both sides in a little hot fat in a heavy skillet.

Mashed Potatoes (Creamed Potatoes)

A good dish of mashed potatoes is as fine as any starchy food ever put on a table. But they are mighty sad if lumpy, grayish looking, or watery.

9 medium potatoes (about 3¼ to 3½ pounds)
6 to 8 tablespoons butter
About ¾ cup hot half and half (half milk, half cream)
Warm milk
Salt

Place potatoes in a saucepan; add water to cover. Bring to a boil and simmer until potatoes are tender. Drain. Peel, mash, and, if desired, put through a ricer.

Heat butter and half and half until butter is melted and cream is hot but not boiling. Beat with a wooden spoon until light and fluffy, adding warm milk as needed for desired consistency. Add salt to taste. Makes 8 or 9 servings.

Note: To have mashed potatoes that are thoroughly hot, place in a casserole. Cover with waxed paper and heat in the microwave. Time depends on quantity and microwave.

Stewed Irish Potatoes

The old Tar Heel cookbook *Mrs. Elliott's Housewife** gives these directions: "Cut up one dozen Irish potatoes in round pieces half an inch thick, nearly cover them with water in a saucepan, cover and let them stew until tender. Drain off the water and let them steam a few minutes, then cover them with milk. Rub a little flour in butter, put it in with salt and pepper, and when the milk comes to a full boil, pour them out in a covered dish."

Another way is to cook chunks of potato in water until done. Add but-

*In 1974 Elizabeth J. Holder, head of the reference department of the Walter Clinton Jackson Library of the University of North Carolina at Greensboro, wrote in response to a query about cookbooks: "The first North Carolina cook book was by Maria Massey Barringer, issued in 1867 and called *Dixie Cookery; or How I Managed My Table for Twelve Years. A practical cook book from Southern housekeepers.* Boston: Loring, 1867. Ms. Barringer was from Concord. We have an 1882 copy bound in with four other titles but have never been able to find a copy of the 1867 edition. The book *Mrs. Elliott's Housewife* followed in 1870.

ter and season with salt and pepper. Mash some of the potato to thicken the liquid.

Albemarle Potato Surprise

This recipe came from Kimsey Perry, former home agent of Perquimans County.

2 cups hot mashed potatoes
1 egg, beaten
1 teaspoon salt
⅛ teaspoon pepper
½ cup grated cheese
Melted butter
Tomato slices, salt, buttered bread crumbs, and grated cheese

Mix mashed potatoes, egg, salt, pepper, and ½ cup grated cheese. Shape into balls and place on a greased baking sheet. Flatten balls slightly. Brush with melted butter. Cover each with a tomato slice. Sprinkle tomato slice with salt and buttered bread crumbs and a sprinkling of grated cheese.

Bake for 15 to 20 minutes in a moderate oven (about 350°). Serve at once. Makes 4 to 6 servings.

Potato Salad

Potato salad in North Carolina is made with cubes of cooked Irish potatoes, diced sweet pickles (always *sweet* pickles), mayonnaise, and celery. Some cooks add a bit of onion and turmeric for a yellow color.

In this recipe, which gives a flavorful salad, the addition of oil and vinegar dressing is not traditional but adds flavor because the warm potatoes tend to absorb the dressing.

6 medium potatoes
2 tablespoons bottled oil and vinegar salad dressing
1 cup celery, diced
½ to 1 cup sweet pickles, diced and drained
1 tablespoon minced onion (optional)
1 teaspoon salt or to taste
¼ teaspoon pepper

1 teaspoon turmeric (optional)
⅛ teaspoon sugar
½ to ⅔ cup mayonnaise
Salad greens

Place unpeeled potatoes in a saucepan; add water to cover. Bring to a boil; reduce heat to simmer and cook until potatoes are done—about 20 minutes. Drain off cooking liquid and discard; place pan with potatoes back on burner, which has been turned off but still has enough heat to cause the water left in the bottom of the pan to evaporate. Immediately pry open each potato with 2 forks; dribble salad dressing into each potato. Let stand until cool enough to handle.

Peel and cube potatoes; add celery, pickles, onion, salt, pepper, turmeric, sugar, and mayonnaise. Cover and chill. Serve on salad greens. Makes 6 servings (generally allow 1 medium potato per serving).

SQUASH

Squash are often stewed with a little water, then mashed with salt, pepper, and butter. Frequently, they are cooked with onions. After the chopped onions are fried in butter or drippings, the sliced squash are added with a little water. The mixture is simmered until done, then seasoned with salt and pepper.

Fried Squash

Another popular way to serve squash is to fry them. Cut the larger portion of crooknecks into slices about ½-inch thick. Coat in flour seasoned with salt and pepper and, if desired, mixed with a little cornmeal. Fry the slices.

Baked Stuffed Squash

For a special meal, you will run into baked stuffed squash. This recipe is especially tasty.

6 small yellow crookneck squash
4 tablespoons butter
½ cup fine bread crumbs

2 tablespoons minced onion
½ teaspoon salt
1 tablespoon minced parsley
⅛ teaspoon black pepper
Pinch of sage
Dash of thyme

Drop the whole squash into boiling salted water and boil for about 10 minutes, or until squash are tender but not soft. Remove from heat, drain, and cool. Slice a portion from the top of the squash, then scoop out pulp and seeds to make a cavity.

Melt butter in saucepan. Add remaining ingredients and stir until bread crumbs are browned. Add chopped pulp from the squash. Pack bread crumb mixture into squash. Place in a baking dish. Bake in a moderate oven (about 375°) for 20 to 25 minutes. Makes 6 servings.

Squash Casseroles

In the *Encyclopedia of Southern Culture* (University of North Carolina Press, 1989), under cookbooks, there appears this statement: "People may not live by squash casseroles alone, but a southern cookbook without a recipe for at least one is rare." A spread of food for a group without a squash casserole is equally rare.

The following recipe is typical. It was contributed by Christine Daniel (Mrs. Louis B. Daniel, Sr.) to a collection of recipes for the Daniel family reunion in 1982.

Christine Daniel's Squash Casserole

2 pounds yellow squash, sliced
1 medium onion, sliced
1 teaspoon salt
½ teaspoon sugar
3 tablespoons melted butter
3 tablespoons flour
2 eggs, slightly beaten
1 cup milk
½ pound grated sharp cheddar cheese
Seasoned salt

Pepper
Buttered bread crumbs

Simmer squash, onion, and salt for 20 minutes. Drain well; mash. Blend thoroughly sugar, melted butter, flour, eggs, and milk; add cheese and seasoned salt and pepper to taste. Combine with squash.

Turn into a buttered casserole. Bake in a 350° oven for 30 minutes, or until firm. Sprinkle with bread crumbs and bake for 10 minutes longer.

Squash Pie

Cut 2 to 3 young yellow squash into thin slices and place in a pie pan lined with unbaked pastry. Sprinkle with 2 tablespoons water, 4 tablespoons sugar, salt, and ginger. Dot with butter. Cover with top crust and bake in a moderate oven (about 350°) until done.

Butternut Squash

Butternut squash can be boiled, mashed, baked, candied, or used as you would use pumpkin to make pie. It is not necessary to steam them, as they cook up dry rather than watery like pumpkin.

Candied Butternut Squash

Slice peeled squash ½ to ¾ of an inch thick. Boil in salted water for 10 minutes or until tender. Drain. Place slices in a pan, sprinkle with brown sugar and cinnamon, and dot with butter. Cook slowly under the broiler for about 10 minutes, or until squash is browned and heated through.

SWEET POTATOES

Tar Heel cooks prepare sweet potatoes in every conceivable manner. At one time countless numbers of sweet "taters" were baked in the ashes of the fireplace. Many a child enjoyed a sweet potato hot from the ashes as a treat before bedtime.

Even after the arrival of wood ranges, many women continued to bake potatoes in the ashes. When the potatoes went into the oven, the old folks baked them at a low temperature (about 250 degrees) for a long time. This process "brings out the candy" in the potatoes. Before putting them in the oven, the potatoes were usually greased with pork drippings to make a softer skin. The hot potato should be gouged open and filled with a pat of butter.

These are some of my favorite yam recipes.

Candied Sweet Potatoes
(Tested)

These might be called glazed sweet potatoes. Whatever the name, the results are delicious.

6 small to medium sweet potatoes
1 cup dark corn syrup
4 tablespoons brown sugar
2 tablespoons butter or margarine
⅓ cup orange juice or water

Wash potatoes and boil until tender but not soft. Drain, peel, and cut into halves lengthwise. Pour syrup, sugar, butter, and orange juice into a heavy skillet. Bring to a boil; add potatoes. Lower heat and simmer until the syrup is thick and the potatoes are well coated. Turn the potatoes gently as they cook. Makes 6 servings.

Sweet Potato Pudding or Pone
(Tested)

This dish is served as a vegetable or a dessert.

2 cups milk
¾ cup brown sugar
2 tablespoons melted butter
1 teaspoon cinnamon
1 teaspoon allspice
½ teaspoon nutmeg
¼ teaspoon ginger
Dash of salt
2 eggs, beaten
3 cups shredded raw sweet potatoes

Add milk, sugar, butter, and seasonings to eggs. Mix with potatoes. Pour into a buttered baking dish and bake in a moderate oven (about 325°) for 1 hour. Serve warm. Makes 8 servings.

Sweet Potato Chips

Slice potatoes very thinly and put in a pan of cold salted water. Dry with a cloth and fry in hot lard. Place on brown paper to drain.

TOMATOES

Tomatoes are served year-round. In the summer, when the fresh ones are in season, it is common to see them served as plain slices or in a bowl with a coating of sugar and vinegar. In the winter, canned tomatoes are often served plain with sugar and maybe with vinegar, unheated—just as they come from the jar.

Today, of course, grocery stores have fresh tomatoes all winter. Little can be said for these hothouse tomatoes except that they are red. Flavorwise, they have no character. You have only to smell a freshly picked North Carolina tomato as you begin to peel it to know what fine flavor it contains.

Scalloped Tomatoes
(Tested)

This recipe came from the former Frances Noble (Mrs. Christopher Bell), who for two years (ca. 1952–53) operated the Old Garden Tearoom in Winston-Salem. Her customers thought that she served the best food in town in the old Dunn house on West Fifth Street at the corner of Broad Street.

1½ cups coarsely broken pieces of stale bread
⅓ cup melted butter
¼ teaspoon salt
6 tablespoons brown sugar
1 pint or 1 can (1 pound) tomatoes

Place bread in a shallow baking dish such as a Pyrex pie plate. Pour melted butter over it and stir to distribute.

Meanwhile, put tomatoes in a saucepan and add salt and brown sugar;

heat to boiling and pour over bread. Stir to distribute tomatoes in bread. Bake in a 425° oven for 30 to 40 minutes, or until well browned. Makes 3 to 4 servings.

Fried Tomato Slices
(Tested)

Firm, underripe tomatoes
Flour, salt, and pepper
Butter
Salad oil

When all the other food for a meal is ready to serve, cut tomatoes in slices ½ to ⅝ inches thick. Coat on both sides in a mixture of flour, salt, and pepper in a shallow pan.

Heat butter and oil (3 tablespoons butter to 1 tablespoon oil) in a black iron skillet. Place tomato slices in the hot fat. Cook until lightly browned on one side; turn and brown on the other side. Turn only once. Serve immediately to prevent sogginess.

Tomato Pudding

Cover the bottom of a baking dish with slices of bread, using little chunks to fill in the whole surface. Cover with a good layer of peeled sliced fresh tomatoes. Dust with cinnamon and sprinkle with brown sugar. Dot liberally with butter. Repeat layers until the pan is filled, ending with tomatoes.

Bake in a 400° oven for 25 minutes, or until browned around the edges.

TURNIPS

A few snips from the pods of red pepper are often added to turnips for stewing. The stewed turnips are seasoned with salt, pepper, and butter or bacon drippings.

Sliced or diced turnips are sometimes cooked with the tops. The seasoning, of course, is salt pork. The combination makes a delicious dish.

· · · · ·

FRUITS

APPLES

In addition to pies, cobblers, bettys, baked apples, and applesauce, apples are likely to show up at any meal from breakfast on as fried apples or candied apples.

Beginning in late June, when little green apples (the kind that give kids a stomachache or the "green apple quick-step," as the old folks call it) begin to appear, they are sliced or quartered and fried, with the peeling on, in a little bacon grease or ham grease. Some cooks meticulously leave the apple rings in pretty circles, but most often the apples are stirred together, for in this case it is the flavor rather than the form that counts. These early green apples have a tart deliciousness not to be found in big, red, ripe apples.

Fried Apples

Wash, core, and slice apples into a little hot grease. Cook over medium heat, stirring gently. Just before they are done, sprinkle sugar over the top to sweeten.

Candied Apples

Wash and peel tart apples and cut into quarters. Place in a shallow baking pan and add a little water and light corn syrup; dot with butter. Sprinkle brown sugar liberally over the top.

Cover and place in a moderate oven (about 350°). Remove cover after about 30 minutes and continue cooking until the apples are tender. They should be clear and transparent. They will be delicious.

Honeyed Peaches

My grandmother used to make these in the oven from the little freckled peaches. She did not peel them. I find that the broiler is better than the oven.

Fill peeled or unpeeled fresh peach halves with honey and dot with butter. Cook under the hot broiler or bake in a moderate oven (about 375°) until brown and bubbly.

· · · · ·

OTHER FAVORITES

GRITS

Grits were prepared by stirring ground whole hominy into boiling salted water and cooking the mixture until done. Now, with the quick-cooking variety, the process takes but minutes.

Fried Grits

These are good for breakfast.

Pour cooked hot grits into a greased loaf pan. Chill until firm. Cut into slices, coat with flour, and brown on both sides in bacon grease in a heavy skillet.

Pickled Eggs

Gallon jars of the pink version of these eggs are often seen in taverns and cafés and at truck stops.

1 cup vinegar
1 cup water
2 tablespoons sugar
1 teaspoon salt
½ teaspoon celery seed
1 clove garlic, minced
2 bay leaves
12 hard-cooked eggs, shelled
Beet juice or red food coloring (optional)

In a saucepan combine vinegar, water, sugar, salt, celery seed, garlic, and bay leaves. Bring to a boil; reduce heat and simmer for 30 minutes. Remove from heat and cool. Add beet juice to tint, if desired. Pour liquid over eggs in a jar or bowl. Refrigerate for 3 to 4 days.

Macaroni Pie

Macaroni pie, a version of macaroni and cheese, is perhaps more a South Carolina dish than a North Carolina one but it is served here.

Cook 1½ cups macaroni in boiling salted water until tender. Drain well.

Beat 2 eggs and blend in 1 teaspoon flour, salt to taste, 1 cup grated sharp cheese, ⅛ pound butter cut into small pieces, and 1 cup cold milk. Add macaroni, mix, and turn into a greased casserole.

Top with additional grated cheese. Sprinkle with black pepper. Bake in a 325° oven until firm and lightly browned. Makes 5 to 6 servings.

Creamed Goobers or Peanuts

This is a favorite of easterners. It is a dish for the world like creamed chestnuts.

Boil young, tender shelled peanuts or goobers in salted water. Drain and serve in cream sauce as a vegetable.

Fried Pumpkin Blooms

Some of the old folks seemed to enjoy this unusual dish.

Remove the hard core in the center of each bloom. Dip in a thin batter. Fry in hot fat until crisp and brown. Serve right away.

E L E V E N

Breads & Sandwiches

Until loaves of commercially baked white bread became plentiful in stores, all bread served in the home was made in the home and generally arrived at the table hot. The white bread, called light bread, was initially regarded as a luxury because it had to be bought at a bakery or grocery store. Loaves of white bread were not sliced at the bakery until modern technology produced a slicing machine. Unsliced loaves were the basis of the popular sandwich loaves frosted with cream cheese for parties.

The following story proves that there are others who, given the opportunity, share a North Carolinian's love of hot breads. A G.I. from another part of the country was asked to be a guest in a Tar Heel home during World War II. He enjoyed the best that the household had to offer, for even with rationing, homes that had hams hanging in the smokehouse and chickens running around in the yard were able to set a fine table.

The soldier went back to camp and talked for days about the delicious "hot 'uns" served at the meal. Finally, someone asked him what in the world was he talking about. He said, "You know, those hot 'uns. Every five minutes during dinner somebody would pass another plate and say 'Have a hot 'un,'" meaning a hot biscuit.

· · · · ·

HOT BISCUITS

In many homes, a pan of hot biscuits was a three-meal-a-day proposition. The old-fashioned cook makes them this way: Unmeasured self-rising flour (flour with leavening added at the mill) is sifted into a large bowl. An unmeasured lump of lard is worked in, with enough buttermilk to make a soft dough.

The cook goes on "the feel" of the dough to know when it is right. It is kneaded lightly on a floured board, and for the family the biscuits are cut with a cutter almost the size of an English muffin. The baked tops are rough and range from golden to a darker brown. The biscuits are usually about an inch thick, though some people like thin ones—with little more than two browned crusts and no feathery light interior. The cook who is unable to serve biscuits hot enough to melt butter is a failure in the biscuit department.

There were those who made baking powder biscuits long before the days when baking powder was available in the grocery store. They made their own baking powder. Here is a recipe I found in the yellowed pages of an old cookbook: "Take a pound of cream of tartar and mix with an even pint of flour. Rub through a sieve three or four times. Put in tins and keep in a dry place. Use 3 teaspoons to one quart of flour."

Soda or Buttermilk Biscuits

2 cups sifted flour
½ teaspoon soda
1 teaspoon salt
3 tablespoons lard
About ¾ cup buttermilk

Inexperienced cooks, and sometimes those with experience, produce soda biscuits that become yellow when baked. This happens because the buttermilk is too sour or too much soda is used.

Sift flour, soda, and salt. Cut in lard. Add enough buttermilk to make a soft dough. Knead lightly on a floured board. Roll out, cut, and bake at 475°.

Self-Rising Flour Buttermilk Biscuits

(Tested)

I have had great success with this recipe. The biscuits are high, white, and almost as light as light rolls.

2 cups sifted self-rising flour
Pinch each of soda and baking powder
⅓ cup lard or shortening
About ¾ cup buttermilk

Heat oven to 450°. Sift flour into a bowl. Add soda and baking powder. Cut in lard (a pastry blender is best for this job) until the mixture looks like meal. Stir in most of the buttermilk. Mix well and add remaining milk to make a soft dough that can be handled.

Turn out on a lightly floured board and knead gently—do not knead too much. Pat out to a ½-inch thickness. Cut with a floured cutter. For soft sides, place close together on an ungreased baking sheet; for crusty sides, place apart. Bake for 10 to 12 minutes, or until done. Makes about 12 biscuits.

HYDE COUNTY BISCUITS AND CREAM

On special occasions the custom around Hyde County is to serve very thick sweet cream instead of butter with hot biscuits and jam.

Naple Biscuits

Beat 8 eggs, 1 pound flour, 1 pound of sugar, and essence of lemon. Bake in a hot oven.

Egg Biscuits

Combine 1 pint cream, 4 eggs, and as much flour as will make the dough stiff. Work smooth and bake in a hot oven.

Dessert Biscuits

Combine ¾ pound flour, ¼ pound sugar, grated peel of a lemon, ½ teacup cream, and the yellows of 2 eggs. Roll them thin and bake in a hot oven.

Ginger Biscuits

Combine 8 ounces flour, 4 ounces butter, 4 ounces sugar, ½ ounce ginger, and 1 egg. Bake in a hot oven.

Sweet Potato Biscuits

2 cups sifted flour
2 teaspoons baking powder
Scant ½ teaspoon soda
2 tablespoons sugar
½ teaspoon salt
2 tablespoons lard
1 cup mashed sweet potatoes
About 1 cup buttermilk

Sift dry ingredients. Cut in lard. Add sweet potatoes and sufficient buttermilk to make a soft dough. Knead gently on a lightly floured board. Roll out and cut. Bake at 450° until golden.

GRAVY SPONGES

A gravy sponge is a sweet potato biscuit that has been made to serve with gravy.

FRIED BREAD

It was a common practice for cooks to fry biscuit dough or pastry in lard or other drippings. Families adopted their own names for this bread. One called it such cakes, whereas another called it fritters. The fried bread was often dusted with sugar and cinnamon.

Chicken Bread

The only menu I have ever seen with chicken bread on it was at the Pinnacle Inn in Banner Elk. A story in one publication, dated May 1926, reported that the name, Pinnacle Inn, had been selected for the summer hotel operated at and by the students of Lees-McRae College. An article about the inn in the July 1953 issue of *The State* magazine indicated that it was still operating at that time. The weekly rates for rooms and meals ranged from \$21 to \$35 per person. The article said that since the early 1900s, the facilities of the college had been used to entertain vacationists in the Elk Valley.

Whatever the specific dates of the inn, I visited there often in the 1930s and especially enjoyed its unique chicken bread, a bread cooked in the fat left from frying chicken. (Plain biscuit dough rolled and cut into squares or rounds can be prepared in the same way.) Along with fried chicken and chicken bread, the fare for Sunday dinner included an abundance of fresh vegetables grown on the college farm. The meal was priced at \$1 per person. The breakfast menu offered buckwheat cakes (for recipe see index), served with syrup, sausage, and bacon or pork chops.

This is the recipe for the chicken bread.

1 ½ cups sifted flour
½ cup cornmeal
3 teaspoons baking powder
1 teaspoon salt
4 tablespoons shortening
¾ cup milk

Sift together dry ingredients. Cut in shortening until the mixture resembles coarse crumbs. Add milk to make a soft dough that can be handled, mixing lightly only until the mixture is dampened.

Turn out on a lightly floured board and knead gently for a few seconds. Roll out to a ⅜-inch thickness; cut into diamond shapes, rounds, or squares.

Fry in a small amount of hot fat left from frying chicken. Cook over medium heat until delicately browned on one side. Turn and brown the other side. The cooking time is about 8 minutes. Serve immediately. Makes 12 to 18 pieces.

A BATCH OF BEATEN BISCUITS

A beaten biscuit is quite different from the usual kind. It is neither tender nor light but requires strong jaws and good teeth. For those who have never seen one, a description is in order. Beaten biscuits are about the size of a fifty-cent piece and one-fourth- to one-third-inch thick. In texture and taste, they are a cross between a soda cracker and a real biscuit.

People used to have a high regard for these biscuits. One old-timer related this story: "When I was a little girl, we, of course, always took our lunch to school. There was a girl in our class who always had beaten biscuits in her lunch. We would willingly trade two choice cookies or cakes for one of her beaten biscuits."

The dough is made without leavening. The beating removes the air and produces a smooth, satiny mass. The old folks claim that it takes a full hour of beating by hand to do the job properly. Cooks would often take the dough out in the yard to a rock, the chopping block, or a leveled stump and beat the "livin' day lights" out of it with a wooden mallet. Others did the beating with the edge of a plate on the dough board in the kitchen.

Because of the time required for the beating, a batch could not be turned out for ordinary meals unless there was a strong and willing cook in the kitchen. Rather, the biscuits were saved for special occasions. Beaten biscuits have not completely disappeared. Now and then a plate of ham-filled ones will turn up at a party.

When the beating begins, crumbs and fragments fly around. The beginner can be easily discouraged at the outset, but with perseverance, all will turn out well. The old recipes say that the dough must be beaten until blisters form and crack. Modern flour must be different from that used years ago, because today it is just about impossible to make the dough blister.

A few families own a beaten biscuit machine, also called a biscuit break. The dough is run through the machine in place of hand beating. Some of the machines are on stands similar to the kind used to support a treadle sewing machine, and the biscuit break is about the same size. The top is covered with a marble slab with rollers at one end. The rollers are like those found on a modern washing machine. A neat little wooden box fits over the rollers when the break is not in use. Other beaten biscuit machines consist merely of two metal rollers.

Some cooks have produced good beaten biscuits by running the dough through the meat grinder six or eight times. After baking, Mrs. Fred G. Ray of the Black Bear Inn near West Jefferson put her biscuits on a Pyrex plate and placed them in a hot warming closet for one hour, which she claimed made them creamy.

The recipe below was edited from the original versions.

Beaten Biscuits

2 cups sifted flour
1 scant teaspoon salt
½ teaspoon sugar (some add it, some do not)
⅓ cup lard
⅓ cup sweet milk
About ⅓ cup water

Sift together flour, salt, and sugar. Cut in lard. Add milk and water to make a stiff dough and knead until dough holds together.

Place on a sturdy surface and start beating or run through a biscuit machine. Beat until the dough becomes smooth and satiny.

Shape with the hands or roll out and cut with a tiny cutter. Stab in several places on top with a fork. Bake at 350° for 30 minutes, or until golden. [One old recipe said: "Bake in a strong, steady oven."] Split open while hot and butter.

A CONFECTION FROM LEFTOVER DOUGH

Although North Carolina cannot claim to be their original home, stickies, a confection made from leftover dough, were once tremendously popular in the state. These pastries are a bit like rugalach, a tradition for the Jewish Hanukkah, especially the ones with cinnamon-sugar filling. But, as in the case of other old favorites, few cooks now make them.

The origin of stickies is obscure but may have the same explanation as that given for Moravian sugar cake. One Christmas, when the Salem College Alumnae Association of Fayetteville was planning to sell sugar cake at a holiday bazaar, a member called to inquire about its origin. No where in the early Moravian records—meticulous though they are—do we find any notation that on a specific day in a specific place a Moravian cook had some yeast dough left from her bread making. Because cooks were thrifty by necessity, the cook probably looked around to see what might be compatible with the leftover dough. Naturally, she had brown sugar, butter, and cinnamon. These she combined with the dough in a baking pan, poking holes in the dough with her fingers. The baked product was sugar cake.

When I was a child, I saw stickies made with leftover scraps of pastry from pies. The scraps were rolled out to the same thickness as piecrust, sprinkled with cinnamon and brown sugar, and dotted with butter. Then the dough was rolled up like a jelly roll, cut into thin slices, and baked.

Stickies

⅔ cup plain flour
⅔ cup self-rising flour
½ teaspoon salt
3 tablespoons shortening
About ⅓ cup sweet milk
1¼ cups brown sugar
½ cup (1 stick) butter
1 teaspoon vanilla
2 teaspoons water

Mix flours and salt with shortening as for pastry; add enough milk to make a firm dough. Roll out thin, spread with sugar, and cut butter into bits over top. Roll up like a jelly roll. Cut into ⅔-inch pieces and place in a greased 8- × 8-inch layer cake pan with cut side down. Bake in a 400° oven until brown. Mix vanilla and water and pour around edges of stickies. Return to the oven for 1 minute, or longer if desired hard.

• • • • •

BAKED BREAD

LOAVES OF SALT-RISING BREAD

Of salt-rising bread, one of the old cookbooks said: "It is the sweetest and most wholesome bread a family can use." As a child I often visited in the home of Cousin Julie Hendrix, who made salt-rising bread fresh each day. I have never known just where Cousin Julie hung on the family tree but, of course, that is the way it sometimes is with southerners and their cousins.

Cousin Julie's Salt-Rising Bread
(Tested)

Once you start making salt-rising bread, each process has to follow the previous one. The time I tested this bread, the baking stage arrived at 12:30 A.M. About an hour later I sleepily pulled the golden brown loaves from the oven and proceeded at that hour to have some with butter—it was just as good as I remembered. This is the recipe I used.

3 medium white potatoes
2 tablespoons sugar
3 tablespoons cornmeal
1 teaspoon salt
4 cups boiling water
2 cups lukewarm milk
¼ teaspoon soda
Sifted flour
4 tablespoons shortening

Peel and slice potatoes and place in a large mixing bowl. Add sugar, cornmeal, and salt. Pour boiling water over mixture. Cover with a dish towel and place in a pan of hot water for 24 hours. (Keep the water hot by leaving the pan on the lowest heat of the stove or in a warm oven.) Near the end of this time the odor of fermentation will be evident and little bubbles will form on the surface.

After 24 hours, remove the potatoes and discard. Add milk, soda, and enough sifted flour to make a stiff sponge. A large amount of flour is required. Return the mixture to the large mixing bowl over hot water and allow to remain 2 to 2½ hours, or until light.

In another large bowl, cut shortening into 2 cups sifted flour. Add previous mixture with sufficient flour to make a soft dough. Knead lightly and quickly so that the dough will stay warm. Shape into loaves and place in greased pans (4 small loaf pans or 3 large ones). Grease tops. Allow to remain in a warm place until doubled in bulk. Bake at 375° for 10 minutes, then reduce temperature to 350° and finish baking.

A LOAF OF BREAD AND A POT OF COFFEE

I do not see how folks live within smelling distance of a bakery without being forever tantalized. The odor of the finest vintage wine has yet to touch the yeasty aroma of bread baking. Use mixes and ready-baked bread when you must, but find enough time one day to make some homemade bread. Put on a pot of coffee, and when the baking is almost completed, open a fresh stick of butter and take the jam pot to the table. Sit down and forget the traffic jams, the blaring of the radio, the blasts of television, and all the urgencies of life.

Dutch Loaf or Potato Bread
(Tested)

Of this Dutch loaf, one reader wrote: "I just wanted you to know that I made the bread by noon the day the recipe came out in the morning paper. My two-and-a-half-year-old son called it cake and just gobbled it up. My husband said it was as good as the bread his mother used to make." A Raleigh woman took several loaves to a bazaar. They were sold right away, leaving quite a few women who wanted a loaf so much that they decided to make their own. For a week requests for the recipe poured into the office of the Raleigh *News and Observer*, which had originally carried it.

I know it sounds as if the bread has to spend a lot of time rising—it does, but that is what produces a fine-grained loaf. Another thing I like about this loaf is that the crust is soft—the loaf cuts like a pound cake. If you do not wish to spoil the folks at your house, pass up this recipe. Once they have tasted it, they will want this kind of bread all the time.

> *1 medium potato, peeled*
> *1 cup milk*
> *1 package dry granular yeast*
> *About 5 cups sifted flour*
> *½ cup shortening and butter, mixed*
> *½ cup sugar*
> *2 eggs*
> *2 teaspoons salt*
> *Melted butter*

Boil potato until soft. Reserve ½ cup potato water. Mash potato. There should be ½ cup but if there is more, go ahead and use it.

Stir yeast into lukewarm potato water and allow to stand for a few minutes. Meanwhile, scald milk and cool to lukewarm. Add lukewarm milk to yeast together with 1½ cups flour and mashed potato. Beat hard for 3 minutes. Cover with a dish towel and put in a warm place to double in bulk (it takes about 1½ hours).

Cream shortening. Add sugar and beat until light. Add eggs and salt. Beat well. Stir eggs into yeast mixture. Add flour to make a very soft dough and mix well. Place in a greased bowl, cover, and allow to rise again in a warm place until doubled in bulk. Turn out on a lightly floured board and punch down. Place the dough in a greased 2-quart casserole dish. Brush the top with melted butter.

Allow to rise again in a warm place until doubled in bulk. Bake in a moderate oven (about 350°) for 50 minutes or until done.

Note: Be sure to make a few slices of this Dutch loaf into toast— spread the slices with soft butter and toast under the broiler until the edges are fringed with brown. There is as much difference between a slice of this toast and the usual pop-up toaster variety as there is between sirloin steak and hamburger.

HOPS, YEAST, AND RIVELS

In the days before the little three-cent cakes of Fleischmann's yeast were available at every corner grocery and drugstore, cooks used "magic" yeast or brewer's yeast to make bread. Magic yeast was a dry cake of yeast about two inches square and half an inch thick. Brewer's yeast consisted of little granules.

Before then, almost everyone had a hops vine in the backyard. This is the way one old cookbook described how to make yeast from hops.

Yeast from Hops

Homemakers probably used this yeast as a starter. When a cook ran out of yeast, she would borrow some starter from her neighbor. Thus, she was back in the bread-making business without going through the difficulty of making her own yeast.

Boil 6 Irish potatoes in 2 quarts of water until done. Boil a pinch of hops in 1 quart of water. Mash potatoes and return them to the water in which they were boiled. Strain the hop water into this, adding ½ cup each of sugar and salt, and put in a jug.

Yeast

When magic yeast came along, it was used with hops in the following manner.

Gather hop blossoms that resemble round roses about 1 inch in diameter with tiny petals. Dry thoroughly in the open and store in a porous bag.

Tie 1 cup of the dried hops in a cheesecloth bag. Peel 2 medium potatoes. Put potatoes and hops in a saucepan and cover with water. Cook until the potatoes are well done and about ½ pint water remains.

Lift out bag of hops and discard. Mash potatoes. Let stand until nearly cold. Stir in ½ teacup magic yeast that has been made into a paste with water. Add flour to make a thick paste. Allow to rise in a warm place until double in bulk—about 2 hours in summer. Stir down and use for making bread.

Rivels

The word *rive* means to split or separate. Rivels, meaning a substance that has been split or separated, were a means of having yeast without driving miles to obtain the commercial product. Peach leaves can be substituted for hop blossoms in the process, but they are not as good.

To make rivels (sometimes called riffles), use the recipe for yeast above. After the yeast mixture has been stirred, add cornmeal until the dough will crumble but is not too dry. Dry these "crumbles" or rivels for several days and store in a dry place. A wooden rival board was also used to dry the mixture.

To use, put ½ cup rivels in ½ cup tepid water and let stand for about 2 hours, or until little bubbles appear on the surface. Proceed to make bread using the rivels as yeast.

LOAF BREADS

In the days before commercial bakeries, North Carolina homemakers, like others, made their own loaves of "light bread." The ingredients and methods were similar to those used elsewhere.

Yeast Loaf
(Tested)

This recipe makes a rich, luscious loaf that is far better than the average everyday loaf.

1 package dry granular yeast
3 tablespoons lukewarm water
1 teaspoon sugar
1 cup hot unseasoned mashed potatoes
½ cup potato water
½ cup scalded milk
¾ cup sugar
½ cup butter
3 eggs, beaten
6 to 7 cups sifted flour
1 tablespoon salt

Dissolve yeast in water according to the directions on the package. Add 1 teaspoon sugar. Mix potatoes, potato water, milk, ¾ cup sugar, and butter and cool to lukewarm. Add yeast mixture and eggs.

Sift 4 cups flour with salt. Add to yeast mixture. Turn out on a floured board and knead in remaining flour. Add sufficient flour to make a stiff dough. Knead thoroughly—none of that quick-mix business. Store in the refrigerator until ready to bake—it will keep for a week.

Turn out on a floured board and knead down. Fill 3 greased loaf pans half full. Place in a warm spot and allow to double in bulk. Brush tops with melted butter. Bake in a moderate oven (about 350°) for 50 minutes, or until done. Makes 3 large loaves.

Superb Yeast Loaf
(Tested)

This recipe makes such a good loaf that it can be sliced and used for sandwiches.

2¼ cups quite warm (almost hot) water
3 tablespoons sugar
1 tablespoon salt
¼ cup shortening
2 packages dry yeast

6½ cups sifted all-purpose flour
¾ cup dry milk powder or powdered milk

Measure warm water into a saucepan or a bowl. Add sugar, salt, shortening, and yeast and stir together. Cover tightly.

Measure flour and milk powder into a 4-quart bowl. Add yeast mixture and stir until well blended. Turn out on a lightly floured board and knead until ingredients are well blended and mixture is smooth and springy (usually this takes no more than 3 minutes).

Place in a warmed bowl that has been liberally greased, turn dough over to grease the top, cover with a damp towel, and place in the oven. Turn on oven to warm for 30 seconds. Turn off heat. (Instead of turning the oven on to preheat, you can place a bowl of hot water in the bottom of the oven to hasten the rising.)

Let rise for 45 minutes—dough will be up to top of bowl—punch down, turn over, and return to oven. Let rise again for 15 minutes. Dough will be not quite to top of bowl.

Turn out on a floured board and divide into 2 parts. Cover dough with a towel and let rest while greasing 2 loaf pans. Shape dough into 2 loaves and place in pans. Return loaves to oven, warming it a little if heat has been lost. Let stay in oven for 15 to 20 minutes—the dough will have doubled in bulk but will not fill pans.

Turn on oven to 400°. From the time the oven is turned on, bake for 35 minutes.

Oatmeal Raised Bread
(Tested)

1 cup scalded milk
½ cup butter or shortening
½ cup brown sugar
1 tablespoon salt
1 cup lukewarm water
1 package dry granular yeast
5 to 6 cups sifted flour
2 eggs
1½ cups rolled oats, uncooked

Pour milk, heated to just below the boiling point, over butter, brown sugar, and salt. Cool to lukewarm. Add water to yeast. Add to milk mixture after a few minutes. Stir in 2 cups flour. Add eggs and beat with egg beater to blend. Add rolled oats. Add enough flour to make a soft dough. Turn out on a lightly floured board and knead until satiny—about 10 minutes.

Round dough into a ball; place in a greased bowl, cover, and let rise in a warm place until light (about 1 hour). Punch down; cover and let rest for 10 minutes. Shape into 2 loaves and place in greased loaf pans. Brush with melted butter, cover, and let rise in a warm place until double in bulk.

Bake at 375° for 1 hour, or until done.

Cheese Loaf
(Tested)

This loaf is well worth making if for no other reason than to produce toasting slices to serve with apple jelly.

1 cup milk
3 tablespoons sugar
1 tablespoon butter
2 teaspoons salt
1 package dry yeast
2 tablespoons lukewarm water
1 egg
2 cups grated sharp cheese
About 4 cups sifted flour
Melted butter

Scald milk and pour over sugar, 1 tablespoon butter, and salt. Cool to lukewarm.

Stir yeast into lukewarm water and allow to stand for a few minutes. Add to cooled milk mixture. Add egg and blend. Add cheese and sufficient flour to make a soft dough. Turn out on a floured board and knead. Allow to rise in a warm place. Knead and place in a greased loaf pan.

Brush the top with melted butter. Allow to rise in a warm place until double in bulk. Bake in a moderate oven (about 350°) for 50 minutes, or until done.

SALLY LUNN

The identity of Sally Lunn has been lost over the years, and now the name is known only as a bread. It seems that the woman called Sally Lunn became famous in her hometown of Bath, England, where she made and sold tea cakes or bread that her neighbors called Sally Lunn.

Sally Lunn may be made with baking powder or yeast. I prefer the yeast kind because of the aroma that fills the house as the bread bakes.

Yeast Sally Lunn
(Tested)

This is an unusually good recipe and one that could not be easier. The crust is delightful—soft and pliable. It is the kind of bread that makes a meal, and an entirely satisfying one, when served with a fresh cake of butter, a jar of jam, a pot of hot coffee, and maybe a slice or two of cheese.

To measure a half package of dry granular yeast, empty the package into a tablespoon and then use half the amount.

½ package cake or ½ package dry granular yeast
2 teaspoons sugar
¼ cup lukewarm water
2 tablespoons lard or shortening
½ teaspoon salt
2 cups sifted flour
½ cup sweet milk
1 egg

Stir yeast and sugar into water. Let stand for a few minutes. Add remaining ingredients and blend well. Cover and let rise in a warm place until about doubled in bulk. The dough will be soft and no additional flour will be required.

Beat down with a spoon and turn into a greased tube pan. Cover and let rise again. Bake in a 400° oven for 25 minutes, or until lightly browned. Serve hot.

Baking Powder Sally Lunn
(Tested)

This is somewhat like a plain one-egg cake only not quite as sweet.

2 tablespoons butter or margarine
3 tablespoons sugar
1 egg, separated
1 cup sifted all-purpose flour
½ teaspoon baking powder
½ teaspoon salt
½ cup milk

Cream butter; add sugar and cream thoroughly. Add the egg yolk and beat well. Sift together flour, baking powder, and salt and add to mixture alternately with milk. Beat well. Fold in the stiffly beaten egg white and pour into a greased 10- × 6- × 2-inch pan.

Bake at 400° for 20 to 25 minutes, or until golden brown. Serve hot. Makes 6 servings.

· · · · ·

HOT ROLLS

Hot rolls were just about as common as hot biscuits. Today, of course, many homemakers serve bakery rolls, but for the truly old-fashioned rolls try one of the following recipes.

Rich Yeast Rolls
(Tested)

2 packages dry granular yeast
½ cup lukewarm water
¼ cup sugar
½ cup milk, scalded
1 teaspoon salt
½ cup butter
3 eggs
4½ cups sifted flour

Stir yeast into water and allow to stand for a few minutes. Add sugar.

Pour hot milk over salt and butter and allow to stand until lukewarm. Add yeast-sugar mixture. Beat eggs and add to mixture. Add enough flour to make a soft dough. Knead slightly on a floured board. Place in a greased mixing bowl and let rise in a warm place until double in bulk.

Turn onto a floured board. Roll out and cut with a small biscuit cutter. Brush with melted butter. Place in baking pans. Allow to double in bulk in a warm place. Bake at 425° for 15 to 20 minutes.

Icebox Rolls

(Tested)

In a large mixing bowl cream ½ cup shortening with ⅓ cup sugar. Mix in 1 egg.

In ⅓ cup lukewarm water, dissolve 1 package dry granular yeast with 1 teaspoon sugar. Sift 2 teaspoons salt with 4 cups flour. Add flour and yeast to creamed mixture alternately with 1 additional cup of lukewarm water. Add more sifted flour to make a soft dough.

Toss onto a lightly floured board and knead briefly. Place in a covered bowl and allow to double in bulk in a warm place. Knead down and make into rolls or store in the refrigerator until about 2 hours before rolls are to be baked. Make rolls and place in a greased pan. Brush tops with melted butter. Allow to double in bulk. Bake in a hot oven (about 425°) for 12 to 15 minutes.

Note: If you are in a hurry, the rolls may be forced after they are shaped by placing the pan of rolls over a pan of boiling water for a few minutes. (*Forced* means that the yeast dough is given a little boost in rising from the added heat of boiling water.)

Sour Dough Rolls

(Tested)

These rolls are not as light as yeast rolls but they do have an intriguing, sour taste.

Flour
2 tablespoons sugar
1 teaspoon salt
2 cups warm water
1 teaspoon soda

To make the starter, sift together 2 cups flour, sugar, and salt into a thick bowl or crock. Stir in water, cover, and place in a warm spot (about 85°) for 2 days. The mixture will become spongy and quite sour to the smell.

To make rolls, sift together ½ cup flour and the soda and add to ¾ of the starter along with additional flour to make a soft dough. Turn out on a lightly floured surface and knead until smooth. Shape into rolls about the size of an egg and place in a greased baking pan. Let rise in a warm place for 1 hour, or until almost double in size. Bake in a 425° oven for 20 minutes, or until done.

To the remaining starter, add more flour, sugar, salt, and water to make a thick batter. Cover and let starter stand. Use as directed above.

Buttermilk Rolls

(Tested)

There are no rolls like buttermilk rolls.

2 cups buttermilk
1 package dry granular yeast
5 cups sifted flour
3 tablespoons sugar
1 teaspoon salt
¼ teaspoon baking powder
¼ teaspoon soda
4 tablespoons shortening

Heat a portion of the buttermilk to lukewarm and use for dissolving yeast. Allow to stand for a few minutes and then mix with remaining buttermilk.

Sift flour with remaining dry ingredients. Cut in shortening. Add buttermilk and blend well. Grease top with butter. Cover and store in the refrigerator.

About 2 hours before serving, take out and make into rolls. Allow to rise in a warm place until double in bulk. Bake at 400° for 12 to 15 minutes, or until done.

Cornmeal Yeast Rolls

(Tested)

Make these with yellow cornmeal for a prettier color—nothing is needed to enhance the delicious flavor and texture.

Cream ½ cup shortening with ⅓ cup sugar. Add 1 egg and mix well. Dissolve 1 package granular yeast in ⅓ cup lukewarm water according to the directions on the package. Add 1 teaspoon sugar to the yeast mixture.

Pour 1 cup boiling water over 1½ cups yellow cornmeal and stir until well mixed. Sift 3 to 4 cups flour with 2 teaspoons salt.

Add cornmeal mixture and flour to creamed mixture alternately with ½ cup lukewarm water. Add additional flour, as needed, to make a soft dough. Place in a bowl, cover, and allow to rise in a warm place until double in bulk.

Make into rolls and brush tops with melted butter. Allow to double in size. Bake at 425° until lightly browned—about 20 minutes.

Cheese Refrigerator Rolls

(Tested)

These are superb when you have ham on the menu.

2 packages dry granular yeast
½ cup lukewarm water
½ cup milk
½ cup butter
4 tablespoons sugar
1 teaspoon salt
3 eggs, well beaten
1 cup grated sharp cheese
About 4½ cups sifted flour

Mix yeast with water according to the package directions. Scald milk and add butter and sugar. Cool to lukewarm. Add yeast mixture to milk with salt and eggs. Mix well.

Add cheese and flour to make a soft dough. Turn out on a lightly floured board and knead until smooth. Place in a greased bowl, cover, and allow to rise in a warm place until double in bulk. Punch down. Grease dough with butter, cover, and store in the refrigerator.

Before shaping into rolls, allow to stand for about 1 hour at room temperature. Make into rolls and place on a greased sheet. Allow to rise until double in bulk in a warm place. Bake at 375° for about 15 minutes, or until brown.

Yam Yeast Rolls
(Tested)

½ package dry granular yeast
¼ cup lukewarm water
¼ cup nonfat dry milk
⅓ cup sugar
1 teaspoon salt
½ cup water
¾ cup sieved cooked sweet potatoes
2 tablespoons melted shortening
About 2¾ cups sifted flour
Melted butter

Soften yeast in lukewarm water. Sift dry milk, sugar, and salt into a large mixing bowl. Add ½ cup water.

Stir in yeast, potatoes, and melted shortening. Add enough flour to make a dough that can be easily handled. Turn out on a lightly floured board and knead until smooth and velvety.

Place in a bowl and brush with melted butter. Cover and allow to rise until dough has doubled in bulk. Knead slightly and shape into rolls. Allow to double in bulk. Bake at 425° for 18 minutes, or until done.

• • • • •

CORN BREAD

Here and there, if you look hard, you may be able to find a North Carolinian who does not like corn bread, but such people are scarce.

Tar Heel cooks do about everything there is to do with cornmeal, which, of course, is most often the old-fashioned water-ground, white variety. The list includes corn bread, crackling corn bread, corn muffins, corn sticks, hush puppies, spoon bread, mush bread, egg bread, ash cakes, hoecakes, corn pone, corn dodgers, cornmeal batter cakes, cornmeal biscuits, cornmeal yeast rolls, and cornmeal waffles.

Crackling Corn Bread
(Tested)

Crackling corn bread lovers never had enough, for the supply of crack-lings lasted for only a short time after the hog killing.

1½ cups cornmeal
1 teaspoon salt
2 tablespoons flour
3 teaspoons baking powder
1 egg, beaten
1¼ cups sweet milk
1½ cups cracklings

Sift together cornmeal, salt, flour, and baking powder. Mix egg and milk and add to dry ingredients. Mix well and add cracklings. Pour into a greased pan and bake in a hot oven (about 425°) for 20 to 25 minutes.

Crackling Dodgers

For crackling dodgers, drop the corn bread batter into plump cakes in a little hot fat in a heavy skillet and cook slowly until well browned on both sides.

All-Corn Muffins
(Tested)

This recipe makes real corn muffins. Split open and filled with butter, they just about melt in your mouth. The method of mixing is a little different but produces excellent results. They are perfect served with summer vegetables.

1 cup cornmeal
1 teaspoon salt
1 cup boiling water
½ cup milk
1 egg
2 teaspoons baking powder
1 tablespoon melted butter

Mix cornmeal and salt. Add water. Stir and then add milk; blend. Add egg and beat lightly.

Just before pouring into greased muffin tins, stir in baking powder and melted butter. Bake at 475° for 12 minutes, or until well browned. Serve at once. Some cooks dust a little sugar over the corn muffins.

Corn Sticks

Prepare corn sticks like corn bread and bake in heavy black iron corn stick pans. For a crisp brown crust, brush the pans liberally with melted shortening or bacon drippings and place in a hot oven to heat while making the batter.

Tony Seamon's Hush Puppies

1 pound fine cornmeal
1 egg
1 tablespoon salt
1 tablespoon sugar
Pinch of soda
1 cup buttermilk

Mix all ingredients, adding water to make a thick batter. Drop by the spoonful into hot fat. Cook at 375° until golden brown.

Cush

Crumble equal parts of corn bread and biscuits. Add a chopped onion and fry all together in meat drippings in a heavy black skillet. Stir until browned.

Mush Bread

Heat 1 pint sweet milk. Add 4 tablespoons butter, ¾ cup cornmeal, and 1 teaspoon salt. Cook until thick. Remove from heat. Add 4 egg yolks and beat well. Fold in 4 beaten egg whites and bake in a moderate oven until done.

Ash Cakes

Mix 2 cups cornmeal and 1 teaspoon salt. Add enough hot water to make a stiff dough. Let stand for 1 hour or more. With the hands, shape into cakes about 1-inch thick.

Lay on hot hearth stones near the fire until the outside crusts up a little. Then cover with hot ashes and bake at least ½ hour or until well browned. Brush off ashes with a cloth. Split with slabs of butter and eat hot.

Hoecakes

These are prepared like ash cakes except that a little more water is added to make a thinner batter.

Grease a hoe [the gardening implement with the metal portion fastened to a handle] or griddle lightly and lay on large spoonfuls of the batter to make cakes about ½-inch thick. Place a clump of butter on top of the cakes before turning. The longer they cook without burning, the thicker the crust, which is the joy of hoecakes.

Corn Dodgers

The batter for corn dodgers is the same as that used for making ash cakes.

Mix 2 cups cornmeal and ½ teaspoon salt. Add enough cold water to make a stiff dough. Shape with the hands into small patties about ½-inch thick. Cook slowly in a heavy black iron skillet containing a small amount of bacon drippings until brown on both sides.

Corn Pone

Though corn pone is essentially the same as corn dodgers, I did run across this interesting recipe, which is different.

Pour 1 quart boiling water over a double handful of cornmeal. Add 1 quart cold water and make a stiff batter. Salt to taste. Set in a moderately warm place overnight or most of the day.

When water begins to rise on this batter, add 1 cup white flour, ½ cup molasses, 2 heaping teaspoons soda dissolved in ¼ cup water. Bake in a covered vessel for 3 hours or more.

Cornmeal Biscuits

Prepare like plain baking powder biscuits using part cornmeal and part flour. Turn out on a lightly floured board and knead gently for a few seconds. Roll out and cut. Bake on an ungreased baking sheet in a hot oven (about 450°) for 12 to 15 minutes.

Scotch Bannochs

This recipe, which came from the Flora MacDonald country, would indicate that the Scots turned out something closely related to spoon bread long before it became so popular in the South.

To prepare, stir ½ cup cornmeal slowly into 1 pint boiling water. Boil until thick. Cook slowly for about 30 minutes. Add 2 egg yolks and 1 teaspoon salt. Fold in 2 stiffly beaten egg whites. Spread in a shallow pan and bake.

Hominy Bread

Mix 2 cups cold hominy grits, 1 tablespoon butter, 1 tablespoon cornmeal, ½ cup sweet milk, 3 well-beaten eggs, and salt to taste. Put into a well-greased deep dish and bake in a hot oven.

Spoon Bread
(Tested)

There are dozens of recipes for spoon bread but this is the one I use. It is a modern version of some of the old-fashioned methods.

2 cups boiling water
1 teaspoon salt
¾ cup yellow cornmeal
3 tablespoons butter
2 eggs, separated
⅔ cup evaporated milk (undiluted)
1 teaspoon baking powder

Add cornmeal to briskly boiling salted water. Boil until just thickened, stirring frequently. Add butter. Cool. Beat egg yolks, add milk, and stir into cornmeal. Fold in stiffly beaten egg whites and baking powder. Turn into a buttered baking dish and bake in a moderate oven (about 375°) for about 40 minutes. Serve at once. Makes 6 to 8 servings.

Green Corn Spoon Bread
(Tested)

2 cups fresh corn
1 quart sweet milk
1 cup cornmeal
1 teaspoon salt
½ cup butter
1 teaspoon sugar
Dash of pepper
2 eggs, separated

Before cutting corn from the cob, cut down the center of each row of kernels. Cut off with two cuttings and scrape the cob. Add corn to 2 cups milk and bring to a boil. Add cornmeal and salt and stir over low heat until thickened. Remove from heat and add butter and sugar. Beat remaining milk and egg yolks, and add to mixture.

Beat egg whites and fold in. Add pepper. Turn into a buttered 3-quart casserole and bake at 325° for 1 hour. Serve at once. Makes about 8 servings.

Corn Lace Bread
(Tested)

Mix ½ cup cornmeal, ½ cup cold water, and ½ teaspoon salt and drop from a tablespoon into a small amount of hot fat in a heavy skillet. Hold the spoon a couple of inches over the fat so the batter will splatter as it drops. If a little clump of cornmeal gathers in the center of the cake, flatten it out with the back of the spoon. Fry on one side until quite brown. Turn and brown on the other side. Drain and serve hot.

Stir the batter each time before dropping a cake. Remove the crumbs that gather in the pan so they will not burn. [I found the cooking of lace bread to be a tedious process.]

Steamed Corn Bread

Mix 1 cup sweet milk, 2 cups buttermilk, 1 level teaspoon soda, 3 table-spoons melted lard, 2 cups cornmeal, 1 cup flour, and 3 tablespoons molasses. When batter is ready to pour, beat in 1 egg. Pour into greased cans with tight lids. Put cans in a kettle with a tight-fitting lid and boil for about 2½ hours.

Hyde County Pone Bread

Mrs. John Howard Patrick of Engelhard contributed this recipe. She said that it took her years to become an expert in making the bread and that only after acquiring an electric mixer did she become really proficient, as the mixing takes so much strength by hand. It may be that Dare County has equal claim to this recipe.

Scald 3 cups cornmeal, 1 cup flour, and 1 cup sugar with enough hot water to make a batter much thinner than a cake mixture (very thin like corn bread batter). Add 1 pint dark bitter molasses and beat until there is not one bubble left in the mixture. Pour into a greased and floured tube pan and bake at 250° for 3 hours.

OTHER CORN BREADS

Egg bread is corn muffin batter that has been cooked in a baking pan. It should be well browned. Some egg bread has a little layer of custard on top with the corn bread on the bottom.

Pot dodgers are balls of cornmeal dough that have been dropped on top of a pot of greens and cooked like dumplings.

Johnny cakes is another name for corn dodgers.

Fried mush is cold cornmeal mush that has been sliced, floured, and fried in bacon grease.

WAFFLES AND GRIDDLE CAKES

Crispy Cream Waffles
(Tested)

This recipe makes the most delicious waffles that I have ever coated with butter. For a special touch, serve them with individual containers of melted butter—much better than a cold, hard square.

1 cup sifted flour
1½ teaspoons baking powder
½ teaspoon salt
2 teaspoons sugar
2 eggs, separated
1 cup heavy cream
2 tablespoons melted butter

Sift together flour, baking powder, salt, and sugar. Stir egg yolks with a fork and add cream. Mix together lightly. Dump in all the dry ingredients and beat only until smooth. Add melted butter and fold in stiffly beaten egg whites. The batter will be thick.

Bake on a hot waffle iron until steam no longer escapes. Makes 4 to 5 average-size waffles.

Self-Rising Flour Waffles

These waffles are wonderfully crisp.

2 eggs
1¾ cups milk
½ cup butter, melted
2 cups sifted self-rising flour
1 tablespoon sugar

Beat eggs. Add remaining ingredients and beat until smooth. Bake on a heated waffle iron. Makes 4 to 8 waffles, depending on the size of your waffle iron.

HOT CAKES

A griddle is made of black iron, the same as a skillet. But the griddle has a heavy bottom and only a thin rim rather than the usual sides found on a skillet. A griddle was often greased by rubbing a meat skin over the surface of the hot pan. (A meat skin is a portion of the skin that has been cut from a slab of salt pork.) Now a pastry brush in melted fat is used.

Light Hot or Flannel Cakes
(Tested)

This recipe has been tried in a modern kitchen and found not to be wanting for one dust of anything—except butter and syrup—for those who love light, puffy hot cakes. Compared to the usual soggy cakes served in restaurants, these cakes might be pictured each with a pair of wings hovering over a plate.

1 cup sifted flour
1 teaspoon soda
1 teaspoon salt
1 egg
1 cup buttermilk
2 tablespoons melted butter, shortening, or lard

Sift together flour, soda, and salt. Break the egg over the dry ingredients. Add buttermilk and butter. Stir until the flour is well dampened. The batter will be lumpy, but leave it that way.

Drop by tablespoonfuls on a lightly greased hot griddle. Spread batter thin and cook until bubbly. Turn and brown on the other side. Serve without waiting around. Pancakes that are not hot enough to melt butter should never be served. Makes enough cakes for 2 hearty eaters or 3 moderate ones.

Buckwheat Cakes

These cakes are light and fluffy.

Before going to bed, dissolve ½ package granulated yeast in ½ cup lukewarm water. Add ½ teaspoon sugar. Mix 2¾ cups buckwheat flour, ½ teaspoon salt, ¼ cup white flour, and 2 cups lukewarm water and blend until smooth. Add yeast, cover, and let stand overnight.

The next morning, stir in 1 tablespoon molasses, ½ teaspoon soda, 1 teaspoon melted butter, and water to thin as desired. Bake on a hot, lightly greased griddle, turning only once.

Save at least 1 cup of the mixture for a starter and each night, add more flour and water. That way you will have buckwheat cakes all winter without adding more yeast.

Grits Griddle Cakes

To leftover grits, add 1 egg, enough milk to make a thin batter, about ½ cup flour, 1 teaspoon baking powder, and salt to taste. Beat until smooth and pour on a hot griddle. Brown on both sides.

Soda Crackers

It seems that the only way folks had soda crackers a few years back was to make them at home. What a troublesome prospect! This is a recipe I found in a cookbook dated 1919.

½ yeast cake
1 scant pint warm water
1½ quarts flour
⅓ cup lard
½ ounce salt
1 teaspoon soda
¼ cup sour milk

In the evening, set a sponge of yeast, warm water, and sifted flour. Let raise [*sic*] overnight. In the morning, work into it the lard, salt, and soda dissolved in the sour milk. Work all well together, using enough additional sifted flour to make a stiff dough.

Pound with a rolling pin and double over. Keep repeating until dough is smooth. Then roll out into a thin sheet and punch holes into it with a large fork. Cut out rounds or squares and place on cookie tins or in large dripping pans. Bake in a hot oven. It takes but a few minutes to bake them.

Note: Have pans heated before putting the crackers on them and do not grease them.

SANDWICHES

The best-known sandwiches in the state are ham biscuits, sausage biscuits, banana sandwiches, pimento cheese sandwiches, tomato sandwiches, and cream cheese sandwich loaves.

A *ham biscuit* is a biscuit filled with a slice of cooked ham. Ham biscuits are served at picnics, potlucks, coffees, teas, and receptions. When the food editor of a Chicago newspaper visited North Carolina in the 1970s, she had ham biscuits for the first time. On returning home, she called to ask for the recipe because she wanted to serve them at a wine tasting.

A *sausage biscuit* is a biscuit filled with a cake of sausage. In the old days, these ingredients were usually left over from breakfast and packed into school lunches.

A *banana* (pronounced ber'nan-ah) *sandwich* consists of slices of banana on slices of white bread spread with mayonnaise.

A *pimento cheese sandwich* is made of pimento cheese on white bread (recipes below).

A *tomato* (pronounced mater) *sandwich* is truly a Tar Heel institution. Made with tomatoes and mayonnaise on white bread, it is a favorite for lunch and picnics. It is an old southern custom to eat a tomato sandwich for lunch while standing by the kitchen sink. When packed into a picnic, a tomato sandwich naturally becomes soggy and tastes all the better.

Cream cheese sandwich loaves were probably invented in the 1920s before loaves of white bread were sliced and after the introduction of cream cheese. Cream cheese was so popular with hostesses that you got the idea some of them would have liked to frost the world with it. The sandwich loaves, made with three horizontal slices of bread and three fillings, are frosted with softened cream cheese and decorated to the hilt. The loaves are beautiful. Cut into slices to serve, they are also delicious.

PIMENTO CHEESE SANDWICHES

Pimento cheese, a southern favorite generally unknown in the North, may not have originated in North Carolina but certainly nowhere is it more popular. Durham novelist Reynolds Price adds to our knowledge of the subject in *The Great American Writers' Cookbook* (1981):

> I've failed in a long effort to trace the origins of pimento cheese, but it was the peanut butter of my childhood—homemade by Mother. I suspect it's a Southern invention (I've seldom met a non-Southerner who knew what it was, though they take to it on contact); in any case, prepared versions can be bought to this day in Southern supermarkets—most of them made apparently from congealed insecticides.
>
> Last year, once I'd acquired a Cuisinart, I rebelled and tried to reconstruct Mother's recipe. I've made a change or two, in the interest of midlife zest; but I think any child of the thirties or forties (from, say, Baltimore down) will recall the glory and bless my name.
>
> Grate a pound or more of extra sharp cheddar cheese. Chop coarsely one jar of pimentoes (four ounces, more if you like) with one or two cloves of garlic. Mix into the grated cheese with plenty of freshly ground pepper and a minimum of salt; then gradually add enough homemade mayonnaise (maybe three tablespoons) to form a stiff chunky paste.
>
> Sometimes I add a little lemon juice or a very little wine vinegar or Tabasco—nothing to disguise the bare cheese and peppers and good mayonnaise. I've been caught eating a pound in two days (though it keeps well) especially if life is hard. On rough brown bread, it's a sovereign nerve-salve.

Some cooks make pimento cheese in the top of a double boiler, but the uncooked version is more widely prepared.

Lula Thigpen's Pimento Cheese

Lula Hackney Thigpen, of Tarboro, like her mother (Lula Hackney Ruffin of Wilson) before her, is famous for her pimento cheese. Because the two women originally made it with homemade mayonnaise that had lemon juice in it, she adds a bit of lemon juice to pimento cheese. "The lemon juice can be tricky," according to Mrs. Thigpen. "You do not really want to be able to taste it, but it does help." This is her recipe.

1½ pounds cheese (½ pound each of medium sharp cheddar,
milk cheddar, and Swiss or mozzarella), grated
2 jars (7 ounces each) pimento,
undrained and chopped
Mayonnaise
Salt, cayenne pepper, and fresh lemon juice

Using, if desired, the medium blade of a hand-turned Mouli grater, mix cheese and pimento with liquid. Add enough mayonnaise to make a spreadable mixture. Add salt, cayenne pepper, and lemon juice to taste. Store in the refrigerator. The cheese will keep for 2 to 3 weeks.

Cooked Pimento Cheese

This recipe was contributed by Mrs. Timothy Parnell of Winston-Salem.

2 eggs, separated
5 to 6 tablespoons sugar or to taste
Pinch of salt
1 teaspoon prepared mustard
1 tablespoon "or so" butter
1 tablespoon vinegar
2 tablespoons milk
1 pound cheese (preferably sharp), shredded
1 can (4 ounces) pimentos

To make the "sauce," blend together beaten egg yolks, sugar, salt, mustard, butter, vinegar, and milk. Heat, stirring, until smooth and hot. Stir the hot mixture into shredded cheese, stirring until smooth.

Drain pimentos, reserving liquid, and dice. Add diced pimentos to cheese mixture and enough pimento liquid to a make mixture of spreading consistency. Beat egg whites until stiff; fold in. Store in the refrigerator.

TWELVE

Though occasionally served for dessert at a family meal, homemade ice cream was often a treat on Sunday afternoon or at an ice cream social, where several kinds of both ice cream and cake were available. It was not until the installation of electric refrigeration in drugstores that it was possible to *buy* ice cream. A popular flavor, named neopolitan, included three flavors—vanilla, chocolate, and strawberry—in one pint. A treat for Sunday dinner was a slice of commercial ice cream on top of a piece of layer cake. When it was time to serve dessert, someone made a quick trip to the drugstore to buy the ice cream.

Popular puddings included bread, rice, apple betty and crisp, tapioca, chocolate, and persimmon in season. Prune whip, made of pureed cooked prunes sweetened with sugar and folded into whipped cream, was piled into stemmed dessert dishes.

Fruits cobblers were common, as were fried apple and peach pies. There seemed to be a never-ending supply of fried pies stored in the warmer atop the wood stove. After school, children headed for that warmer and pies so large that two filled a dinner plate.

Pies, no doubt the most favorite dessert, might easily be on the menu every day and with a bake-sale quantity offered on Sunday. The top choices were fruit pies and egg custard.

Cakes—towering, luscious layer cakes—belonged to the weekend. A weekday cake might be a one-egg cake baked as cup cakes and served with warmed chocolate sauce, or it might be warm gingerbread. Strawberry shortcake turned up frequently when the berries were in season.

The custom of serving hot bread at every meal also provided dessert when the bread was combined with other items that were always on the table: butter and sweets of some sort, such as honey in the comb, jam, jelly, preserves, and molasses. No matter how lavish a meal, including the dessert, many men routinely topped off the whole thing with a hot biscuit spread with butter and preserves.

. . . . .

FREEZER ICE CREAM

Freezing ice cream was a social event as well as an occasion for providing the most popular dessert. In the heyday of the ice cream freezer, a dish of homemade ice cream was *something*, for it was not possible to go to the corner drugstore or reach into the home freezer for readymade ice cream. "Let's make some cream" was always a happy invitation.

Making freezer ice cream was an outdoor activity. It started with a visit to the icehouse. The "cream" was usually a rich mixture of pure cream, eggs, and sugar, with fruits added as desired. The freezing container was about three-fourths filled with the mixture and fastened into the center of the freezer. Layers of chipped ice were packed around the freezing container alternately with layers of ice cream salt until the freezer was filled. (A dasher or paddlelike stirrer rotates in the center of the freezer container, mixing the ice cream mixture.)

Then the cranking began—it went fast at first. You could just breeze along but once the cream started to freeze, the turning became harder. When the crank would not go around another turn, water from the melted ice was poured out a little hole in the side of the freezer and the whole thing was firmly repacked with ice and salt. Over the top went a folded tow sack (burlap bag).

Despite the joyful prospect of having a dish—or three or four dishes— of ice cream, it had to "ripen" for about an hour. Then came the opening. It was the favored member of the family who got the dasher to lick while the ice cream was being served.

It is almost heresy for me to say that commercial ice cream is a better, smoother, more delicious product than the homemade freezer kind ever was. It is true, but how can the joy of opening a cardboard carton ever compare with the fun of cranking the freezer?

Lick-the-Dasher Ice Cream
(Tested)

2 cups sugar
¼ cup cornstarch
¼ teaspoon salt
4 cups milk
4 eggs, beaten
2 tablespoons vanilla
4 cups half and half (half milk, half cream)
Whipping cream in any proportion (the more heavy cream that is added, the creamier the ice cream)

Mix sugar, cornstarch, and salt in the top of a double boiler. Blend in milk gradually and cook over hot water, stirring, until mixture is thickened—about 12 to 15 minutes. Do not overcook or it will curdle.

Blend a small amount of the hot mixture into the beaten eggs, then stir all the eggs into the rest of the mixture. Cook for 4 to 5 minutes more, stirring constantly. Chill the custard.

Add vanilla and chilled half and half and whipping cream. Fill a gallon freezer container no more than two-thirds full (the recipe fits a gallon container perfectly) and freeze in hand-cranked or electric freezer with a mixture of 1 part ice cream salt to 6 parts crushed ice according to freezer directions.

When the mixture is frozen, the electric motor will stop or the hand crank will no longer turn. Remove the dasher and repack the freezer with ice and salt—8 parts ice to 1 part salt. Cover with a rug or blanket and let ice cream ripen in the freezer for several hours.

• • • • •

PUDDINGS

Snow Cream

To a large pan of clean, fluffy white snow stir in enough chilled boiled custard to make it about the consistency of ice cream. Flavor to taste with vanilla. Serve at once.

For an easier snow cream, stir evaporated milk into clean snow with sugar and vanilla to taste.

Boiled Custard

(Tested)

Boiled custard is not boiled.

6 eggs
1 cup sugar
1 pint half and half (half milk, half cream)
1 pint (2 cups) whole milk
Pinch of salt
1 teaspoon vanilla

Beat eggs in an electric mixer, adding sugar gradually, and continue to beat until thoroughly mixed. Meanwhile, heat half and half and whole milk over low heat until the mixture begins to steam or has reached a not-quite-scalded state. Pour into egg and sugar mixture, stirring constantly.

Pour mixture into the top of a double boiler and cook over boiling water, stirring, until it coats a spoon. Watch to prevent overcooking or it will curdle. When lifting the spoon to see if the custard is cooked, lift out the top of the double boiler because in that much extra time it may overcook. Cool. Add vanilla.

DIP

Dip is boiled custard. In some homes it was the custom to serve a punch cup of dip with blackberry, huckleberry, dewberry, strawberry, or cherry pie or cobbler. The combination of chilled custard and the slightly warm or maybe even hot pie is unrivaled by the creation of any French chef and will impress modern-day guests.

PUTTING THE PERSIMMON INTO PUDDING

Persimmon pudding is as characteristic of North Carolina as any dish there is. The fall day when frost nips the persimmon tree is the day a lot of puddings go into the oven.

Finding a recipe on which all persimmon pudding lovers will agree is difficult. Some insist that the pudding must have eggs; others would not dream of putting an egg into it. Grated sweet potatoes are a necessity for some; others stick to plain persimmons. Cornmeal goes into some puddings but is ignored for others. Sometimes heavy spicing kills the flavor of the persimmon. A few cooks add fresh coconut.

Whatever is in the pudding, it is not likely that you will jump up and down and scream with joy at the first taste. You almost have to be raised on the stuff to love it. There is nothing odd in that fact—whoever but a New Englander was born liking Indian pudding?

Our cook used to bake the pudding in a big black bread pan, and sometimes she used two pans. Its spicy aroma was related to that of gingerbread but in place of the molasses smell, there was the almost winey aroma of persimmons. Many is the time I stood out in the cold bleak weather of November in mud to my shoe tops picking persimmons for our cook to make pudding (the ones on the ground are softer than the ones on the tree). She always served it warm—I guess it was because it never had a chance to get cold. This is her recipe.

Persimmon Pudding
(Tested)

2 to 3 cups persimmon pulp
3 eggs, beaten
1 ¼ cups brown sugar
1 large sweet potato, peeled and shredded or grated
1 cup flour
½ cup cornmeal
1 teaspoon baking powder
1 teaspoon salt
¼ cup melted butter
2 cups buttermilk
1 teaspoon cinnamon
½ teaspoon ginger
½ teaspoon nutmeg

The best way I have found to make persimmons into pulp, which is not an easy job because of the numerous large seeds, is with a Foley food mill. Mix all the ingredients well. Pour into a greased baking dish so the mixture will be only about a good inch thick.

Bake in a moderate oven (about 350°) for 1 hour, or until firm. Serve plain or with whipped cream. Makes about 12 to 16 servings.

Mrs. M. C. Myatt's Persimmon Pudding

The late Pete Ivey, writer and publicist of Chapel Hill, was one of the state's leading proponents of persimmon pudding. He claimed that Mrs. M. C. Myatt made the best. This was her recipe.

1 quart persimmons, making about 2 cups persimmon pulp
1 pint milk
½ pound butter, melted
1 pint (2 cups) flour
1½ cups brown sugar
4 teaspoons baking powder, dissolved in a little warm water
½ teaspoon salt
½ teaspoon cinnamon

Mix ingredients, stir, and pour into a well-buttered baking dish. Bake in a 325° oven for about 1 hour. Serve hot or cold with whipped cream. Makes 6 to 8 servings.

Queen of Puddings

1 quart sweet milk
1 pint bread crumbs (half biscuit and half light bread)
1 cup sugar
2 tablespoons melted butter
4 eggs, separated
Grated rind of 1 lemon
Glass of grape or other tart jelly
½ cup sugar
Juice of 1 lemon

Pour milk over bread crumbs and soak until soft. Add 1 cup sugar and melted butter to beaten egg yolks. Mix well. Add to crumb mixture with lemon rind. Pour into a buttered baking dish. Bake at 325° until set and brown. Spread jelly over the top.

Make a meringue of 4 egg whites and ½ cup sugar and lemon juice. Spread over all and brown at 375°.

Rice Pudding
(Tested)

Just why the old folks made rice pudding without eggs I do not know, but that is the way they did it using this kind of recipe. It is delicious. A couple of beaten eggs may be added, if you wish.

1 quart milk
⅓ cup raw regular rice
⅓ cup sugar
⅛ teaspoon nutmeg
¼ teaspoon salt
1 teaspoon vanilla
½ cup seedless raisins

Heat milk but do not allow it to boil. Add to remaining ingredients and pour into a buttered shallow Pyrex dish. Place in a 250° oven and bake for 2 hours. Stir pudding about every 20 minutes. Serve with lemon sauce.

Lemon Sauce

Mix 2 tablespoons flour, ½ cup sugar, and pinch of salt. Add 1 cup hot water and blend. Cook over low heat, stirring, until thick and clear. Add 1 teaspoon grated lemon rind, 2 tablespoons lemon juice, and 2 tablespoons butter. Serve hot or cold.

Ambrosia

Ambrosia is a favorite throughout the year but appears most often around Christmas with fruit cake. The simplest ambrosia is made with fresh orange sections combined with fresh grated coconut. If desired, crushed pineapple, sliced cherries, halves of grapes, diced bananas, and diced marshmallows may be added.

12 oranges
1 fresh coconut
2 pounds white grapes
2 pounds red grapes
1 can (about 20 ounces) Royal Ann cherries
1 package (8 ounces) dates

3 bananas
12 marshmallows
1 can (20 ounces) crushed pineapple
1 can (20 ounces) pineapple chunks

Peel oranges, remove pulp from each section, and chop. Grate coconut. Seed and chop grapes, cherries, and dates. Cut bananas and marshmallows into small pieces. Combine all ingredients and let stand in the refrigerator for several hours.

THREE RECIPES FOR HEAVENLY HASH

Mrs. James Atwell's Heavenly Hash

This recipe comes from *Out of the Kitchen*, published by the Elkin Junior Woman's Club.

Whip 1 pint heavy cream. Whip in 24 marshmallows cut fine, 1 cup chopped walnuts, a few candied cherries, and a small amount of drained crushed pineapple. Chill in the refrigerator for several hours. Serve in sherbet glasses or on plain cake.

Mrs. Walker's Heavenly Hash

From *The Wilson Cook Book*, published in 1941 by the Woman's Society of Christian Service of Wilson, comes this recipe of Mrs. N. Gan Walker.

Blanch ¼ pound almonds and split. Cut 1 can (20 ounces) sliced pineapple and ½ pound marshmallows. Put all ingredients into a bowl and pour a little cream over them. Chill in the refrigerator for several hours. Whip 1 pint heavy cream; fold into mixture and serve in parfait glasses.

Scovia Poston's Heavenly Hash

I like the procedure of this recipe from *The Quaker Cook Book*, published by the Woman's Auxiliary of High Point Friends Meeting.

Whip 2 cups whipping cream and put half in the bottom of a casserole. Add 1 cup broken nuts, the diced drained contents of 1 can (20 ounces) crushed pineapple, and 1 cup seeded diced grapes. Top with remaining whipped cream. Place in the refrigerator.

SLUMPS, GRUNTS, BETTYS, COBBLERS, AND DUMPLINGS

Slumps and grunts are homespun New England desserts. To make a slump, you drop dabs of soft biscuit dough into a pan partially filled with bubbling hot, syrupy sweet fruit or berries. The blobs of dough steam to the fluffy tender doneness that southerners associate with the dumplings served with chicken.

Fruits used for slumps include blueberries, cherries, blackberries, apples, apricots, peaches, and plums. On Cape Cod, blueberry slump for some reason is known as blueberry grunt. Steamed berry puddings are also called grunts.

The southern counterpart of a New England slump or grunt would be a betty, cobbler, or fruit dumpling.

Irish Potato Pudding

This pudding, which is served as a dessert, is a popular dish at wheat threshings in Orange County.

Cream together 1 cup butter and 2 cups sugar. Add 4 eggs, one at a time, and beat well after each. Stir in 2 cups mashed potatoes, 2 cups milk, ½ teaspoon salt, and 1 teaspoon vanilla. Pour into a buttered baking dish and bake in a 350° oven for 1 hour.

Cornmeal Pie (Really a Pudding)

This is a Tar Heel version of a pudding similar to the New England Indian pudding. It is really quite good—better than any Indian pudding I have ever tasted.

Mix 1 cup cornmeal and 1 cup cold water. Add 2 cups hot water and cook for about 15 minutes on top of the stove, stirring. Remove from heat and add 2 well-beaten eggs, ½ cup molasses, ½ cup brown sugar, 1 teaspoon vanilla, ½ teaspoon salt, and 1 pint sweet milk. Pour into a greased baking dish. Cover and bake at 250° for about 5 hours, stirring occasionally. Serve with cream.

Whim Wham

This old recipe sounds a lot like the ones for trifle.

Sweeten 1 quart cream. Mix with it a teacup of white wine and the grated peel of a lemon. Whisk the liquid to a froth, drain on a sieve, and put into a glass dish.

Cut some cake as thin as possible. Make layers of cake, currant jelly, and froth, finishing with the froth.

Marmalade Soufflé
(Tested)

This is a recipe I developed from one in a little cookbook called *Everybody Eats*, written by the late Selina Lewis of Tryon. Ms. Lewis with her Thousand Pines Inn gained a reputation around Tryon for producing superb food.

This soufflé is one of the most tasty desserts I have ever eaten, especially if served after a heavy meal. Its lightness and ethereal quality have an effect that is similar to that of drinking a tiny glass of Cointreau.

3 egg whites
¼ cup sugar
⅓ cup orange marmalade
½ teaspoon orange or lemon extract

Beat egg whites until foamy. Add sugar gradually. Continue beating until stiff and glossy. Fold in marmalade and extract.

Pour into the top of a double boiler that has been buttered—butter the lid, too. Place over simmering water and cook without lifting the lid for 1 hour. Serve right away. If you do not remove the lid, it will keep for 10 minutes or so. Serve with orange sauce.

Orange Sauce

Beat 3 egg yolks (left from soufflé). Combine ¼ cup sugar, 1 tablespoon flour, and a pinch of salt and add to the yolks. Add 1 cup orange juice and blend. Cook over low heat, stirring, until smooth and thick. Serve warm. Flavor with rum, if desired.

Bird's Nest Pudding

This was the recipe of Mrs. C. B. Watson as given in *The Twin-City Housewife*, published in 1920:

Peel and core enough apples to fill a pudding dish; fill the centers with raisins, currants and citron; flavor with cinnamon, and after sprinkling with sugar, pour in water and let bake, not too soft. When done make a sponge cake batter, flavor with vanilla and pour on top. Let this bake; then serve with any good, rich sauce.

Note: I tried this idea by pouring cake batter made from a yellow cake mix around the baked stuffed apples and then baked it. Served warm with whipped cream, it was different and delicious.

Kiss Pudding

Here is another old recipe:

Boil one quart sweet milk in custard kettle, stir into it four heaping tablespoons sugar and four of cornstarch dissolved in a little cold water or milk and add to the well-beaten and strained yolks of 4 eggs. Have the whites of eggs beaten to a stiff froth with a cup of pulverized sugar and a teaspoon vanilla.

Pour custard into a pudding dish or small custard cups, place in oven and let remain until set. Spread whites over top and return to oven until a delicate brown.

Meringue Crumb Pudding

This dessert has also been called Carolina pudding and rock garden pudding.

1½ cup graham cracker crumbs
1 teaspoon cinnamon
⅛ teaspoon nutmeg
⅛ teaspoon cloves
¼ teaspoon allspice
½ cup melted butter
3 eggs, separated
⅓ cup flour

½ cup sugar
2 cups milk
Pinch of salt
6 tablespoons sugar
½ teaspoon cream of tartar

Mix crumbs, spices, and melted butter. Blend well. Reserve 2 tablespoons of the crumb mixture for the top. Pack remaining crumb mixture into the bottom of an 8- or 9-inch-square pan that has been coated lightly with salad oil. Place in a 375° oven and bake for 8 minutes. Chill.

Beat egg yolks. Mix flour and ½ cup sugar and add to the yolks. Blend. Add milk and salt. Cook over boiling water, stirring, until thickened. Cool to room temperature and pour into crumb-lined pan. Chill well.

Make meringue of 6 tablespoons sugar, cream of tartar, and egg whites. Spread on top of the pudding and sprinkle with reserved crumbs. Brown in a 375° oven. Cool before serving. Cut into squares to serve. Lift out squares with a pancake turner. Makes 9 servings.

Jeff Davis Pudding

Sift together 3 cups sifted flour, 1 teaspoon soda, ½ teaspoon cinnamon, 1 teaspoon grated nutmeg, and ½ teaspoon allspice. Add 1 cup sorghum, 1 cup finely chopped beef suet, 1 cup buttermilk, 2 beaten eggs, 1 cup currants, and 1 cup raisins. Mix well and pour into a large greased mold. Cover tightly and steam for 4 hours.

Carrot Pudding

In a pudding pan make a hot syrup of 1 cup brown sugar, 2 cups water, and 1 cup currants or raisins. In a separate dish sift together 1¾ cups flour, 1 teaspoon baking powder, ½ teaspoon cloves, ½ teaspoon cinnamon, ½ teaspoon salt, and ½ teaspoon soda.

Cream 4 tablespoons shortening. Add 1 cup white sugar and cream well. Blend in 1 egg. Add 1 tablespoon lemon juice, ½ grated lemon rind, and 1 cup grated raw carrots. Add sifted ingredients and blend well. [The recipe called for no additional liquid, which may or may not be correct.]

Pour mixture into the pudding pan, being careful not to mix with the hot syrup. Cover tightly with a lid or foil tied firmly in place. Bake in a moderate oven.

Tipsy Pudding

Cut sponge cake into slices, dip in sherry wine, and over it pour a boiled custard flavored with brandy. On top put whipped cream flavored with wine. Over all spread almonds that have been blanched and chopped very fine.

Baked Apples

Fine North Carolina apples are cooked and served for breakfast, as a vegetable, or as dessert. There are dozens of ways of baking an apple but this way gives the best I have ever tasted.

Mix dark corn syrup and water (3 parts corn syrup to 1 part water) and pour into a baking dish. Have syrup ⅓- to ½-inch thick.

Peel and core apples or peel only about ⅓ of the way down. Place peeled portion in syrup. Fill centers liberally with brown sugar, sprinkling some over the top. Dust with cinnamon.

Place apples in the baking dish and cover. If the dish does not have a cover, use aluminum foil squeezed tightly around the edges of the dish. Bake at 350° for 30 minutes. Remove cover and turn apples over. Sprinkle with additional brown sugar and continue baking until tender.

Little Phoenix Apple Torte*

1 egg
1 cup sugar
3 tablespoons flour
½ teaspoon salt
1 teaspoon baking powder
½ teaspoon cinnamon
1 cup chopped tart apples
¾ cup chopped nuts (pecans and black walnuts mixed)
½ teaspoon vanilla

*Little Phoenix Lodge was in a storybook setting near West Jefferson.

Beat egg; add sugar. Sift flour, salt, baking powder, and cinnamon. Add to chopped apples and nuts. Combine with egg and sugar. Add vanilla.

Pour into a buttered baking dish and bake in a moderate oven (about 350°) for about 45 minutes. Serve with whipped cream. Makes 4 servings.

Banana Pudding
(Tested)

North Carolina natives think of banana pudding as a dessert that is served everywhere. It was not until I received a request for the recipe from New York City many years ago that I began to realize that it is distinctive to this section of the country.

½ cup sugar
Pinch of salt
3 tablespoons flour
4 eggs
2 cups milk
Vanilla wafers
Bananas
6 tablespoons sugar

Blend ½ cup sugar, salt, and flour. Add 1 whole egg and 3 yolks and mix. Stir in milk. Cook over boiling water, stirring, until thickened. Remove from heat and cool.

In a baking dish, arrange a layer of whole vanilla wafers, a layer of sliced bananas, and a layer of custard. Continue, making 3 layers of each.

Make a meringue of the remaining 3 egg whites and 6 tablespoons sugar. Spread over banana mixture and brown in a 375° oven. Serve cold, not chilled. Makes 8 servings.

Blackberry Pudding

Mix 1 pound sugar, ½ pound butter, ½ pound flour, and 6 eggs and place in the oven to bake. When the mixture is hot, stir in 1 quart blackberries.

Blackberry or Dewberry Roll
(Tested)

The memory of this blackberry roll goes back to the days when the kids were sent out early in the morning to pick blackberries. If we returned with lots of berries, there was likely to be blackberry roll for dinner.

Our cook baked two or three of these juicy rolls in the big black bread pan. Before she put the roll in to bake, she made what she called a "rolling fire"—you get a rolling fire by filling the firebox with small sticks of wood and opening the damper up wide. The flames literally rolled up the chimney, making the stove mighty hot, not to mention what it did to the kitchen.

This is the recipe. The bright reddish-purple juice oozes out into the pan as the roll bakes.

2 cups sifted flour
2 teaspoons baking powder
1 teaspoon salt
2 tablespoon sugar
⅓ cup butter
1 egg
⅓ cup milk
4 tablespoons soft butter
Blackberries

Sift together flour, baking powder, salt, and sugar. Cut in ⅓ cup butter with a pastry blender. Beat egg with milk. Add and mix lightly. Turn out on a lightly floured board and knead just enough to make the dough cling together.

Roll out to a thickness of about ¼ inch. Spread with 4 tablespoons soft butter. Cover with sweetened blackberries—the dough will take a good pint and it takes ⅔ to ¾ cup sugar to sweeten them.

Roll up like a jelly roll. It is a good idea to roll out the dough on waxed paper—otherwise, it is difficult to lift it to the baking pan. Place the roll in a greased baking pan. Bake at 400° for 25 minutes, or until brown. Cut into slices and serve plain or with berry sauce. Makes 6 to 8 servings.

Berry Sauce

Grandmother used to make a berry sauce something like jam. It is delicious and looks pretty over a blackberry roll.

Mix 1 cup berries with ¾ cup sugar and the juice of half a lemon. Cook over low heat, stirring to prevent burning, until thickened.

Sack Dumplings

Make a small sack from unbleached domestic, a cotton fabric used for curtains, aprons, and other items. Dip the sack in a pot of boiling water. Coat inside of sack with flour.

Mix 1 quart fresh blackberries, 1 cup flour, ½ teaspoon baking powder, pinch of salt, and sugar to taste. Put mixture in the sack and tie tightly with string at the top. Place the sack in boiling water and cook for 1 hour. Serve hot with hard sauce.

Caramel Dumplings

This is a wonderful dessert.

1½ cups sifted flour
1 teaspoon baking powder
Salt
2 cups sugar
Milk
1 teaspoon vanilla
1 cup finely chopped pecans
3 cups hot water
1 tablespoon butter

Sift together flour, baking powder, pinch of salt, and ½ cup sugar. Add sufficient milk to make a stiff batter. Add vanilla and pecans.

Meanwhile, caramelize ½ cup sugar in a heavy skillet. Add water, 1 cup granulated sugar, butter, and a pinch of salt. Boil for 5 to 10 minutes. Pour into a baking dish and drop batter by the teaspoonful into the boiling hot syrup. Place in a hot oven (about 400°) and bake about 15 or 20 minutes, or until puffed up and brown. Serve hot.

Old-Fashioned Molasses Cookies
(Tested)

In some homes cookies of this kind were stored by the dozens in crockery jars. They have just the right spicy flavor.

1 cup shortening
1½ cups molasses
¼ cup granulated sugar
1 egg
4 cups sifted flour
1½ teaspoons salt
2 teaspoons ground cinnamon
2 teaspoons ground ginger
½ teaspoon ground cloves

Melt shortening and pour into a large bowl. Add molasses and sugar and blend well. The mixture may not blend at first but will after a little beating. Cool, then beat in egg.

Sift dry ingredients and add to shortening mixture. Mix well. It will be a stiff dough. Drop by the teaspoonful on a greased baking sheet. Bake at 350° for 10 minutes, or until the cookies barely begin to brown. Remove from the oven and run a spatula under them so they will be easy to remove from the baking sheet. Makes about 4 dozen cookies.

●　●　●　●　●

PIES

PASTRY

Standard pastry was made most often with lard, because most cooks had their own supply and for those who did not, it was cheap. What is more, lard makes the best pastry—it is more flaky than pastry made with shortening, for my taste.

The old folks made pastry the same way they did biscuits—by throwing a clump of lard into the flour. My grandmother, who could make six pies while the stove was getting hot enough to bake them, always said that pastry dough should be rolled only on one side as turning it over made it tough. So to this day, I would not think of turning over a piece of pastry dough while rolling it.

King-size, extra deep pies and cobblers are widely popular, of course, especially in large families or when there is a large group to be fed.

Favorite Pastry
(Tested)

1 whole egg
10 tablespoons tap water
2 teaspoons vinegar
3 cups straight [all-purpose] flour
1 teaspoon salt
1¼ cups shortening [half lard for a more flaky crust]

Beat egg, water, and vinegar lightly. Sift together flour and salt. Using hands, crumble shortening into flour mixture until coarse crumbs form. Pour in water mixture and stir with a fork. Roll out on a lightly floured board. Bake by pie directions. Makes 3 or 4 piecrusts.

SURRY COUNTY'S SONKER

Sonker is a well-known name in and around Dobson, the seat of Surry County, but no one seems to know how it originated. Like other items made with dough, chances are a thrifty cook simply put together biscuit or other dough and fruit or sweet potatoes to make a dessert.

The main point about a sonker is that it is bigger than a pie, indicating that it was designed to feed a group such as the hands who brought in the harvest. Several readers interviewed on the subject mentioned that it was made in a bread pan. A bread pan, unknown in modern kitchens, was a baking pan some three to four inches deep and big enough to fill the oven of a wood stove. It was used three times a day to hold hot biscuits.

In 1980 a woman named Anne Clarke wrote that her receipts (the old spelling of recipes) were old Catawba County ones that had been in her family for over 150 years: "We used leftover biscuit dough to make both sonker and stickies. My grandmother was Scottish."

In a 1987 interview, Maxine Dockery, who with her husband owns the Lantern Restaurant in Dobson, said that she had been making sonker as long as she could remember. In 1986 columnist Jerry Bledsoe had called Mrs. Dockery "The Julia Child of Sonker." This is the way she makes it.

Maxine Dockery's Sweet Potato Sonker

6 to 8 sweet potatoes, cooked and peeled
3 to 4 cups sugar
3 to 4 cups self-rising flour
½ pound (1 cup) butter
Pastry to cover top of pan
Topping

Use a baking pan 11 × 13 inches and 3 or more inches deep. Cover the bottom of the pan with a layer of sliced sweet potatoes. Sprinkle with sugar and flour and dot with butter. Continue making layers until the pan is filled. Top with a layer of pastry. Bake in a 400° oven for 40 minutes, or until the pastry is done.

TOPPING

Stir ½ cup or more of granulated sugar into 1 to 2 cups sweet milk; heat, stirring. Remove from heat and add 1 teaspoon vanilla. Pour the hot topping over the hot sonker. Serve warm.

Blackberry Sonker

Another reader said that for a blackberry sonker, line the sides of a baking pan with buttermilk biscuits rolled like pastry for pie. Place blackberries in the pan; sprinkle with 1 cup sugar and 1 stick of butter cut into small pieces. Add 1 cup or more of water. Cover berries with a layer of dough rolled thin and cut into strips 1½ inches wide and as long as the pan.

Cover with a crust as for a cobbler. Sprinkle the crust with sugar and dot with butter. Bake in a 400° oven for 40 minutes, or until done.

Apple Sonker

To make apple sonker, still another reader said to peel and slice apples into a big baking pan; sweeten to taste with brown sugar. Sprinkle with some flour and cinnamon. Cover with a pastry crust. Spread the crust with soft butter and sprinkle with granulated sugar and a little cinnamon. Bake at 350° until done.

FRUIT AND VEGETABLE PIES

Apple pie is a favorite. It is special when made with June apples, which are green and have just the right amount of tartness.

Ruby Brooks's Apple Pie

This recipe has won at least two top prizes in the apple pie contest at the Dixie Classic Fair, a regional event. Ruby Brooks prefers magnum bowman apples, an old variety. If unavailable, try stayman or winesap.

2 cups plus 1½ tablespoons all-purpose flour
Salt
¾ cup vegetable shortening
¼ cup cold milk
1 teaspoon vinegar
5 apples, peeled, and sliced about ¼-inch thick
Sugar
Dash of salt
¼ teaspoon cinnamon
¼ stick butter

To 2 cups flour, add ½ teaspoon salt. With pastry blender, cut in shortening to make small, even particles. Combine milk and vinegar and add to flour mixture. Stir to form a ball. Divide ball in half. Roll out on a lightly floured board for a double piecrust. Fill pie pan with bottom crust.

To make filling in the bottom crust, layer apples and a mixture of remaining 1½ tablespoons flour, sugar, salt, and cinnamon. Dot with butter. Top with gashed pastry. Bake in a 400° oven for 8 to 10 minutes; reduce heat to 350° and continue baking for 40 minutes, or until done.

Apple Stack Pie

This is truly an old combination.

Roll out regular pastry and cut into circles the size of a pie pan and place on baking sheets. Bake the circles in a hot oven (about 425°) until golden brown.

Have about 7 or 8 pastry circles. Take to the table stacked up one on top of the other together with a bowl of spicy applesauce and a bowl of whipped cream. At the table top each pastry circle with a layer of applesauce and one of whipped cream. Stack all the layers like a layer cake. To serve, cut in wedges like a cake.

Dewberry and Blackberry Pies

Dewberries make a prettier pie (it is redder) than blackberries, and some claim that the flavor is better. I agree. Do try serving it with dip, a cup of chilled boiled custard (for recipe see index).

Cherry Pies

Use sour cherries for the pie and for a prettier one, add a few drops of red food coloring.

Strawberry Pie
(Tested)

This is the old-fashioned way of making a strawberry pie. My! What flavor the juice in this pie has!

Line the pie pan with unbaked pastry. Fill with sliced fresh strawberries. Over the top sprinkle a mixture of 1 cup sugar and 3 tablespoons flour. Dot liberally with butter. Bake at 450° for 10 minutes, then reduce heat to 350° and continue baking until the crust is golden brown.

Glazed Strawberry Pie
(Tested)

This recipe preserves more of the fresh strawberry color and flavor.

1 quart strawberries
1 cup sugar
3 tablespoons cornstarch
Baked pie shell
Whipped cream

Wash berries before capping. Cap and put half the berries in the bottom of a pie shell. Slice if extra large.

Mash remaining berries and bring to a boil. Add sugar that has been mixed with cornstarch. Cook slowly for about 10 minutes, stirring to prevent burning. Remove from heat and pour over raw berries in the pie shell. Chill in the refrigerator. Top with whipped cream.

Rhubarb for Pies

I have never heard of anyone canning rhubarb, also called pieplant. For that reason, in the days before frozen food the pies had to be enjoyed while the plant lasted. In making rhubarb pies, mothers used to tell daughters: "Put in as much sugar as you would for any fruit pie and then add that much again. Turn your back and throw in another handful."

Candied Rhubarb Pie
(Tested)

1⅓ cups sugar
Flour
Salt
¼ cup butter
2 tablespoons melted butter
1 egg, beaten
4 cups fresh rhubarb, cut into 1-inch lengths
Unbaked 9-inch pastry shell

Mix ⅓ cup sugar, ½ cup flour, and ⅛ teaspoon salt for topping. Cut in ¼ cup butter until the mixture is like coarse cornmeal. Set aside.

Combine remaining 1 cup sugar, 3 tablespoons flour, ⅛ teaspoon salt, melted butter, egg, and rhubarb and turn into pastry shell. Sprinkle with topping.

Bake in a 425° oven for about 40 minutes, or until filling bubbles up and pastry and topping are browned—to prevent spillover in the oven, place pie in a shallow baking pan. If the topping and pastry brown too fast, reduce heat to 375° to complete cooking.

Rhubarb or Pieplant Pie

Mix 1 cup (maybe even more) sugar, 4 tablespoons flour, pinch of salt, a dust of nutmeg, and 1 teaspoon grated lemon rind. Sprinkle ⅓ of this mixture on the bottom of an unbaked pastry shell. Add enough 1-inch lengths of rhubarb to make a good deep pie. Sprinkle with the remaining sugar mixture. Add big hunks of butter to the top.

Top with gashed crust or lattice work. Bake at 450° for 10 minutes. Reduce heat to 350° and continue baking until the pastry is browned.

Muscadine Grape Pie

This is a good pie but certainly a dilly to make.

Heat the grapes gently and then peel and seed. Fill an unbaked pie shell. Sprinkle with sugar and flour and dot liberally with butter. Bake in a hot oven.

PUMPKIN PIES

Pumpkin is widely served from the time the first ones are ripe. I have found that baking a fresh pumpkin is easier than stewing it and the resulting product is far less watery.

Baked Pumpkin

Cut pumpkin in half and remove seeds and membrane. Place, cut side down, in ¼ inch of water in a large baking pan. Bake at 300° until tender. Cool and scoop out pulp with a spoon. Strain to remove excess liquid.

Pumpkin Custard Pie

3 cups well-drained pumpkin pulp
3 eggs, beaten
1 cup sugar
1 cup milk
1 teaspoon vanilla
Unbaked pastry

Mix all ingredients and pour the mixture into a pan lined with the unbaked pastry. Place in 450° oven for 10 minutes. Reduce heat to 300° and continue baking until the filling is firm—about 1 hour.

Pumpkin Pie
(Tested)

This is my favorite pumpkin pie recipe. It is a better product when made with the commercially canned pumpkin than with the home-cooked variety.

2 cups pumpkin pulp, canned or well drained
1 cup plus 2 tablespoons light brown sugar
2 tablespoons flour
2 teaspoons cinnamon
1 teaspoon ginger
¼ teaspoon salt
½ teaspoon powdered cloves
4 eggs, well beaten
2 tablespoons molasses
2 cups half and half (half milk, half cream) or undiluted evaporated milk, heated
Unbaked pastry for a 9-inch pie

Mix all ingredients except the last two. Stir in hot half and half. Pour into pie pan lined with the unbaked pastry. The pan should be a good 1¼ inches deep.

Place in a 450° oven for 12 minutes. Reduce heat to 300° and bake for 1 hour. The high temperature cooks the crust; the low temperature cooks the filling.

Eggless Pumpkin Pies

Many an old-fashioned cook made her pumpkin pie without egg in the filling. The reason is that with eggs, the filling—after baking and cooling—will shrink a little toward the center, leaving a crack between the filling and the crust. Without the eggs the filling clings right to the crust, making a more attractive pie.

Squash Pie

Mix 2 cups cooked squash, 1 egg, grated rind of 1 lemon, ⅓ cup cream, ⅔ cup sugar, 1 teaspoon salt, and dash each of ginger and cinnamon. Pour into a 9-inch unbaked pie shell. Bake at 400° for 10 minutes. Reduce heat to 350° and continue baking until firm and brown.

Sliced Sweet Potato Pie
(Tested)

The custom was to bake sliced sweet potato pie in a "dirt" dish, the kind of pottery made from red dirt by potters such as the late Jacques Busbee in the Sandhill area. The color of dirt dishes is called tobacco spit. The dish is about two inches deep. A casserole about that deep can be used instead.

Unbaked pastry for a 2-crust, 10-inch pie
2 to 3 medium sweet potatoes
Juice of ½ lemon
⅔ cup granulated sugar
⅓ cup brown sugar, packed
½ teaspoon cinnamon
⅛ teaspoon salt
1 stick (½ cup) butter
1 teaspoon vanilla
1 egg white
2 teaspoons water

Line a pie dish about 2 inches deep with pastry. Peel potatoes; slice thinly and blanch with boiling water to which lemon juice has been added to reduce discoloration. Drain potatoes. Fill pastry with layers of potatoes sprinkled with sugars, cinnamon, and salt. Dot each layer with butter. Dribble top layer with vanilla.

Cover with remaining pastry, gashed to allow steam to escape. Crimp edges to seal. Beat egg white and water slightly—only until mixed. Brush with a pastry brush over top of pastry.

Bake in a 350° oven for 45 minutes, or until done. To test for doneness, stick a knife through the pie. If the potatoes are done, the knife will slip in easily. Best served slightly warm.

Sweet Potato Custard Pie
(Tested)

Sweet potato custard pie is likely to turn up any day there are sweet potatoes to be had. As with pumpkin pie, the old folks often made the custard without eggs so the filling would not shrink from the crust and leave a small canyon around the edges. Some cooks flavor the pie with bourbon whiskey.

This is my recipe. I use eggs and add spices with a rather heavy hand.

1 cup mashed sweet potatoes
¼ cup melted butter
3 eggs
¼ cup brown sugar
1½ cups milk
Dash each of nutmeg, cinnamon, and cloves
Unbaked pie shell

Add butter to sweet potatoes. Separate eggs. Beat yolks with sugar. Add potatoes, milk, and spices. Beat egg whites until stiff and fold into mixture. Pour into a pie shell that has been brushed with slightly beaten egg whites and then allowed to stand for a while—this helps prevent sogginess. Bake in a moderate oven (about 350°) until the mixture is set and lightly browned.

For a luscious topping, before baking sprinkle the pie with a mixture of 4 tablespoons butter and about ⅓ cup each of brown sugar and flour blended together until crumbly.

Green Tomato Pie

4 to 5 medium green tomatoes
1 lemon, sliced
2 tablespoons cornstarch
¾ cup sugar
¼ teaspoon salt
½ teaspoon cinnamon
2 tablespoons butter
Pastry for double-crust pie

Slice tomatoes. Add lemon and water. Cook until clean and transparent. Make a paste of cornstarch and a small amount of cold water. Add to tomatoes with butter, sugar, salt, and cinnamon. Stir until thickened. Pour into unbaked pie shell and top with upper crust. Bake in a hot oven (about 425°) until golden brown.

Damson Plum Pie

Many claim that no fruit has a finer flavor than a damson plum. These plums are most often made into preserves but many old cooks use them for pies. The reddish-purple color of the pie is as beautiful as the most beautiful bottle of sparkling Burgundy wine ever produced. Cutting the fruit from the pits is not easy, but with time and patience it can be done.

2 tablespoons flour
1 cup sugar
1 quart fresh damson plums, seeded
2 tablespoons butter
Dust of cinnamon
Unbaked pastry

Blend flour and sugar and mix well with the plums. Turn the mixture into a pie pan lined with pastry. Dot with butter and sprinkle with cinnamon. Cover with strips of pastry. Bake for 10 minutes at 425°. Reduce heat to 325° and continue baking for 30 minutes, or until pastry is lightly browned.

For an extra-special treat, bake this pie with an egg custard hypocrite topping (see hypocrite pie below).

Yum Yum Pie

1½ cups flour
2 tablespoons shortening
1 teaspoon salt
1 cup sugar
2 teaspoons baking powder
Milk
2 cups fruit (blackberries, peaches, blueberries,
apples, or applesauce)

Mix flour, shortening, salt, sugar, and baking powder. Add enough milk to make a soft batter. Pour batter into a baking dish and sprinkle fruit over it. Cover generously with sugar and dot with butter.

Bake at 400° for about 25 minutes. If necessary, during the last 10 minutes increase heat to 450° to brown top. The batter rises to the top and forms a nice crust.

Hypocrite Pie
(Tested)

The reason for the name is that a custard topping covers a layer of dried fruit, giving the impression that the pie is a custard pie when all the time it is not. The camouflage makes a good pie.

1 8-inch unbaked pastry shell
2 cups cooked, mashed, and sweetened dried apples
1 egg, beaten
¾ cup milk
3 tablespoons sugar
½ teaspoon vanilla

Spread apples in a layer to cover bottom of pastry shell. To beaten egg, add milk, sugar, and vanilla; blend well. Pour over apples. Bake in a 425° oven for 10 minutes; reduce heat to 350° and bake for about 40 minutes longer, or until the custard is set.

Hypocrite Pudding

Make just like hypocrite pie except without the pastry. Bake throughout at 325° until the custard is set.

Fried Half-Moon Pies

I have seen stacks of 18 or 20 of these pies disappear at one meal as if they were sheets of paper in a draft.

Cook dried peaches or apples with water until soft. Add sugar to sweeten and mash the two together with the potato masher to make a pulp.

Make a regular pastry and roll out, as for piecrust, into circles 6 or 7 inches in diameter. Put a layer of the sweetened fruit pulp about ½-inch thick on half of the pastry. Fold over the other half and cut away excess pastry. I have seen the old-time cooks do it by running a saucer around the edge.

Crimp edges together with a fork. Slip gently into a heavy black iron skillet that contains about ½ inch hot lard. Fry until brown on one side. Turn gently and fry on the other side. Serve hot or cold.

Fried Apple Jacks

1 pound dried apples
1 cup sugar
Sprinkling of cinnamon
Piecrust dough
Shortening for frying
Powdered sugar (optional)

Cook apples in water to cover until soft; add sugar. Simmer until there is little juice left, then mash thoroughly. Add cinnamon. Remove from heat and cool.

Roll out the dough into saucer-sized rounds; place saucer on dough and cut around with a sharp knife. Wet edges with water all around. Put a tablespoon of the apples on half of the dough, then bring the other half over and seal the edges.

Have all the pies ready on a piece of waxed paper before starting to fry them. Heat shortening ¼ to ½ inches deep in a skillet. Fry until brown on one side, then turn carefully and brown on the other side. Sprinkle with powdered sugar if desired. Makes 10 pies.

• • • • •

CUSTARD PIES

Egg Custard Pie
(Tested)

Not even apple pie is a greater favorite than egg custard. When it comes to baking an egg custard, an old wood stove has it all over the modern range. If you place the pie almost on the bottom of the oven, the crust will bake just about crisp—sometimes it will be really crisp. But that is next to impossible to do in a modern range—I have been trying for years.

Some modern cooks advise baking the filling separately and then slipping it into a baked pie shell. That has always seemed like too much trouble to me. By following this recipe, you will get a crust much less soggy than most.

½ cup sugar
1 tablespoon flour
4 eggs
1 cup whole rich milk
1 tablespoon butter
1 teaspoon vanilla
⅛ teaspoon nutmeg
1 unbaked pastry shell

Mix sugar and flour. Add to well-beaten eggs and mix well. Heat milk and butter to scalding point but do not boil. Add with vanilla and nutmeg to egg mixture and mix well.

Meanwhile, stick a pie pan lined with pastry into a hot oven (about 450°) for 5 minutes. Remove pastry from the oven and reduce heat to 325°. Leave the oven door open for a few minutes to allow it to cool slightly. Pour warm egg mixture into the hot pie shell and continue baking until a knife, when inserted, emerges clean.

Deluxe Egg Custard Pie

There has never been one better than this.

Line a 10-inch pie pan with pastry. Over the pastry sprinkle ½ cup packed brown sugar.

Heat 3 cups heavy cream over boiling water until just hot (do not scald). Add ⅓ cup sugar and pour hot mixture over 6 slightly beaten egg yolks. Add 1 teaspoon vanilla and pour over brown sugar in the pie shell. Bake in a 350° oven for 35 minutes, or until almost set. The custard will be firm when cold.

Strawberry Egg Custard Pie

In a pan lined with unbaked pastry, place 2 layers of whole strawberries. Sprinkle generously with crumbs made of flour and butter. Add sugar to sweeten.

Beat 2 eggs slightly. Add sugar to taste and enough milk to fill the crust when poured over the berries. Bake in a 375° oven until done.

Coconut Custard Pie

Coconut custard pie is also popular.

Stir 1 cup shredded coconut into the egg custard mixture given above and bake as you would an egg custard pie. Some cooks add a grated whole fresh coconut to the mixture.

Deluxe Coconut Custard Pie
(Tested)

4 eggs
2 tablespoon sugar
¼ cup flour
½ cup (1 stick) melted butter
5 ounces flaked coconut
1 pint light corn syrup
Unbaked deep 9-inch pastry shell

Beat eggs until mixed. Blend sugar and flour and add to eggs with remaining ingredients. Pour into pastry shell. Bake in a 450° oven for 8 minutes, then reduce temperature to 300° and continue baking for 40 minutes, or until the filling is firm.

Fresh Coconut Pie
(Tested)

This recipe makes quite a pie. It could scarcely help being good with a whole grated coconut and a half cup of butter in it.

1 9-inch unbaked pie shell
6 egg whites
Pinch of salt
¼ teaspoon cream of tartar
¾ cup sugar
½ cup melted butter
1 fresh coconut, grated

Bake pie shell in a 450° oven for 5 minutes. Remove shell from oven and reduce heat to 325°.

Beat egg whites, salt, and cream of tartar until foamy. Add sugar gradually and continue beating until stiff. Fold in butter and coconut. Turn into pie shell and bake at 325° for 1 hour, or until firm and browned.

CREAM PIES AND OTHER FAVORITES

Any assortment of pies will always include cream pies—coconut cream, chocolate cream, lemon meringue, banana, and butterscotch. I have found that these recipes produce superb pies.

Butterscotch Pie
(Tested)

The method of preparing this butterscotch pie is a little different from the usual cream pie, but the pie has a real butter and brown sugar flavor in place of the kind usually made like a cream pie with brown sugar substituted for white. The filling cuts "clean," too.

1 cup brown sugar, firmly packed
3 tablespoons water
1 tablespoon butter
Pinch of salt
⅛ teaspoon soda
½ cup flour
1½ cups cold milk
3 eggs, separated
6 tablespoons granulated sugar
Prepared piecrust

Add water, butter, and salt to brown sugar and bring to a boil. Remove from heat while adding the soda to keep it from bubbling over. Cook to the hard-ball stage.

Meanwhile, blend the flour with some of the milk to make a smooth paste and gradually add the remaining milk. Add to beaten egg yolks and cook over boiling water, stirring constantly, until smooth and thick.

Pour hot brown sugar mixture into flour mixture and beat well to blend. Cool just slightly and pour into cooled prepared crust.

Make meringue with 3 egg whites. Beat until foamy and gradually add sugar. Continue beating until shiny and the mixture stands in stiff peaks. Spread to edge of crust and twirl on top. Brown at 375°.

Lemon Light Bread Pie

This is an old recipe. Wet fresh white bread is used in place of flour to thicken the filling for lemon meringue pie. The wet light bread is prepared by removing the crust from light bread and dipping it in a bowl of water until wet. The excess liquid is then squeezed out.

Mix 1 cup wet light bread, 1 cup sugar, the juice and rind of 1 lemon, and 3 egg yolks. Cook over boiling water, stirring, until thick. Add butter the size of a walnut. Stir and cool.

Pour lemon mixture into a prepared pie shell. Top with meringue made of 3 egg whites and 6 tablespoons sugar. Brown the meringue.

Lemon Jelly Pie or Tarts
(Tested)

Lemon jelly pie is full of lemon flavor and buttery goodness.

¼ pound butter
Grated rind of 2 lemons
Juice of 3 lemons
Pinch of salt
1½ cups sugar
3 egg yolks
4 whole eggs

Melt butter. Add lemon rind and juice, salt, sugar, egg yolks, and whole eggs that have been beaten slightly. Cook over boiling water, stirring constantly, until thick and shiny. Cool. Fill baked pie or tart shells. Top with whipped cream, if desired.

Lemon Cheese
(Tested)

This is not, of course, a cheese. It is a filling for cakes or tart shells.

½ pound butter
2 cups sugar

6 eggs
4 lemons

Melt butter in the top of a double boiler. Stir in sugar. Beat eggs and add with grated rind and juice of the lemons. Cook over hot water, stirring, until smooth and thickened. Cool and use.

Pecan Pie
(Tested)

A pecan pie is rich but it is delicious. This is my favorite recipe.

½ cup butter
1 cup dark brown sugar, firmly packed
1 cup dark corn syrup
4 eggs
1 teaspoon vanilla
Pinch of salt
Unbaked pie shell
Pecan halves

Cream butter and brown sugar together. Add corn syrup and blend well. Beat eggs only until well mixed and add to butter-sugar mixture. Add vanilla and salt. Pour into pie shell and top with pecan halves. Bake at 375° until crust is browned and filling is set—about 40 minutes.

Black Walnut Pie

Follow the recipe for pecan pie and top with black walnuts in place of pecans.

Lemon Cornmeal Chess Pie
(Tested)

This pie has a lovely flavor. The filling is firm even before it is entirely cold.

2 cups sugar
2 tablespoons cornmeal
1 tablespoon flour
4 eggs

¼ cup melted butter
¼ cup milk
¼ cup lemon juice
4 teaspoons grated lemon rind
Unbaked pastry

Mix sugar, cornmeal, and flour. Add eggs, one at a time, and beat well after each. Stir in butter, milk, and lemon juice and rind. Mix well.

Pour mixture into a pie pan that has been lined with the unbaked pastry. Bake at 350° on the lower shelf of the oven for 45 minutes, or until done. Cool before cutting.

Peanut Pie

You run into this pie in the eastern part of the state, which is peanut country.

2 eggs, beaten
1 cup dark corn syrup
1 teaspoon vanilla
1 cup white sugar
2 tablespoons melted butter
1 cup salted peanuts
Unbaked pie shell

Combine eggs, corn syrup, vanilla, sugar, and melted butter. Blend thoroughly. Stir in peanuts. Pour into pie shell. Bake in a moderate oven (about 350°) for 45 minutes to 1 hour, or until firm.

Origin of Chess Tarts

A chess tart is a first cousin of pecan pie. It is an old, old tart that may have obtained its name from the town of Chester, England. Or the name may have come from the fact that the filling resembles something the English called a "cheese," which is not a cheese of the kind we know today.

Then there is the story about the cook who was asked what she put in the pie. The cook replied: "Anything in your chest." Or the one who was asked what kind of pie it was. The answer was "Oh, jes' pie."

Wherever refreshments are served, you are likely to find chess tarts.

Many cooks bake them in tiny little tart shell pans, which make about two bites. But there is one thing about those two bites: you will never have any that are more delicious.

Chess Tarts

(Tested)

½ stick (¼ cup) butter
1½ cups brown sugar, firmly packed
1 tablespoon flour
2 eggs
2 tablespoons water
1 teaspoon vanilla
Unbaked pastry

Cream butter thoroughly with brown sugar and flour. Add eggs, which have been beaten with 1 tablespoon water. Add the other tablespoon of water and vanilla. Mix well and let stand while you are making the pastry.

Line fluted tart shell or pie pans with pastry and then fill two-thirds full. Top with pecans, if desired. Bake at 375° for 30 minutes, or until done. Makes 12 to 14 tarts.

Chess Cakes

(Tested)

Many folks call chess tarts or pies chess cakes. This recipe is from the cookbook, *The Twin-City Housewife*, published in 1920. I edited the recipe after testing it to make it easier to follow. It really does make a product that melts in your mouth.

7 egg yolks
1½ cups brown sugar, packed
1 cup granulated sugar
½ pound butter less 1 tablespoon
1 teaspoon lemon extract
Unbaked pastry

Mix egg yolks, sugars, butter, and lemon extract, blending with two knives or a pastry blender. Do not beat. Pour into tart shell pans lined with unbaked pastry, filling about two-thirds full.

Brown Sugar Pie
(Tested)

Cooks whip up a brown sugar pie at the drop of an egg. Some like to add a little milk to the usual brown sugar, butter, and eggs, as in this recipe.

3 eggs
3 cups brown sugar
½ cup milk
½ teaspoon salt
½ cup butter, melted
1 teaspoon vanilla
Unbaked pastry for 2 pies

Beat eggs. Add brown sugar, milk, salt, melted butter, and vanilla and divide between 2 pie pans that have been lined with unbaked pastry. Bake at 450° for 5 minutes. Reduce heat to 325° and bake for 30 minutes, or until the filling is firm.

Brown Sugar Pie
(Tested)

This is Mrs. Jack Lovelace's recipe from *The Wilson Cook Book*, published in 1941 by the Woman's Society of Christian Service of Wilson. The pie is rich but luscious—just the kind to satisfy the demands of a sweet tooth. I prefer this recipe to the one with milk in it.

½ cup (1 stick) butter
2 cups brown sugar, packed
3 eggs
1 teaspoon vanilla
Unbaked pastry

Cream butter. Add sugar and blend well. Add eggs, one at a time, and blend well, but do not beat more than absolutely necessary. Add vanilla and pour mixture into a 9-inch pie pan lined with unbaked pastry. Bake at 450° for 5 minutes. Reduce temperature to 325° and bake for 25 minutes longer, or until the filling is firm.

Andrew Jackson Pie

This wonderful pie tastes a lot like a brown sugar pie made with white sugar.

Whip 5 eggs until foamy. Mix 2 cups sugar and 3 tablespoons flour and add to eggs. Beat well, then add 2 tablespoons melted butter, ⅔ cup milk, and ⅛ teaspoon nutmeg. Blend ingredients thoroughly and pour into an unbaked piecrust. Bake at 450° for 8 minutes and then at 350° until done.

Raisin Nut Chess Pie
(Tested)

The old cookbook in which I found this recipe failed to point out that the filling made by the amounts suggested was for two pies instead of one. I poured the whole recipe into one pie shell and the pie had not been in the oven 3 minutes when the odor of burning food filled the kitchen. Even the fallen mixture, when it finally emerged from the oven, was delectable.

I tried the recipe again after cutting it down and editing it a little. This recipe is for one pie. The day after the recipe appeared in the *Winston-Salem Journal*, a man stopped me on the street to say that he had read the recipe and because it sounded so much like a pie his mother used to make, he made it himself and thought it was delicious. It is also called "Osogood Pie."

¼ cup (½ stick) butter
1 cup granulated sugar
2 eggs
1 teaspoon vanilla
1 tablespoon vinegar
½ cup medium raisins
½ cup broken pecans
Pastry-lined pie pan

Cream butter and sugar together. Add eggs and beat well. Add vanilla and vinegar.

Pour boiling water over raisins to plump them. Drain well, cool, and add with pecans to creamed mixture. Pour into the unbaked pastry shell. Bake at 450° for 8 minutes, or until the pie begins to brown. Reduce heat to 300° and continue baking for 25 to 30 minutes, or until the filling is firm.

Raisin Pie
(Tested)

1 cup sugar
3 tablespoons flour
Pinch of salt
1 cup boiling water
1½ cups seedless raisins
1 tablespoon grated lemon rind
¼ cup lemon juice
1 tablespoon butter
1 8-inch pastry shell, unbaked
Additional pastry for lattice
1 egg white
1 teaspoon water

In the top of a double boiler, combine sugar, flour, and salt. Add boiling water slowly, stirring constantly. Cook over hot water, stirring, until thick and clear. Add raisins, lemon rind and juice, and butter. Heat.

Pour into pastry shell. Cover with strips of pastry to make a lattice crust. Beat egg white and water slightly; brush over the lattice with a pastry brush. Bake in a 425° oven for 15 minutes, or until the pastry is done.

Sour Cream Pie

This is a recipe from the Nu-Wray Inn in Burnsville.

Mix ¾ cup sugar and 1 cup sour cream. Add 2 beaten eggs, pinch of salt, 1 teaspoon cinnamon, ½ teaspoon nutmeg, ½ teaspoon cloves, and ½ cup pecans. Pour into an unbaked pie shell and bake in a hot oven (about 425°) for 20 minutes. Reduce heat to 325° and bake for 20 minutes longer.

Buttermilk Pie

3 eggs
2 cups buttermilk
¼ cup melted butter
1 teaspoon vanilla
3 tablespoons flour
1 cup sugar
Pinch of salt
Unbaked pie shell

Beat eggs until light and lemon colored. Add buttermilk, butter, vanilla, flour, sugar, and salt. Blend well. Pour into the pie shell.

Bake in a hot oven (about 450°) for 5 minutes. Reduce heat to 325° and continue baking until a knife, when inserted, emerges clean. Cool before cutting.

Sugar Pie

Make sufficient pastry for 3 single-crust pies. Roll out enough pastry to line a 9-inch pie pan. Fill pan. Roll the remaining pastry very thin and sprinkle with a mixture of 1 cup brown sugar, ½ teaspoon cinnamon, and 4 tablespoons butter cut into fine pieces. Roll up like a jelly roll and cut into half-inch slices. Place these slices cut side up around the pastry in the pie pan.

Pour ½ cup milk over the whole. Bake at 400° for 30 minutes, or until lightly browned.

Molasses Pie

Beat 4 to 6 eggs until light. Add 2 cups molasses, 1 cup sugar, 1 table-spoon cornmeal, 1 tablespoon flour, 1 teaspoon vanilla, and ½ cup melted butter. Blend well and pour into an unbaked pie shell. Bake in a slow oven until firm.

Transparent or Jelly Pie

1 jelly glass [1 cup] tart jelly
1 cup butter
1 cup sugar

3 eggs, well-beaten
1 teaspoon vanilla
Unbaked pastry

Line a pie pan with unbaked pastry. Spread jelly over the pastry. Cream butter and sugar together until light and fluffy. Add eggs and beat well.

Pour over jelly. Put in 450° oven for 5 minutes. Reduce heat to 350° and continue baking for 30 minutes, or until the filling is set.

Transparent Pie—Another Version

Combine 1 cup white sugar, ¼ cup butter, 5 egg yolks, and 1 teaspoon vanilla. Pour into 2 pastry-lined pans. Bake and cover tops with meringue.

STACK PIES

There have been occasions when a woman has stacked three or four transparent or other pies right on top of each other to transport. These are called stack pies and are cut like a layer cake to serve.

No-Nothing Pie

A no-nothing pie was what folks made when the hens were not laying and milk was scarce. The pie does not call for eggs, and water may be substituted for milk.

1 unbaked 8-inch piecrust
½ cup sugar
⅓ cup flour
½ teaspoon cinnamon
1⅓ cups milk or water
1 tablespoon butter

Sprinkle sugar, flour, and cinnamon into the pie shell. Pour in milk. Dot with butter. Bake in a 375° oven for 15 minutes. Reduce temperature to 325° and continue baking until the pie is set.

Vinegar Pie

3 eggs, separated
1 cup sugar
3 tablespoons flour
Pinch of salt
1½ cups boiling water
¼ cup vinegar
1 teaspoon lemon flavoring
6 tablespoons sugar
Baked pie shell

Beat egg yolks until thick. Mix 1 cup sugar with flour and salt and add to the yolks. Blend well. Add boiling water slowly, stirring. Add vinegar. Cook over hot water, stirring, until smooth and thick.

Remove from heat and add lemon flavoring. Cool. Pour into the pie shell. Make a meringue of egg whites and 6 tablespoons sugar. Spread over the top. Brown in a slow oven (about 325°).

Jeff Davis Pie

Mix 1 cup sugar, 3 tablespoons flour, 1 whole egg, and 2 egg yolks. Add 1 cup sweet cream and 1 cup sweet milk. Cook over boiling water, stirring, until thick. Remove from heat and add 1 teaspoon cinnamon, ¼ teaspoon nutmeg, ¼ teaspoon cloves, 1 teaspoon vanilla, and 2 tablespoons butter. Pour into a baked pie shell.

Top with meringue made from 2 egg whites and 2 tablespoons sugar. Brown the meringue.

Note: In some Jeff Davis pies, nutmeg is the only spice used.

Rose Leaf Pie

The old recipe said: "This dessert was accounted very dainty and delicate."

Gather petals from white roses to make 2 quarts or thereabouts. Wash and dry with a clean napkin. Mash thoroughly and place in a pastry-lined pan. Sugar the petals properly. Tuck them under a fluffy top crust and bake in a hot oven.

CAKES, FROSTINGS, AND FILLINGS

When it comes to cakes, those made by North Carolina cooks are second to none in quality, size, variety, and abundance. Anybody who has grown up without seeing the outlay of homemade cakes at a Sunday school picnic and missed the chance of sampling them has just missed it. And even at an average funeral, the collection of cakes still looks almost like the day's run at a commercial bakery, not to mention the lineup at church suppers and family reunions. Because all the family would gather at the homeplace on Sunday (many families still continue the practice), Saturday's work was not finished until the sideboard was filled with a supply of pies and cakes. Not just two or three, but easily a dozen. The prettiest cakes were displayed on stemmed cake stands.

Back in the pioneer days when women were strong enough to beat their own cakes without the help of a mixer, cakes had three layers instead of the modern family size of two. An old-fashioned cook tested a cake with a broom straw—she never thought of doing it any other way. She, of course, selected a clean straw from the top of the broom.

Undoubtedly, the most widely used recipe was (and probably still is) the one for the 1, 2, 3, 4 cake. It is a plump three-layer cake. The old procedure for making this cake goes like this: A woman sat down with a big bowl in her lap. In the bowl was a half-pound cake of butter. By her side she had a pint cup of sugar. She sat and creamed the butter with her hands, gradually adding the sugar and creaming the two together until she could no longer feel the grains of sugar. If you do not think that is a neat feat by hand, try it someday when you have a few unscheduled hours.

1, 2, 3, 4 Cake
(Tested)

Using this recipe you can beat the batter by hand or in the mixer. It produces a luscious, fork-tender cake. With the mixer, I cream the butter and sugar together until the two are like whipped cream. I then add the eggs and continue beating in the mixer. But when the time comes to add the flour and milk, I take the bowl from the mixer and continue with a wooden spoon. Overbeating of the flour in the mixture will give a tough cake.

1 cup butter
2 cups sugar
3 cups cake flour, sifted
4 eggs
3 teaspoons baking powder
1 teaspoon salt
1 cup milk
1 teaspoon vanilla

Cream butter. Add sugar gradually and cream together until light and fluffy. Add eggs one at a time and beat thoroughly.

Sift flour two times with baking powder and salt. Add alternately with milk to creamed mixture, beginning and ending with the flour. Add vanilla. Pour batter into 3 greased and floured cake pans and bake at 375° until the cake shrinks from the edges of the pan.

Note: The cake is not inclined to stick but as a precaution, line the bottoms of the pans with circles cut from brown grocery bags. Grease and flour the paper, too.

Fresh Coconut Cake

Use the recipe for 1, 2, 3, 4 cake. Cool layers, fill, and frost with boiled white frosting. Coat liberally with grated fresh coconut; pat and press into the frosting. For a more moist cake, dribble a bit of the coconut milk over the cooled cake layers before frosting.

Note: A trick in preparing the coconut is to heat it in a 375° oven for 8 minutes after it has been cracked. This makes the meat easier to pull from the shell. I find that the easiest way to grate fresh coconut is in the food processor. The consistency of the coconut will not be lost and yet it will be sufficiently fine.

Scraped Coconut Cake

Some cooks made what they called a scraped coconut cake. To prepare it, they scraped fresh coconut into thin curls that resembled wood shavings. They found that the best implement for the job was an old silver spoon with edges worn sharp and thin.

The cake covered with the white shavings was a beauty and made about the best coconut cake I have ever tasted.

Old-Fashioned Pound Cake
(Tested)

Sharing almost equal popularity with the fresh coconut and 1, 2, 3, 4 cakes, which can be frosted in numerous ways, is the old-fashioned pound cake, which is served most often unfrosted. The old recipes call for 1 pound butter, 1 pound sugar, 1 pound or 1 dozen eggs, 1 pound flour, and often a wine glass of brandy for flavoring.

Old-time cooks turn out perfect pound cakes every time with the old recipes and tedious creaming, but I have had better luck with the recipe given here. It provides the same (if not better) flavor and moist texture as the old-fashioned ones, and the method is more dependable for the modern cook. Was there ever any cake better than a slice of pound cake oozing with the richness of butter and eggs?

2 cups butter (no substitute)
3 cups unsifted all-purpose flour
½ teaspoon soda
3 cups sugar
3 tablespoons lemon juice
1 tablespoon vanilla
10 large eggs, separated
¼ teaspoon salt
2 teaspoons cream of tartar

Use a small portion of the butter to grease a tube pan (the large kind used for fruit cakes and angel cakes). Dust additional flour over the butter and tap the pan gently against the table to remove excess.

Sift flour, soda, and half the sugar into a large mixing bowl. Add butter, softened to room temperature, but not melted or runny. Mix with the fingers until well blended. Add lemon juice, vanilla, and egg yolks, one at a time, blending well after each.

Beat egg whites with salt until soft peaks are formed. Add remaining sugar gradually and beat thoroughly after each addition. Gently fold in cream of tartar. Pour beaten whites over first mixture and mix gently by hand, lifting and folding the whites into the batter until they are completely folded in. Pour into a prepared pan and smooth top.

Bang the pan hard against the table to remove air holes. Place pan on the middle rack of a 300° to 325° preheated oven. Bake for 1 hour and 15 minutes without opening oven door. Then test cake without removing it from oven. Stick straw all the way through cake. If no crumbs cling, turn off heat and close oven door. Let cake remain in oven for 10 to 15 minutes longer, or until it seems to shrink from sides of pan. If crumbs or batter cling to the straw, bake cake for 10 to 15 minutes longer, or until done. Let it remain in the oven as directed above.

Remove cake from oven and allow it to sit in the pan for 10 minutes. Loosen and turn out.

Skillet Pound Cake

Spread slices of pound cake with soft butter and brown evenly in a hot skillet.

Chocolate Pound Cake

½ pound butter
½ cup shortening
3 cups sugar
5 eggs
3 cups sifted flour
¼ teaspoon salt
½ teaspoon baking powder
½ cup cocoa
1¼ cups milk
1 teaspoon vanilla

Cream butter and shortening with sugar. Add eggs one at a time and blend well after each. Sift together dry ingredients and add alternately with milk. Add vanilla.

Pour batter into a greased and floured tube pan. Bake in a 325° oven for 1 hour and 25 minutes, or until cake tests done.

ROTATION CAKE

Many old cookbooks contain what is called a rotation cake. As far as I can tell, it is about the same as a pound cake.

White Pound Cake

(Tested)

White pound cake is not as popular as the regular pound cake, but quite a few cooks take great pride in the white version. This recipe makes an excellent cake.

4 cups sifted flour
1½ tablespoons baking powder
1½ teaspoons salt
8 egg whites
¾ cup sugar
1 cup shortening
2 cups less 2 tablespoons sugar
1⅓ cups milk
1 teaspoon vanilla

Add baking powder and salt to flour and sift together three times.

Beat egg whites until foamy, add ¾ cup sugar gradually, and continue beating only until the mixture will hold up in soft peaks. Set aside.

Cream shortening. Add remaining sugar gradually and cream together until light and fluffy. Add flour mixture alternately with milk, a small amount at a time, beating after each addition until smooth. Add vanilla and egg whites and mix thoroughly into batter.

Pour into a greased 9-inch tube pan, the bottom of which has been lined with greased brown paper. Bake in a moderate oven (about 350°) for about 1 hour, or until done.

White Mountain Cake

(Tested)

This is a favorite for birthday cake. It is served with white boiled frosting.

¾ cup butter
2 cups sugar
1 teaspoon lemon flavoring
3 cups sifted cake flour
2 teaspoons baking powder
¼ teaspoon salt
1 cup milk
6 egg whites, beaten stiff but not dry

Cream butter thoroughly. Add sugar gradually and cream well together. Add lemon flavoring.

Sift flour, baking powder, and salt together three times and add alternately with milk to creamed mixture. Fold in egg whites and blend well.

Pour into a greased 9-inch tube pan, the bottom of which has been lined with greased brown paper. Bake in a moderate oven (about 350°) for about 1 hour, or until done.

OTHER FAVORITES

Then there are caramel cakes, angel food cakes, sponge cakes, spice cakes, marble cakes, and gingerbread. None of these is particularly different from similar cakes described in this chapter. About making a sponge cake, one old cookbook said: "For a perfect sponge cake every time, use equal weights of sugar and eggs and half weight of flour."

A marble cake might be made by stirring 2 squares of melted chocolate into the 1, 2, 3, 4 cake or, in some cases, by stirring a mixture of spices into about 2 tablespoons of molasses and then adding that mixture to the batter.

Gingerbread
(Tested)

1 cup shortening or cooking oil
1 cup dark brown sugar, packed
1 cup dark molasses
1 tablespoon ground ginger
1 teaspoon cinnamon
½ teaspoon nutmeg
3½ cups flour
2 teaspoons soda
½ teaspoon salt
1 cup buttermilk
Whipped cream

In a bowl, combine shortening, sugar, molasses, and spices. Beat well until syrupy. Add flour, soda, and salt, sifted together, alternately with buttermilk. Pour into a greased 8- × 12-inch baking pan. Bake in a

325° oven for 40 minutes, or until it tests done. Serve warm with whipped cream.

Lady Baltimore Cake
(Tested)

A Lady Baltimore cake is in the special-occasion department. This recipe makes three big luscious layers. The cake is white and feathery light. It is one of my favorites.

3½ cups sifted flour
4 teaspoons baking powder
1 teaspoon salt
1 cup butter
2 teaspoons vanilla
1½ cups sugar
1 cup milk
1 cup egg whites (7 or 8)
½ cup sugar

Sift flour, baking powder, and salt together three times. Cream butter until light and fluffy. Add vanilla. Add 1½ cups sugar gradually and cream together until like whipped cream. Add flour and milk alternately in small amounts, beginning and ending with flour. Mix thoroughly after each addition.

Beat egg whites until stiff, gradually adding ½ cup sugar. Beat until glossy. Fold egg whites into batter and mix thoroughly.

Turn into 3 prepared deep 8-inch or 9-inch layer pans. It is a good idea to line the greased pans with greased and floured brown paper. Bang the filled pans against the table to remove the large air bubbles. Bake at 375° for 25 minutes, or until done. Cool in the pans a few minutes before turning out.

Lady Baltimore Frosting
(Tested)

1½ cups sugar
½ teaspoon cream of tartar
½ cup water

3 egg whites
1 teaspoon vanilla
½ cup each of chopped nuts, seeded raisins, dates,
and candied cherries

Mix sugar, cream of tartar, and water. Bring to a boil and stir until sugar is dissolved. Cook, without stirring, to the soft-ball stage, or to 240° on the candy thermometer.

Meanwhile, beat egg whites until stiff and gradually pour hot syrup over the egg whites and continue beating until mixture will stand in soft peaks. Add vanilla.

Remove about a third of the frosting and to it add the nuts and fruits. Use this part for the filling.

Magnolia Cake
(Tested)

This one is a lot like a Lady Baltimore cake but even better, I think. Black walnuts and pecans in the batter could not help but make a cake good.

3 cups sifted flour
3 teaspoons baking powder
1 teaspoon salt
1 cup chopped black walnuts
½ cup broken pecans
1 cup butter
2 cups sugar
4 eggs
2 egg yolks
1 cup sweet milk
1 teaspoon vanilla
Frosting

Sift together flour, baking powder, and salt. Add nuts to flour mixture.

Cream butter, adding sugar gradually. Cream together until light and fluffy. Add eggs and yolks, one at a time, and beat well after each.

Add dry ingredients to creamed mixture alternately with milk, beginning and ending with flour mixture. Add vanilla. Blend well. Turn into 3 layer pans that have been greased and lined with greased and floured brown paper. Bake at 375° for 20 to 25 minutes, or until done. Turn out and cool. Cover with the following frosting.

Magnolia Frosting

(Tested)

1 cup water
2 cups sugar
1 tablespoon vinegar
2 egg whites
¼ pound soft marshmallows, diced
1 cup chopped raisins
1 cup chopped dried figs
1 fresh coconut, grated

Cook water, sugar, and vinegar, without stirring, to 240° on a candy thermometer.

Meanwhile, beat egg whites until stiff and add diced marshmallows. Pour hot syrup slowly over egg whites and continue beating until frosting will stand in soft peaks. Add fruits and coconut. Spread between layers and on top of the cake.

Orange Date Nut Cake

(Tested)

1 package (6 ounces) dates
1 cup chopped pecans
4 cups sifted flour
1 teaspoon baking powder
1 teaspoon soda
¼ teaspoon salt
2 cups (1 pound) margarine
2 cups sugar
4 eggs
1½ cups buttermilk
2 tablespoons grated orange rind
1 cup orange juice
1½ cups sugar

Chop dates finely and add pecans. Add 1 cup of the flour and blend.

Sift remaining flour with baking powder, soda, and salt. Cream margarine and add 2 cups sugar; cream until light and fluffy. Add eggs, one at a time, beating well after each.

Add sifted dry ingredients alternately with buttermilk, blending well. Add floured dates and pecans and orange rind and mix. Pour into a large tube pan that has been greased and floured. Bake in a 300° oven for 1½ hours, or until done.

Meanwhile, add orange juice to 1½ cups sugar in a saucepan and bring to a boil. Pour hot sauce over hot cake when it comes from the oven. Cool in pan and then turn out. It turns out beautifully if allowed to cool, but do not try it while the cake is still hot.

Queen Elizabeth's Cake
(Tested)

1 cup boiling water
1 package (8 ounces) dates, chopped
1 teaspoon soda
¼ cup butter
1 cup sugar
1 egg, beaten
1 teaspoon vanilla
1½ cups sifted flour
1 teaspoon baking powder
½ teaspoon salt
½ cup nuts
Frosting

Pour boiling water over dates and soda. Let stand while mixing cake.

Cream butter and sugar. Add beaten egg and vanilla. Blend in dry ingredients, which have been sifted together. Stir in nuts and date mixture. Blend well and pour into a greased and floured 9- × 12-inch pan. Bake in a 350° oven for 35 minutes, or until done. Cool and frost.

FROSTING

In a saucepan combine 1⅓ cups brown sugar (packed), 1 small can evaporated milk, and 2 tablespoons butter. Stir to mix. Bring to a boil and then boil for 3 minutes. Cool slightly.

Sprinkle chopped nuts and flaked coconut over top of cake. Pour frosting over all—it will be thin. Spread to distribute. The frosting does not get hard. It is more like a thick custard.

Black John Cake
(Tested)

This luscious recipe came from Mrs. M. R. Ingram of Taylorsville. She pointed out that no other nuts should be substituted for black walnuts. The cake is actually better when two or three days old. Be careful not to overcook the filling. It should be a rather thin syrup that penetrates the cake. Before the turn of the century syllabub was the traditional accompaniment for this cake.

1 cup butter
1 cup brown sugar, packed
1 cup molasses
3 eggs
3 cups sifted flour
1 teaspoon ginger
1 teaspoon cinnamon
½ teaspoon salt
1 teaspoon soda dissolved in 3 tablespoons cold water
1 cup buttermilk
Filling

Cream together butter and brown sugar. Blend in molasses—the mixture may look curdled but do not be concerned. Add eggs one at a time, blending well after each. Sift together flour, spices, and salt and add to creamed mixture alternately with soda-water mixture and buttermilk. Blend well and pour into 2 greased and floured 9-inch cake pans. Bake in a 350° oven for 25 minutes, or until done. Turn out and cool. Make the filling.

FILLING
Boil together 2 cups brown sugar (packed), ½ cup sweet milk, and 4 tablespoons butter until thick. Remove from heat and add ½ cup chopped raisins, ½ cup shredded or flaked coconut, 1 cup chopped black walnuts, and 1 teaspoon vanilla.

Velvet Cake
(Tested)

I received this recipe in 1950 from a ninety-year-old woman who said it belonged to her mother. It is the moist, crumbly type of cake that really does just disappear in the mouth. There is no better cake recipe in this book. I like to bake it in a large pan about two inches deep and then frost it with chocolate frosting and cut it into squares.

1 cup butter
2 cups sugar
2 egg yolks
2 whole eggs
1 cup buttermilk
¾ teaspoon soda
2½ cups sifted flour
1 teaspoon vanilla

Cream butter. Add sugar and cream well together. Beat in egg yolks and mix well. Add whole eggs, one at a time, beating well after each.

Stir soda into buttermilk and add to creamed mixture alternately with flour, blending well. Add vanilla. Pour into 3 greased layer cake pans and bake at 375° for 20 to 25 minutes, or until done. Cool and frost with white frosting made with the egg whites left from the 2 yolks used in the recipe. If baked in a 13- × 9½- × 2-inch pan, bake at 325° until done.

Whipped Cream Cake
(Tested)

The cream serves as the shortening.

2¼ cups sifted cake flour
1½ cups sugar
2 teaspoons baking powder
½ teaspoon salt
1½ cups heavy cream
3 eggs, beaten
1 teaspoon vanilla

Sift together flour, sugar, baking powder, and salt. Whip cream until stiff and fold in beaten eggs gently. Fold in dry ingredients and vanilla.

Pour into 2 greased and floured cake pans. Bake at 350° for 30 minutes, or until done. Turn out and cool. Frost as desired.

Sponge Cake
(Tested)

This recipe came from Mrs. S. F. Clark of Wilson. It makes a very good cake.

1 cup sifted cake flour
1 teaspoon baking powder
¼ teaspoon salt
3 eggs, separated
1 cup sugar
3 tablespoons hot water
1 teaspoon lemon or vanilla extract

Sift together flour, baking powder, and salt. Beat egg whites until stiff with half the sugar. Add water and extract to yolks and beat until light and fluffy, gradually adding remaining sugar.

Sift in flour mixture and mix gently. Add beaten egg whites. Fold batter for a very light cake and beat for a finer-grained cake. Turn into a shallow ungreased jelly roll pan or a small tube pan and bake at 325° until the cake springs back when touched.

Robert E. Lee Cake
(Tested)

This cake is an old southern favorite and is quite appropriate to include in this book since one of the state's most outstanding hotels was the Hotel Robert E. Lee in Winston-Salem, now demolished. This is a modernized version of the old recipe.

2¼ cups sifted cake flour
1½ cups sugar
1 tablespoon baking powder
1 teaspoon salt
½ cup salad oil
6 eggs, separated
¾ cup cold water

2 teaspoons vanilla
½ teaspoon cream of tartar

Sift together into a bowl flour, sugar, baking powder, and salt. Make a well in the center and add oil, egg yolks, water, and vanilla. Beat with a spoon until very smooth.

Beat egg whites with cream of tartar until extremely stiff. Pour egg yolk mixture over beaten whites. Carefully fold the two together until well blended. Do not stir or beat.

Pour into 4 ungreased 8- or 9-inch layer cake pans. Bake at 325° for 20 to 25 minutes, or until the tops spring back when touched. Invert pans on cake racks and leave that way until cold. Remove layers from pans and fill with lemon jelly filling.

Lemon Jelly Filling
(Tested)

3 tablespoons butter
Grated rind of 1 lemon
Juice of 2 lemons
Pinch of salt
1 cup sugar
2 tablespoons flour
2 whole eggs
2 egg yolks

Melt butter in the top of a double boiler. Add lemon rind and juice and salt. Mix sugar and flour and add to slightly beaten whole eggs and yolks. Add to butter mixture.

Cook over boiling water, stirring, until smooth and thick. Cool and use between layers. Frost the cake with golden orange frosting (see index).

Devil's Food Cake
(Tested)

For years I tested devil's food cakes, but this was the first recipe that produced the kind of cake it should.

4 squares unsweetened chocolate
½ cup sugar

½ cup buttermilk
2½ cups sifted cake flour
1½ teaspoons baking powder
¾ teaspoon soda
½ teaspoon salt
½ cup butter
1¼ cups sugar
3 eggs, well beaten
1 cup buttermilk
1 teaspoon vanilla

Melt chocolate over boiling water. Add ½ cup sugar and ½ cup buttermilk and stir over boiling water until well blended. Cool until it is time to use.

Sift flour with baking powder, soda, and salt three times. Cream butter, add 1¼ cups sugar gradually, and cream together until light and fluffy. Add eggs and beat well.

Add about one-fourth of the flour mixture and mix thoroughly. Add chocolate mixture and blend. Add remaining flour alternately with buttermilk, a small amount at a time, beating thoroughly after each addition. Add vanilla.

Pour into 3 layer cake pans that have been greased and lined with greased and floured brown paper. Bake at 350° for 25 minutes, or until done. Cool and frost with white frosting.

Chocolate Layer Cake
(Tested)

This is the best chocolate cake recipe I have ever tried. The cake is moist and delicious.

2 cups flour
1 teaspoon baking powder
1 teaspoon salt
½ cup cocoa
⅔ cup butter
1½ cups sugar
1 teaspoon vanilla
3 eggs, separated

½ teaspoon soda
¾ cup buttermilk

Sift together flour, baking powder, salt, and cocoa. Cream butter. Add sugar and cream well together. Add vanilla. Beat in egg yolks and blend well. Add sifted dry ingredients alternately with buttermilk into which soda has been stirred, beginning and ending with flour mixture.

Beat egg whites until stiff and fold in gently but thoroughly. Pour into 2 greased and floured 9-inch layer cake pans. Bake at 350° for 25 minutes, or until done.

PAYNIE'S CHOCOLATE CAKE

Jessie Payne (Paynie) worked for a number of Lexington families and operated her own catering business. She presided over the kitchen for many of Lexington's important social events. Some years ago the late Mrs. J. F. Spruill and the late Mrs. Stokes Adderton of the Lexington Sorosis Club compiled a cookbook of her recipes. This wonderful cake came from that book. It has three parts—chocolate buttermilk cake, chocolate filling, and soft caramel icing.

Chocolate Buttermilk Cake
(Tested)

1 cup butter
2 cups sugar
2 eggs
3½ cups sifted cake flour
3⅓ tablespoons cocoa
2 teaspoons soda
1 teaspoon salt
2 cups buttermilk
1 teaspoon vanilla

Cream butter. Add sugar and cream together until light and fluffy. Add eggs, one at a time, and beat well after each.

Sift together flour, cocoa, soda, and salt and add to creamed mixture alternately with buttermilk. Blend thoroughly. Add vanilla and pour into a greased and floured jelly roll–size pan.

Bake in a 350° oven for 45 minutes, or until done. Turn out and cool.

To give the cake Paynie's treatment, spread the following filling over the top of the cake.

Paynie's Favorite Chocolate Filling
(Tested)

4 whole eggs
2 cups sugar
½ cup (1 stick) butter
4 squares unsweetened chocolate
1 tablespoon vanilla
About 1 cup toasted rolled pecans

Place eggs, sugar, butter, and chocolate in the top of a double boiler and cook over hot water, stirring constantly, until thickened. Add vanilla and set aside to cool. Spread over top of cake. Sprinkle generously with pecans.

Allow the cake to stand until firm and then spread or dribble with caramel icing.

Caramel Icing
(Tested)

This icing is creamy and delicious. It is also easy to prepare. Make a double quantity for a layer cake.

2 cups light brown sugar, packed
5 tablespoons light cream
½ cup (1 stick) butter
½ teaspoon baking powder
½ teaspoon vanilla

Mix brown sugar, cream, and butter and bring to a boil over medium heat. Boil for 2 minutes, stirring. Remove from heat and add baking powder and vanilla. Beat well until smooth and creamy. Spread on cake.

Cut the cake in squares to serve.

CHOCOLATE POTATO CAKE

Quite a few of the old cooks used mashed potatoes and sometimes yeast in chocolate cakes. Those recipes I tested seemed inferior in texture and taste to cakes made in other ways and so are not included in this book.

$100 Waldorf Astoria Cake
(Tested)

This recipe appears in just about all the club, church society, and auxiliary cookbooks. It did not originate in North Carolina and probably not at the Waldorf Astoria Hotel either, but regardless of its origin, it was made in just about every community in the state.

½ cup butter
2 cups sugar
4 squares unsweetened chocolate, melted
2 eggs, beaten
2 cups sifted cake flour
2 teaspoons baking powder
1 teaspoon salt
1½ cups milk
1 cup chopped nuts
2 teaspoons vanilla
Frosting

Cream butter and sugar together. Add chocolate and eggs and blend well. Sift together flour, baking powder, and salt and add to creamed mixture alternately with milk. Add nuts and vanilla. Bake in a greased loaf pan at 350° degrees for 1 hour, or until done. Cool.

FROSTING

Melt ½ cup butter and 2 squares unsweetened chocolate. Add 1 well-beaten egg. Stir in 1½ cups sifted confectioners' sugar. Add 1 teaspoon vanilla, 1 teaspoon lemon juice, and ½ cup chopped nuts. Beat until smooth and spread on cake.

Black-Eyed Susan Cake
(Tested)

This is a special-occasion cake.

4 squares unsweetened chocolate
½ cup hot water
½ cup sugar
2 cups sifted cake flour
1 teaspoon soda
1 teaspoon salt
½ cup butter
1¼ cups sugar
3 eggs
¾ cup milk
1 teaspoon vanilla

Combine chocolate and water in the top of a double boiler; cook and stir for 2 minutes. Add ½ cup sugar and blend well. Remove from heat. Cool to lukewarm.

Add soda and salt to flour and sift together three times. Cream butter, add 1¼ cups sugar gradually, and cream together until light and fluffy. Add eggs, one at a time, beating thoroughly after each. Add half of the flour and beat until smooth. Add milk and remaining flour, alternately, in small amounts, beating after each addition until smooth. Then add vanilla and chocolate mixture and blend.

Turn batter into two 9-inch layer pans 1½ inches deep or into three 8-inch layer pans. Bake in a moderate oven (about 350°) for 30 to 35 minutes. Cool cake in pans for about 5 minutes before removing. Frost with the following golden orange frosting.

Note: I would suggest that you grease and line the cake pans with brown paper. Grease and flour again so the cake will come out easily.

Golden Orange Frosting

Cream together ⅓ cup butter, 1½ tablespoons grated orange rind, and ¼ teaspoon salt. Add 1 unbeaten egg yolk and mix well. Add 1 pound sifted confectioners' sugar alternately with 2 teaspoons lemon juice and sufficient orange juice to make the proper consistency.

Decorate the top of the cake with black-eyed Susan designs, using thinly sliced orange rind for petals and chocolate chips for the centers of flowers.

Brown Front Cake

Brown front cake is a favorite. It may or may not have originated in this state.

Add 1 cup boiling water to 3½ tablespoons cocoa. Set aside to cool. Cream 1 cup soft butter with 2 cups sugar. Add 4 slightly beaten eggs and blend. Sift 1 teaspoon salt with 3 cups sifted cake flour. Add flour to creamed mixture alternately with 1 cup buttermilk in which 2 teaspoons soda have been dissolved. Bake in 3 greased floured layer cake pans in a moderate oven (about 350°) until done. Cool.

ICING

Stir 1 cup butter, 1 cup milk, and 2 cups sugar over moderate heat until the sugar melts. Cook at low heat until a small amount forms a soft ball in cold water. Remove from heat, beat until creamy, and spread on the cooled cake.

Banana Cake
(Tested)

Banana cake is quite popular.

½ cup butter
1 cup sugar
2 eggs, well beaten
1 cup (3 medium) mashed ripe bananas
1 teaspoon vanilla
2 cups sifted flour
2 teaspoons baking powder
¼ teaspoon salt
¼ cup buttermilk
1 teaspoon soda

Cream butter. Add sugar gradually and cream well together. Add eggs and mix well. Add mashed bananas. Add vanilla.

Sift together flour, baking powder, and salt. Add to creamed mixture alternately with buttermilk into which the soda has been stirred. Pour into 2 prepared 9-inch layer cake pans and bake at 350° for about 25 minutes, or until done. Cool and frost as desired.

Applesauce Cake
(Tested)

Applesauce cake turns up during all seasons of the year. It is more a family cake than a church picnic or party cake. It is often served unfrosted and perhaps warm from the oven.

½ cup shortening
1½ cups sugar
2 eggs
1½ cups thick applesauce
2½ cups sifted flour
1 teaspoon salt
1 teaspoon cinnamon
¼ teaspoon ginger
½ teaspoon cloves
½ cup chopped nuts
1 teaspoon soda dissolved in 2 tablespoons hot water

Cream shortening and sugar together. Add eggs, one at a time, and mix well. Add one-third of the applesauce and blend. Sift flour with salt and spices. Mix nuts with flour. Add with remaining applesauce to creamed mixture and blend.

Add soda-water mixture. Blend well. Pour into a large greased loaf pan. Bake in a moderate oven (about 350°) for about 1 hour, or until done.

Note: If desired, add 1 cup chopped seedless raisins with the nuts. For a spicier cake, substitute apple butter for the applesauce.

Haywood County Prune Cake with Buttermilk Icing
(Tested)

This recipe came from Mary Cornwell, former home demonstration agent for Haywood County, where it was developed. You may think that both the title and the ingredients sound unusual. I did and almost included the recipe as an untested one before my curiosity got the best of me. I tried it and found it to be delicious.

This cake is moist, rich, and old-fashioned. The icing forms a glaze over the top instead of the usual coating of frosting.

1½ cups sugar
1 cup vegetable oil
3 eggs
2 cups sifted flour
1 teaspoon soda
1 teaspoon cinnamon
1 teaspoon nutmeg
1 teaspoon allspice
¼ teaspoon salt
1 cup buttermilk
1 teaspoon vanilla
1 cup nuts
1 cup prunes, cooked, seeded, and chopped

Blend sugar and oil. Add eggs. Sift dry ingredients together and add alternately with buttermilk. Add vanilla, nuts, and prunes. Pour into a greased Pyrex pan 11 × 7 × 2 inches deep and bake at 300°. When the cake is done, remove from the oven and while still hot cover with the following buttermilk icing.

Buttermilk Icing
(Tested)

1 cup sugar
½ cup buttermilk
½ teaspoon soda
1 tablespoon white corn syrup
¼ cup butter
½ teaspoon vanilla

Boil mixture in a deep pan until it forms a soft ball. Pour over hot cake without beating. Leave the cake in the pan until ready to cut into blocks for serving.

Burnt Sugar Cake
(Tested)

2¼ cups granulated sugar
1 cup boiling water
⅔ cup butter
3 eggs
1 teaspoon soda
1 tablespoon hot water
3 cups sifted flour
1 teaspoon baking powder
½ teaspoon salt
1 cup milk
1 teaspoon vanilla

Place ¾ cup sugar in a heavy skillet and cook over medium heat, stirring, until melted and dark brown in color. Add boiling water gradually. Cook slowly until syrup is thick like molasses. Remove from heat and set aside to cool.

Cream butter with remaining 1½ cups sugar. Add eggs one at a time, blending well after each.

Add soda to 1 tablespoon hot water and cool. Add to creamed mixture alternately with sifted dry ingredients, sugar mixture, and milk. Add vanilla. Pour into three 8-inch greased and floured layer cake pans lined with greased and floured brown paper.

Bake in a 375° oven for 25 minutes, or until done. Remove from pans, cool, and frost as desired.

Blackberry Jam Cake
(Tested)

This recipe produces a light, tender jam cake, which is a great deal more than I can say of many I have tested.

⅔ cup shortening
1½ cups sugar
3 eggs, beaten
1 cup blackberry jam
3 cups sifted flour
1 teaspoon baking powder

1 teaspoon soda
1 teaspoon salt
1 teaspoon ground cinnamon
1 teaspoon ground cloves
1 cup buttermilk

Cream shortening until light and fluffy. Add sugar and cream well together. Beat in eggs and blend well. Mix in blackberry jam.

Sift together flour, baking powder, soda, salt, cinnamon, and cloves. Add dry ingredients to creamed mixture alternately with buttermilk, beating until smooth after each addition.

Turn into 3 greased and floured layer cake pans and bake in a moderate oven (about 350°) for 30 minutes, or until done. Cool and frost with white boiled frosting.

HICKORY NUT CAKE

Any type of cake batter to which hickory nut goodies have been added might be called a hickory nut cake. There does not seem to be a special recipe for this cake.

Prince of Wales or Prince Albert Cake
(Tested)

Information about this cake turned up in Stanly County and in Bethania, the old Moravian settlement in Forsyth County. No doubt it was also prepared in other sections of the state. It was a special treat around Christmastime in place of or in addition to the regular fruit cakes.

This cake is wonderfully tender and is luscious put together with lemon filling and coated with white frosting or filled and frosted with white frosting flavored with lemon. Some Prince of Wales cake recipes have two spicy layers and one yellow layer. This recipe makes three 8-inch layers but if you wish, bake the batter in two 9-inch pans and use a golden layer in between.

1 cup butter
1 cup sugar
4 eggs
1 cup minus 2 tablespoons molasses
2½ cups sifted cake flour

1 teaspoon soda
2 teaspoons cinnamon
2 teaspoons ginger
1 teaspoon nutmeg
½ teaspoon cloves
½ teaspoon allspice
1 cup buttermilk

Cream butter and sugar until light and fluffy. Add eggs, one at time, blending well after each. Blend in molasses.

Sift flour with soda and spices. Add to creamed mixture alternately with buttermilk. Blend well and pour into 3 greased and floured 8-inch layer pans. Let stand for 3 to 5 minutes to allow bubbles to rise. Bang pans against the table to remove bubbles.

Bake at 375° for 25 minutes, or until done. Cool and frost as desired.

Dolly Varden Cake

About one hundred years ago the name of Dolly Varden, which originally belonged to one of Dickens's characters, became widely popular—even to the extent of being given to a cake.

It would seem from this recipe, taken from an old cookbook, that a Dolly Varden cake is very similar to a Prince of Wales cake.

For the dark layers, mix ½ cup butter, 1 cup sugar, and ½ cup syrup. Add 4 egg yolks. Sift together 2 cups flour, 2 teaspoons baking powder, 1 teaspoon cloves, 1 teaspoon cinnamon, and ½ teaspoon freshly grated nutmeg. Add to creamed mixture alternately with ⅔ cup milk. Add 1 cup chopped raisins and ½ cup currants.

For the light layer, mix ½ cup butter and 1½ cups sugar. Sift 2 cups flour with 2 teaspoons baking powder and add alternately with 1 cup milk. Add 2 teaspoons vanilla. Beat 3 eggs stiff and fold in.

Bake in three 8-inch greased and floured cake pans and put together in alternate layers with jelly between. For the top, make a frosting of the remaining egg whites and 1 cup powdered sugar.

CHRISTMAS CAKES

At Christmastime, the traditional white and dark fruit cakes are about equally popular.

Light Fruit Cake
(Tested)

Many who have made and eaten this light fruit cake claim it is the best that they have ever tasted. I share that opinion. Probably the best way to add the flavor of brandy is to soak the fruits in brandy overnight before making the cake.

Use the old-fashioned pound cake recipe (see index) for the batter, removing 1 cup of the flour to use for coating the fruits. Prepare the pans by greasing and lining with greased brown paper cut to fit. The batter fills one angel cake tube pan and four 1-quart loaf pans.

Have ready the following fruits and nuts:

1 pound red candied cherries
1 pound green candied cherries
1 pound candied pineapple, diced
2 pounds pitted dates, thinly sliced
1 box (15 ounces) white raisins
1 pound citron, finely diced
2 pounds mixed candied fruits, diced
2 packages (6 ounces each) blanched and peeled almonds
4 packages (6 ounces each) pecan halves

Sprinkle the cup of flour over fruits and nuts. Mix well with the hands. Pour batter on top of fruits and mix well.

Fill pans. Place a sheet of aluminum foil over the top of each pan and squeeze down around the edges. Place a shallow pan of water in the bottom of the oven.

Bake at 275°. The large cake takes 3½ hours. The loaf cakes take 2 hours. Bake until a toothpick inserted emerges clean. Remove the foil for the last 15 minutes of baking to allow the cake to dry on top.

Cool in pans. Turn out and wrap well in aluminum foil. If possible, age the cakes for 4 weeks. During the aging open the foil occasionally, if desired, and sprinkle with brandy or wine.

There are those who like to add a grated fresh coconut to the fruits used in light fruit cake.

Dark Fruit Cake

(Tested)

This recipe produces the best dark fruit cake I have ever made.

1 pound raisins
1 pound pitted dates
1 pound citron
1 pound currants
1½ pounds candied cherries
½ pound candied pineapple
¼ pound candied orange peel
¼ pound candied lemon peel
1½ pounds shelled nuts
1 pound butter
1 pound light brown sugar
12 eggs
4 cups sifted flour
1 teaspoon soda
½ teaspoon nutmeg
½ teaspoon mace
½ teaspoon cloves
1 tablespoon cinnamon
1 tablespoon allspice
1 teaspoon salt
1 cup molasses

Cut fruits into small pieces and break nuts. Cream butter and sugar together. Beat eggs and add to creamed mixture. Blend well. Sift dry ingredients together and add to creamed mixture alternately with molasses. Add batter to fruits and nuts. Mix thoroughly, using hands if necessary.

Pour batter into 2 large tube pans that have been greased and lined with greased brown paper cut to fit. Cover tops with aluminum foil squeezed tightly down around the edge of the pans.

Place a pan of hot water in the bottom of the oven. Bake at 275° until done. I baked mine for 4 hours and 30 minutes and they were perfectly done. Test the cakes with a toothpick to determine doneness, as ovens and pans will make the time vary. Remove the foil for the last 30 minutes or so to allow tops of cakes to dry out. Makes about 15 pounds of cake.

Note: If desired, pour 1 cup brandy over the fruits the night before baking.

Japanese Fruit Cake
(Tested)

This cake is a definite part of the old-fashioned celebration of Christmas.

1 cup butter
2 cups sugar
4 eggs, separated
3¼ cups sifted flour
1 teaspoon baking powder
1 teaspoon salt
1 scant cup milk
1 teaspoon vanilla
1 teaspoon cinnamon
1 teaspoon allspice
½ teaspoon cloves
¼ pound finely chopped raisins
Filling

Cream butter and sugar together. Add egg yolks and mix well. Sift together flour, baking powder, and salt. Add to creamed mixture alternately with milk. Fold in stiffly beaten egg whites. Add vanilla.

Divide batter into two parts with more in one part. To the smaller part add spices and raisins.

Make the white part in two layers and the spiced layer in one. Bake at 350° for 25 to 30 minutes, or until done. Make the filling.

FILLING

Combine the juice of 2 lemons, the rind of 1 lemon, 1 grated large fresh coconut, 2 cups sugar, and 1 cup boiling water. When the mixture begins to boil, remove from heat and stir in 2 tablespoons cornstarch that has been dissolved in ½ cup cold water.

Continue to cook, stirring constantly, until the mixture drops in a lump from the spoon. Cool and spread between the layers. Cover the top with white frosting.

Hermit Cake
(Tested)

This cake is a Christmas favorite in Virginia and, like many other good recipes, it found its way to North Carolina. Traditionally, it is baked in a heavy pan of the Dutch oven type. I baked it in a large pudding pan without a hole in the center. Unlike many fruit cakes, the Hermit cake can be sliced as thin as nut bread.

4 packages (7 ounces each) pitted dates
4½ cups shelled pecans
1 pound butter
3 cups brown sugar, packed
6 eggs
5 cups sifted flour
2 teaspoons baking powder
2 teaspoons cinnamon
1 teaspoon nutmeg
Grated rind and juice of 1 large lemon
4 teaspoons vanilla

Chop dates and mix with pecans. Cream brown butter and sugar together. Add eggs, one at a time, and blend well after each. Sift flour with baking powder, cinnamon, and nutmeg and add to creamed mixture with lemon rind and juice and vanilla. Add date-pecan mixture. The batter will be stiff.

Pour into a large pan that has been greased and lined with greased brown paper. Bake uncovered at 275° for 2½ to 3 hours, or until cake tests done. Cool in pan.

Christmas Cake
(Tested)

This cake was brought to my attention by Mrs. Hugh Salmons, of Elkin, who developed it from Mrs. J. S. Atkinson's recipe in the *Elkin Junior Woman's Cook Book*. There is no leavening in the recipe—the batter is the pound cake type. It makes a wonderful cake.

1 cup butter
1⅔ cups sugar
5 eggs

2 cups sifted flour
½ pound shelled pecans
½ pound shelled black walnuts
1 pound candied cherries
1 can (4 ounces) moist-style shredded coconut

Cream butter until light and fluffy. Add sugar gradually and cream well together. Add eggs one at a time, beating in each with a wooden spoon.

Coat nuts and cherries with a portion of the flour. Stir remaining flour into creamed mixture. Add nuts, cherries, and coconut and mix. Turn into a tube pan that has been greased and lined with greased brown paper. Bake at 250° for 3 hours and 30 minutes, or until done.

Date and Nut Cake

(Tested)

This recipe makes an excellent cake. Personally, I like the combination of dates, nuts, and cherries a lot more than the other candied fruits usually found in fruit cakes.

2 pounds pitted dates, chopped
4 cups nuts, slightly broken
1 cup candied cherries, cut in half
½ teaspoon soda dissolved in ½ cup boiling water
½ cup butter
1 cup sugar
4 eggs
1 cup sifted flour
½ teaspoon salt
1 teaspoon baking powder
1 teaspoon vanilla

Mix dates, nuts, and cherries. Pour soda mixture over them and set aside while mixing the remaining ingredients.

Cream butter and sugar together. Add eggs one at a time, mixing well after each. Sift flour with salt and baking powder. Add with vanilla to creamed mixture and blend well.

Add date mixture and mix well—use hands if necessary. Pour batter into a large tube pan that has been greased and lined with greased and floured brown paper. Cover top with aluminum foil squeezed around the edges. Place a pan of water in the bottom of the oven. Bake at 275° for 3½ hours, or until cake tests done. Remove foil for the last 30 minutes of baking.

Stack Fruit Cake

This is really an old recipe and I am sure there are many variations of it. The cake consists of thin layers of baked cookie dough—almost like pancakes—with a filling of mashed sweetened dried fruit between each layer. The combination stands for several hours or overnight to ripen before cutting. Some cakes have as many as fourteen layers but seven layers is considered quite an achievement. The cake looks for the world like a Sacher cake, that distinctive Viennese favorite.

When I made the cake, I baked eight thin circles of ginger cookie dough about eight inches in diameter. For the filling, I used a mixture of cooked mashed dried apples and peaches sweetened with honey. The cake had a lot of flavor but seemed soggy.

Mrs. J. T. Stroud of Jonesville gave me the following directions for this old favorite plus a sample of one of the cakes. I kept the sample in my freezer for five years.

Make the kind of dough you would use for old-fashioned ginger bread with molasses and spices. Add enough flour to make a dough that can be rolled like cookies. Roll out thin on a lightly floured board. Using a plate or a pie pan as a pattern, cut the dough into circles.

Lay circles gently into a heavy skillet that contains a scant covering of lard. Brown slowly and carefully on both sides. (The layers may also be baked in the oven like cookies.)

Cool and put together with cooked dried apples that have been mashed to a pulp and sweetened. Some of the old folks used honey to sweeten the cake. The cake may be eaten right away, but the flavor is far more mellow after about a week.

Ellen Cheek's Stack Cake

⅓ cup butter
1 cup dark brown sugar, packed
⅓ cup molasses
2 eggs

2⅔ cups all-purpose flour
1 teaspoon baking powder
1 teaspoon soda
1 teaspoon salt
1 teaspoon ginger
Filling

Cream together butter, brown sugar, molasses, and eggs. Sift together dry ingredients; blend into creamed mixture. Cover dough and chill thoroughly.

Divide dough into 6 parts. Roll each part out to make an 8-inch circle. Place on greased 8-inch cake pans. Bake in a 400° oven for 8 to 10 minutes, or until done. Turn out; cool.

Stack and fill layers. Refrigerate for 24 hours to allow them to become mellow and moist. To serve, cut into wedges.

FILLING

1 pound dried apples, cooked and mashed
1 cup brown sugar, packed
1 cup granulated sugar
2 teaspoons cinnamon
½ teaspoon allspice

Mix all ingredients and spread between layers.

Shoe Box Cake

Although the origin of this cake is a mystery, the reason for its name is simple—the cake is baked in a shoe box.

1 pound graham crackers
6 eggs
2 cups milk
2 cups sugar
½ pound melted butter
1 cup black walnuts
2 cups pecans
½ pound grated coconut
2 teaspoons baking powder

Roll crackers to make fine crumbs and blend with remaining ingredients. Line a shoe box with waxed paper and fill with cake mixture. Bake in a 250° oven for 3½ hours.

Sally White Cake

A Christmas tradition in Wilmington, this cake is named for its originator, Sally White.

1 pound butter
2 cups (1 pound) sugar
12 eggs
4 cups (1 pound) flour
2 teaspoons mace
2 teaspoons nutmeg
2 pounds shelled almonds
1 pound citron, finely chopped
2 fresh coconuts, grated

Cream butter and sugar together. Add eggs one at a time, blending well after each. Sift together flour, mace, and nutmeg and add a portion of flour mixture to almonds, citron, and coconut. Add to creamed mixture and blend. Bake in a tube pan lined with greased and floured brown paper in a 250° oven for 2 hours, or until done.

Farmers Fruit Cake

This recipe came from Mrs. Ethelyn Richardson, of Laurel Springs, who had been making it for twenty-five to thirty years. She pointed out that since this cake contains no nuts, it is especially appreciated by older people.

2 cups dried apples, packed tightly
2 cups molasses
2 cups raisins
1 scant teaspoon each cloves, allspice, cinnamon, and nutmeg
1½ cups butter or shortening
2 cups sugar
1 cup milk
4 eggs

5 cups flour
4 teaspoons baking powder

Soak apples overnight in water; drain and chop finely. Simmer in molasses until tender. Add raisins, spices, butter, sugar, milk, and eggs. Mix all together and add flour sifted with baking powder.

Fill prepared loaf or tube cake pans about three-fourths full, crimp foil over the tops, and bake in a slow oven as for any fruit cake. After 1 hour, remove foil and let tops brown.

Note: For a decorative touch, place pecan halves, candied cherries, and almonds in the bottom of the greased brown paper-lined pans.

Raised Fruit Cake

Mix 2 cups bread sponge, ¾ cup butter, 1 cup molasses, 1 teaspoon each of cinnamon and allspice, 2 eggs, ½ cup sugar, ½ teaspoon soda, ½ teaspoon cloves, and 1 cup chopped dried fruit with raisins and currants that have been stewed in molasses. Add flour to make a stiff batter.

Dried Apple Fruit Cake

This cake was made at Christmastime because it was less expensive than some other kinds. It was also made at other times of the year when the ingredients were available.

Cover 2 cups dried apples with water and cook until soft—all the water should be gone. Mash and stir 1 teaspoon soda into hot apples. Cool.

Cream 1 cup butter and 2 cups sugar. Add 3 eggs, one at a time, and blend well. Sift 3 cups sifted flour with 1 teaspoon salt, 1 teaspoon cloves, 1 teaspoon cinnamon, and 1 teaspoon allspice. Add 1 pound seedless raisins, 1 pound chopped dried figs, and ½ pound black walnut goodies. Add flour mixture to butter mixture alternately with apples and 1 cup strawberry preserves. Blend well.

Turn into a greased tube pan with the bottom lined with greased brown paper. Bake at 275° for 4 hours, or until done.

LAYER FRUIT CAKE

This cake is an old one and a big one. The fruit cake layers are stacked with Japanese fruit cake filling (for recipe see index) between each layer.

Mincemeat Cake
(Tested)

In the days after the Christmas fruit cakes were baked but were not yet ready to eat, it was customary in some households to whip up a mincemeat cake. This modern version makes a better cake than some of the dried, overbaked, underfruited cakes I have tasted.

½ cup shortening
1 cup sugar
2 eggs
2 cups sifted flour
2 cups prepared mincemeat
½ pound seedless raisins
1 cup broken nuts
1 teaspoon vanilla
1 teaspoon soda dissolved in 1 tablespoon hot water

Cream shortening and sugar together. Add eggs and blend well. Add remaining ingredients and mix thoroughly. Pour into a greased loaf pan, filling about three-fourths full. Bake at 325° for 1½ hours, or until done.

OLD-TIME CAKE RECIPES

Hard-Times Cake

When there were no eggs, no milk, and no butter for cake making, thrifty homemakers turned to this recipe. It was used long before World War I but was quite popular then. It has also been called Economy Cake, Poverty Cake, Poor Man's Cake, and Mother's Minus.

2 cups brown sugar
2 cups hot water
4 tablespoons lard
1 pound seedless raisins, cut up

3 cups sifted flour
2 teaspoons baking soda
2 teaspoons salt
2 teaspoons cinnamon
2 teaspoons cloves

Simmer together for 5 minutes brown sugar, water, lard, and raisins. Set aside to cool. Sift dry ingredients together, add to the first mixture, and beat until smooth. Pour into 2 well-greased and floured loaf pans and bake in a 325° oven for about 1 hour and 30 minutes.

Nothing Cakes and Cheap Cakes

For these recipes, my source listed the ingredients but gave no directions:

1. 1 egg, ¾ cup sugar, lump of butter the size of an egg, 1 pint sweet milk, 1 pint flour, and 1 teaspoon yeast powder.

2. 1 egg, 1 cup sugar, butter the size of an egg, ½ cup sweet milk, 1 pint flour, soda, and cream of tartar.

Sit-in-the-Sun Cake

This is one of the most interesting old cake recipes I have discovered. The directions do not explain the reason for placing the cake in the sun or indicate whether it is a loaf or a layer cake.

Cream ¾ pound butter with ¾ pound sugar. Add 2 egg yolks and mix well. Add ¾ pound flour alternately with 10 egg whites beaten to a froth. Flavor to taste.

Cover and place in the hot sun until bubbles form on the top—about 2 hours. Bake.

Break Cake

You have heard of breaking bread, but have you ever heard of Break Cake?

Combine 2 tablespoons butter, ½ cup sugar, 1 egg, ¼ cup sweet milk, ¾ cup flour, 1 teaspoon baking powder, ¼ salt, and vanilla flavoring just as you would for any cake. Bake and "break" it off to serve it.

Composition Cake

Mix 1 pound flour, 1 pound sugar, ½ pound butter, 7 eggs, ½ pint cream, and a gill [4 ounces] of brandy.

Black Cake

This cake calls for 2 pounds currants, 2 pounds raisins, 1 pound citron, cinnamon, mace, 1 glass wine or brandy, 1 pound flour, 1 pound sugar, 1 pound butter, and 12 eggs. Bake 4 hours in a loaf.

Bread Cake

Combine 1 cup butter, 3 cups sugar, 1 cup light sponge, 3 eggs well beaten, 1 teaspoon soda, spices, raisins, figs, and flour to make it stiff.

Pork Cake

This one is a favorite around hog-killing time.

Cook 1 pound fresh pork fat in boiling water until tender and then drain and mash well. Add 2 cups sugar, 4 eggs, 4 cups flour, grated whole nutmeg, 1 teaspoon cinnamon, 1 pound seedless raisins, 1 cup molasses, and 1 teaspoon soda stirred into 1 cup buttermilk. Bake in a tube pan.

Rochester Cake

Cream ½ cup shortening with 1½ cups sugar. Add alternately with 1½ cups sour milk, 2 eggs, 3 cups flour sifted with 1 teaspoon salt, 1½ teaspoons soda, 2 teaspoons cinnamon, 1 teaspoon cloves, and 1 teaspoon nutmeg. Bake in 2 layers.

FILLING

Cook 2 tablespoons cornstarch, ¾ cup sugar, 1 cup water, and ¾ cup raisins until thick and clear. Add 2 tablespoons butter and ½ cup chopped black walnuts. Cool and spread between layers and on top.

Jenny Lind Cake

Mix ½ cup butter, 1½ cups sugar, 3 eggs, 1 teaspoon soda, 2 cups flour, and ½ cup sweet milk. Bake it either as a loaf or a layer cake.

Railroad Cake

Mix ½ cup butter, 2 cups sugar, 3 eggs, 1 teaspoon soda, 2 teaspoons cream of tartar, 3 cups flour, and 1 cup milk.

Dover Cake

Mix ½ pound butter, 1 pound sugar, 1 pound flour, 6 eggs, 2 teaspoons baking powder, 1 cup milk, and 1 teaspoon vanilla.

Almond Cake

This one should certainly be tasty.

Combine 1 pound butter, 1 pound sugar, 1 pound flour, 9 eggs, 2 cups finely chopped almonds, ½ pound finely chopped citron, and the grated rind and juice of 1 lemon.

FROSTINGS AND FILLINGS

A good many old-time cooks followed the practice of dribbling sugar syrup over baked and cooled layers of cake and allowing it to harden before covering with frosting. The syrup was made by combining and boiling equal parts of sugar and water. Sometimes the syrup treatment was used in place of frosting. It helps make and keep the cake moist.

Boiled Frosting
(Tested)

White boiled frosting is undoubtedly the most widely used. I have followed this recipe in all kinds of weather and have never had a failure. It will cover a 2-layer cake.

1½ cups sugar
2 tablespoons white corn syrup

¼ cup water
2 egg whites
1 teaspoon vanilla

Mix sugar, syrup, and water. Boil until it spins a thread, or to 238° on a candy thermometer. Beat egg whites until stiff but not dry. Gradually add boiling syrup to egg whites, beating vigorously. Add vanilla and continue beating until of a proper consistency to spread.

Seven-Minute Butter Frosting
(Tested)

The late Mrs. I. I. Cohen, of Winston-Salem, who gave me this recipe, said: "It is just out of this world. You'll think it is whipped cream." I tried the recipe and agreed fully with Mrs. Cohen. It does not get hard on the cake but holds its shape beautifully. It is wonderful on fresh coconut cake.

This is enough frosting for a 2-layer cake.

1 cup sugar
½ teaspoon cream of tartar
3 tablespoons water
2 egg whites
1 stick butter
2 teaspoons vanilla

Mix sugar, cream of tartar, water, and egg whites in the top of a double boiler. Cook over boiling water, beating constantly, until the mixture stands in soft peaks. Remove from heat and cool to room temperature.

Whip butter until light and fluffy. Add cooled mixture by the tablespoon to the butter and continue beating until all is added. Add vanilla. Frost cake.

Caramel Frosting
(Tested)

This is the old-fashioned way to making caramel frosting. It is sweet to the taste but does not curdle, which is more than can be said of caramel frosting when the cream is cooked with the sugar. The frosting is enough for a 2-layer cake.

3 cups brown sugar, packed
1 cup water
2 tablespoons butter
1 teaspoon vanilla
Cream

Cook brown sugar and water to the soft-ball stage, or to 238° on a candy thermometer. Add butter and vanilla. Remove from heat and beat until thick and creamy. At first, it looks as if it will not cream but it will. Add a little cream to make it easy to spread on the cake.

Fudge Frosting
(Tested)

This recipe makes a melt-in-the-mouth frosting.

2 squares (1 ounce each) unsweetened chocolate
3 cups sugar
3 tablespoons light corn syrup
Pinch of salt
1 cup milk
4 tablespoons butter
1 teaspoon vanilla

Combine chocolate, sugar, corn syrup, salt, and milk. Cook over low heat, stirring, until sugar is dissolved. Cook to the very soft-ball stage, or to 232° on the candy thermometer.

Remove from heat. Add butter and cool until just warm, or to 110°. Add vanilla and beat until mixture is of proper spreading consistency. It may look sugary when you first start beating but it comes out smooth in the end.

Seafoam Frosting
(Tested)

Seafoam frosting is often used on spice or devil's food cake. This is the best recipe I have ever tried.

2 egg whites
1½ cups brown sugar, firmly packed
Dash of salt

⅓ cup of water
1 teaspoon vanilla

Combine egg whites, brown sugar, salt, and water in the top of a double boiler. Place over rapidly boiling water and beat at high speed for 7 minutes, or until the mixture will stand in stiff peaks. Add vanilla and beat until thick enough to spread.

Rocky Mountain Filling

Boil 2 cups sugar and ½ cup water until the mixture spins a thread. Pour hot syrup over 3 stiffly beaten egg whites. Continue beating. Add a grated fresh coconut and a package each of chopped seedless raisins, currants, figs, and dates. Add nuts as desired—for example, try a combination of pecans, English walnuts, black walnuts, and Brazil nuts.

Persimmon Filling

Add chopped ripe persimmons to white frosting.

Minnie Ha Ha Filling

Cook 2 cups sugar and ½ cup water until mixture spins a thread. Pour slowly over 2 stiffly beaten egg whites. Add a grated fresh coconut, ½ box raisins, 2 cups finely diced apples, 2 finely diced oranges, 1 cup pecans, and ½ cup walnuts.

THIRTEEN

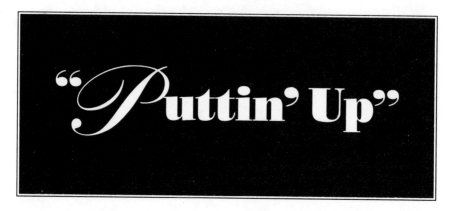

"*Puttin' Up*"

In the days before commercially canned foods, women had to make
like squirrels all summer and busy themselves with a lot of "puttin'
up." The winter supply of food depended largely on their summer's work.
A new daughter-in-law was judged, in part, by the amount of food she
put up during the first summer of her marriage. Those who flitted around
doing things other than filling fruit jars were regarded in the same way
as the lazy grasshopper was compared to the busy little ant.

Before fruit jars were available, food was preserved by drying, salting,
and brining. Then came the fruit jar, which was every bit as welcome, I
am sure, as the freezer was when it came along.

The first fruit jars were a far cry even from the greenish glass ones
with a glass lid—the lid clamped down over a rubber with the help of a
wire contraption, which sometimes worked and sometimes did not. The
early fruit jars were but one step from the stone crocks used for brining
and as a container for foods. These first jars were also made of glazed
pottery and looked very similar to a glazed dirt dish. The tops of the
jars—pottery as well—consisted of a circle topped with a knob. Inside
the jars was a groove around which the homemaker placed melted beeswax when the jars were filled and then stuck the tops into the beeswax
to seal the contents—or at least in an effort to seal them. When these
jars first appeared, they were regarded as great news in the food preservation field. Often, they were called Arthur's Jars, because it seems
they were introduced and promoted by an ad in *T. S. Arthur's Home
Magazine* about 1850.

After glass fruit jars became plentiful, it was routine for a woman to fill as many as five hundred jars in a season. From the time the first English peas and strawberries were ripe until the last of the fresh pork was processed, putting up was almost a daily proposition. Modern cooks with electric ranges and home freezers have no idea what it was like to spend hot day after hot day in July and August over the wood stove filling fruit jars.

For instance, when the beans were ripe, that meant getting up at the crack of dawn to gather them. Then there were hours and hours of breaking, stringing (the beans had strings in those days), and packing them into the jars before the endless processing in a hot water bath. The beans that did not go into jars were shelled and placed in the sun to dry.

During the peach season, you might wake up to find three bushels of peaches ready to be peeled, canned, or dried. And there are those who yearn for the good old days?

Some of the old favorite recipes for putting up appear, below.

· · · · ·

PICKLES

In making pickles, the old folks frown on the practice of placing cucumbers in a jar and covering them with spiced vinegar. They claim that a pickle is not a true pickle unless it has been brined. Here is the way it is done in a lot of cases.

12-Day Pickles

Place 1 peck medium cucumbers in a stone jar and cover with brine made of 1 pint salt to 1 gallon boiling water. Let stand for 1 week, then pour off brine.

Cover with clear boiling water and add 1 tablespoon alum or ½ cup lime to every gallon of water. Let stand for 24 hours, then pour off.

Cover with clear boiling water, let stand for 24 hours, and pour off.

Boil together 1 cup sugar to each quart vinegar with pickling spices to taste. Have enough vinegar to cover the pickles. Split or chunk cucumbers. Pour hot vinegar over them, let stand for 24 hours, and pour off.

Boil the same vinegar, adding 1 cup sugar to each quart vinegar. Pour over cucumbers, let stand 24 hours, and pour off.

Boil the same vinegar, adding 1 cup sugar to each quart vinegar.

Pack pickles into hot sterilized jars. Pour hot vinegar to cover and seal immediately.

Grape Leaf Pickles

A grape leaf pickle is one of the finest pickles in the world. I remember with great delight the ones that used to turn up at Sunday school picnics. Was there ever any greater pickle pleasure than that of biting into a crisp whitish grape leaf pickle?

Use a stone crock or jar. In the bottom place a layer of cucumbers, a layer of grape leaves, and so on until the jar is full. Add a few green grapes occasionally.

Fill the jar with salt brine heavy enough to float an egg. Weight down cucumbers with heavy stone and cover the jar with cloth tied on tightly. The cucumbers will be pickled in about 6 days. Use right away, as they will not keep like other pickles.

Grape Leaf Pickles in Jars

Wash and dry cucumbers. Pack into quart jars. Add 2 tablespoons salt to each quart. Fill jars with cold water, seal, shake well, and let stand for 3 days.

On the third day, empty the jars and discard any cukes that happen to be soft. Rinse. Place a grape leaf in the bottom of each jar. Fill half full with cucumbers. Add another leaf and 6 green grapes. Fill with cucumbers. Add another grape leaf, 6 more grapes, and 1 tablespoon salt. Fill with water and seal.

Bread and Butter Pickles
(Tested)

30 cucumbers (1 inch in diameter)
10 medium onions
4 tablespoons salt

Slice cucumbers and onions. Sprinkle with salt. Let stand for 1 hour. Drain in a cheesecloth bag. Make a spiced vinegar using the following ingredients:

5 cups vinegar
2 teaspoons celery seed
2 teaspoons ground ginger
4 cups sugar
1 teaspoon turmeric
2 teaspoons white mustard seed

Bring spiced vinegar to a boil. Add cucumbers and onions and return to a boil. Reduce heat and simmer for 10 minutes. Seal in sterilized jars.

Crisp Cucumber Pickles

Called the best by many, this recipe was contributed by Mrs. Rush Thompson.

Wash and slice 7 pounds cucumbers. Soak for 12 to 14 hours in lime water (2 cups builder's lime with enough water to cover).

Wash and soak for 4 hours in salt water (1½ cups salt with enough water to cover). Drain and soak for 2 hours in cold water.

Drain and bring to a boil in alum water, using ½ cup powdered alum with water to cover. Drain and rinse in boiling water.

Drain and put into boiling syrup made with 4 pounds sugar, 7 cups vinegar, 1 cup water, and ½ box mixed pickling spices. Simmer for 30 minutes, cool, and pack in sterilized jars. Seal.

Icicle Pickles

These pickles are superb.

Soak cucumbers for 1 to 2 weeks in brine made of 1 cup salt to 2 quarts water. Wash and cut through centers. Discard any that are soft. Soak in alum water (2 tablespoons alum to 1 gallon water) overnight. Wash and drain.

Boil together for a few minutes 4 quarts sugar, 1 quart vinegar, 1 table-spoon whole cloves, 2 sticks cinnamon, and 1 teaspoon whole allspice. Pour hot liquid over cucumbers. Do this for 4 mornings. On the fourth morning, pack in jars and seal.

Company Pickle Chunks

These get rave notices.

20 medium cucumbers
8 cups sugar
2 tablespoons mixed pickling spices
5 teaspoons salt
4 cups cider vinegar

Cover cucumbers with boiling water. Let stand until the next morning. Drain. Repeat this procedure for the next 3 days. On the fifth day, drain and slice into ½-inch pieces.

Combine remaining ingredients. Bring to a boil and pour over cucumbers. Let stand for 2 days. On the third day, bring to a boil and seal in hot sterilized jars.

Cucumber Pickles

Mrs. A. C. Farthing of Lenoir called these "the best in the world."

Soak large cucumbers (6 inches long or more) in very cold water for 5 hours. Then cut lengthwise, without peeling, into about 5 pieces.

Pack very closely into quart jars with 3 stalks of celery and 3 slices of onion to each jar. Drain off any water after packing.

Heat together to boiling 1 quart vinegar, 1 cup sugar, ½ cup water, and ⅓ cup salt and pour over cucumbers. Seal at once.

Ripe Cucumber Pickles

These are made from cucumbers that have turned yellow. Some call the pickles "slippery jacks."

Peel ripe cucumbers, remove the seeds, and soak the meat in alum using any good recipe for watermelon rind pickle.

Ann Geis's Grandmother Ford's Green Tomato Pickles

Of this recipe, the late Hilda Boyette wrote:

I searched through many cook books at the library for pickle recipes using green tomatoes . . . also some of my own books plus those of friends, etc. I experimented with combining recipes, etc. . . . Finally, I called Ann Geis. She told me her grandmother's recipe was the best one she had found anywhere. She was right. It is the best.

I made 25 quarts from green tomatoes from the Farmer's Market last fall. By Christmas, all but one quart had been inhaled! My hat's off to Grandmother Ford.

This is the recipe.

7 pounds green tomatoes, sliced
2 gallons water
3 cups dehydrated lime for pickles
5 pounds granulated sugar
3 pints vinegar
3 drops green food coloring
1 teaspoon cloves
1 teaspoon cinnamon
1 teaspoon mace
1 teaspoon allspice

Cover sliced tomatoes with 2 gallons water and lime; cover and let stand for 24 hours. Drain; rinse with cold water at least four times to remove the lime.

In a large pot boil sugar, vinegar, food coloring, and spices tied in a bag until syrup becomes slightly thick. Add rinsed tomatoes. Remove from heat and let stand, covered, overnight. The next morning, heat only until the tomatoes are glazed (about 20 minutes). Do not boil or overcook (see note below). Put into hot sterilized jars, cover with syrup, and seal.

Note: This recipe is also good for watermelon rind pickles, but use ginger instead of mace and omit the green coloring. Do not cook tomatoes or watermelon rind in the syrup too long or you will have "pickled mush."

Pickled Stuffed Peppers

This recipe is a blue-ribbon winner contributed by the late Mrs. Austin Burke.

2 dozen sweet bell peppers
1 large head of cabbage, finely shredded
¼ cup salt
2 tablespoons white mustard seed
2 tablespoons celery seed
3 cups white vinegar
1 cup water
½ cup granulated sugar

Select peppers of uniform size. Cut off the tops and the stems. Remove seeds and white sections.

Make a brine of 1 cup additional salt to 1 gallon of water. Place peppers in brine and allow to stand overnight. Drain and soak in cold water for 1 hour.

Mix cabbage, salt, mustard seed, and celery seed and stuff peppers. Place stuffed peppers in sterilized jars. Fill jars with a solution of boiling vinegar, 1 cup water, and sugar. Process packed jars for 10 minutes.

Pickled Stuffed Peppers

This recipe, which came from the late Mrs. Stokes Linville of Winston-Salem, has won many a blue ribbon at North Carolina county fairs. Several people who have tried the recipe say it produces the best pickled stuffed peppers. The old folks always reattached the tops of the peppers with string.

2 medium heads of cabbage, finely chopped
2 teaspoons salt
1 medium onion, chopped
1 tablespoon white mustard seed
1 tablespoon celery seed
2 dozen sweet bell peppers
Salt
1 quart strong vinegar
1 quart boiling water
1 cup sugar

Mix cabbage, 2 teaspoons salt, onion, and seeds. Cover and let stand for 48 hours.

Meanwhile, wash peppers. Cut off tops and reserve. Remove seeds. Make a brine of ½ cup salt for each 2 quarts of water. Place peppers in brine. Cover and weight down to keep peppers in brine. Allow to stand for 48 hours.

Wash peppers well in cold water and drain. Drain cabbage mixture well and fill peppers firmly with it. Put tops on peppers and tie in place with string.

Fill jars with peppers standing upright. Cover with a solution of boiling vinegar, water, and sugar. Seal at once. The peppers will be ready to eat in about 3 weeks.

Sweet Pickled Peaches

9 pounds peaches
1 quart cider vinegar
4 pounds sugar
1 tablespoon allspice
1 tablespoon cloves
4 sticks cinnamon, broken

Peel the peaches and place in a stone jar or large mixing bowl. Make a syrup of the vinegar, sugar, and spices. After the syrup has been brought to a boil, pour over the peaches. For each of the following 8 mornings, drain the syrup off the peaches, bring to a boil, and pour back over the peaches. On the ninth morning, pack the peaches in sterilized jars, pour the hot syrup over them, and seal.

Jerusalem Artichoke Pickles

In 1966 the *Winston-Salem Journal* conducted a Pickles and Pound Cake Contest in nineteen counties in northwestern North Carolina and central Virginia. The winning pickle recipe in the Wilkes County contest was for artichoke pickles prepared by Margaret Motsinger (Mrs. M. E. Motsinger). They were and still are the best.

About 2 gallons Jerusalem artichokes
Pods of red pepper
1 gallon vinegar

3 cups sugar
½ cup salt
2 teaspoons turmeric
1½ teaspoons celery seed
2 tablespoons mustard seed
Hot pepper to taste

Wash and scrub artichokes; dry thoroughly with a cloth. Cut into bite-size chunks. Pack into hot, sterile jars, adding red pepper pods to taste.

Bring other ingredients to a boil, reduce heat, and simmer for about 5 minutes. Cover artichokes with hot, spiced vinegar. Seal. Process in a boiling water bath for 15 minutes.

Saul Gold's Delicatessen Pickles

For many years the late Saul Gold ran the Cake Box in Rocky Mount, a food specialty shop that also did catering for "all of Eastern North Carolina." Each year when I had cucumbers in the garden, I filled several gallon jars with these pickles, our favorite.

Freshly picked cucumbers, about 3 to 4 inches long,
preferably picked the day of pickling
Fresh garlic cloves
Pickling spices
Red pepper pods
Heads of fresh dill
1 cup vinegar
½ cup noniodized salt
1 gallon water

Wash cucumbers; cut off blossom end and discard. Pack into gallon jars. To each jar add 1 garlic clove, 1 teaspoon of pickling spices, 1 pod of red pepper, and 1 head of fresh dill.

Combine vinegar, salt, and water; bring to a boil. Pour over cucumbers. Cover and let stand in the refrigerator for 5 to 6 weeks. Do not eat before that time because the taste will be terrible.

Watermelon Rind Pickles

5 pounds prepared watermelon rind
3 tablespoons alum
1 quart cider vinegar
½ cup water
⅛ teaspoon oil of cinnamon
⅛ teaspoon oil of cloves
8 cups sugar

Cut watermelon rind in any shapes desired. Cover rind with water and bring to a boil. Reduce heat and simmer until rind is easily pierced with a fork. Add alum to rind in kettle and let stand overnight. Drain, rinse, and drain again.

Mix vinegar with ½ cup water, oils, and sugar and bring to a boil. Add rind and return to a boil. Let rind stand in syrup overnight. Bring to a boil the next morning. Repeat for the next 4 mornings. Pack hot rind into hot sterilized jars and cover with hot syrup. Seal.

Note: The oils make light-colored pickles. If desired, substitute 1 tablespoon whole cloves and 2 cinnamon sticks, or ½ teaspoon ground cloves and 1 teaspoon ground cinnamon, for the oils.

Pickled String Beans

Some recipes suggest pouring a spiced vinegar solution over cooked string beans in a jar to make pickled beans. These are not true, old-fashioned pickled beans. The beans should be brined so they will pickle naturally like sauerkraut.

The old folks started the pickling process in early fall. That way the summer heat did not cause the beans to sour. If prepared in the summer, they may be packed after pickling in sterilized jars and processed.

This recipe came from Mrs. W. M. Ball, a home economist.

Prepare beans and break. Cook in simmering water until tender. Drain off water and turn beans out on a sterilized towel on a table top. Drain well and fill a sterilized cloth bag. Tie up bag.

Place bag in a crock that contains brine made with sufficient salt to float an egg. Use pure salt for making brine, not the iodized variety.

Weight beans down so they will stay under the brine. Store in a cool place. They are pickled in about 5 to 6 weeks, the same time required to pickle cucumbers. To serve, season with meat drippings and heat.

Dilly Beans

2 pounds small, tender green beans
1 teaspoon red pepper
4 cloves garlic
4 large heads of dill
2 cups water
¼ cup pickling salt
2 cups white vinegar

Wash and string green beans and pack uniformly in hot sterilized jars. To each pint, add ¼ teaspoon red pepper, 1 clove garlic, and 1 head of dill. Heat together water, salt, and vinegar. Bring to a boil and pour over the beans. Seal. Makes 4 pints.

Pickled Cabbage

With pickled cabbage, vinegar provides the tart taste, as compared to the flavor of sauerkraut, which is produced by natural fermentation.

Chop cabbage finely to make 4 gallons. Place in an enamel vessel or stone crock. Sprinkle with 1 cup salt and add 1 gallon water. Cover and let stand overnight. The next morning squeeze liquid from the cabbage with the hands, a handful at a time.

To 1 gallon vinegar, add 4 pounds sugar and 1 cup mustard seed and bring to a boil. Cool thoroughly and pour over cabbage. Seal in glass jars.

Note: Be sure the vinegar solution is absolutely cold before pouring over cabbage. If hot, it will cook the cabbage.

The Speases' Pickled Turnips

The late Mr. and Mrs. Grady Speas, who lived a couple of miles north of Bethania on Route 1 out of Rural Hall, made pickled turnips for years. According to Mrs. Speas, both the Speases and the Capps in that area had pickled turnips for generations.

I sampled some of the Speases' pickled turnips. Served raw, they were as tasty a relish as any. Mr. Speas cut the turnips on a cutter that he had designed and made. It was like a kraut cutter, except that one blade sliced and an auxiliary set of small blades shredded the raw turnips into julienne strips.

This is the way the Speases pickled turnips.

Shred or cut raw turnips into thin strips. Toss strips in a dishpan with salt—do not use quite as much salt as you would in making sauerkraut. Place in a stone crock and weight down. Let stand as you would kraut until the natural fermentation ceases—turnips take a little longer than kraut and, of course, the time depends on the weather.

Remove from crock, pack in fruit jars, and seal. Serve raw or cook like fresh turnips and season with a little sugar and lard.

Mrs. Ragland's Pickled Turnips

Pickling turnips is an old routine with Lebanese cooks, according to Mrs. Edward T. Ragland of Winston-Salem. This is her recipe.

Use 1 quart of water to 2 quarts of vinegar. Use 1 tablespoon of salt to 1 quart of liquid.

Peel raw turnips and cut into slices about ½-inch thick. Put slices into fruit jars. Fill with cold liquid and seal. To make turnips pink, use juice drained from pickled beets as part of the liquid or add red food coloring. The turnips will be ready to eat in about 2 weeks.

Poke Stalk Pickles

In the spring when poke stalks get about 2 feet tall, cut off at ground level and strip off leaves. Cut into lengths about 4 inches long.

Boil in salted water (more salty than water used for cooking vegetables but not salty like a brine) for about 15 minutes, or until the skins "turn loose." Peel.

Drain and soak in cold water for 30 minutes. Drain. Cover with cold water and soak for another 30 minutes. Sprinkle black pepper over the stalks and serve like you would fresh cucumbers, or heat vinegar to boiling and pour over stalks that have been placed in sterilized jars and seal.

Pickled Walnuts

Gather walnuts when you can stick a pin through them. Lay them in salt water for 2 weeks. Remove from water and scrape off soft skin, rub with a coarse towel, and place in fresh water for 3 days, changing the water daily. Drain. Combine garlic, allspice, and black pepper with vinegar, bring to a boil, and pour boiling liquid over walnuts. If they are rather old and hard, scald them in an iron pot.

• • • • •

RELISHES

Relishes are served throughout the year, and especially in the winter months, to accompany meats. The most widely used is the wonderful Dixie relish.

Dixie Relish

1 quart chopped cabbage
1 pint finely chopped white onions
1 pint finely chopped sweet red peppers
1 pint finely chopped sweet green peppers
½ cup salt
4 tablespoons mustard seed
2 tablespoons celery seed
1 tablespoon whole allspice
1 stick cinnamon
1 quart vinegar
1½ pounds granulated sugar

Place chopped vegetables in an enamel kettle or crock and sprinkle salt over them. Allow to stand for 5 to 6 hours, or overnight. Squeeze in a cheesecloth bag to remove juice.

Tie spices in a bag and add to remaining ingredients in a kettle. Bring to a boil. Add vegetables and cook for 10 minutes. Pour into hot sterilized jars and seal.

Chowchow

Dixie relish shares its popularity with chowchow, which is a very similar product.

1 medium head of cabbage
4 medium onions
3 sweet green peppers
1 to 2 hot peppers
3 tablespoons salt
1½ cups vinegar
1 pound brown sugar
2 tablespoons celery seed
1 tablespoon mustard seed
1 tablespoon turmeric

Grind vegetables and mix well. Add salt. Let stand for 30 minutes. Squeeze out excess water. Bring to a boil vinegar, brown sugar, seeds, and turmeric. Pour over mixture and seal.

Sweet Red Pepper Relish

This recipe has a lovely red color and fine flavor.

3½ cups sweet red bell peppers
1 tablespoon salt
2 cups vinegar
3 cups sugar

Remove the seeds and run peppers through a food chopper. Sprinkle with salt and let them stand for 3 to 4 hours. Add vinegar and sugar and cook until thick. Fill sterilized jars and seal.

Vegetable Relish

This recipe makes another very good relish.

4 cups ground onions
1 medium cabbage (about 4 cups ground)
10 green tomatoes (about 4 cups ground)
12 sweet green peppers
6 sweet red peppers

½ cup salt
6 cups sugar
1 tablespoon celery seed
2 tablespoons mustard seed
1½ teaspoons turmeric
4 cups cider vinegar
2 cups water

Grind vegetables, using coarse blade of grinder. Sprinkle with salt and allow to stand overnight. Rinse and drain. Combine remaining ingredients and pour over vegetables. Bring to a boil, reduce heat, and simmer for 3 minutes. Seal in hot sterilized jars. Makes 8 pints.

Pear Relish

1 peck firm keiffer pears
3 sweet red peppers
3 sweet green peppers
5 medium onions
2 tablespoons mixed pickling spices
2 pounds granulated sugar
1 tablespoon turmeric
1 tablespoon salt
4 cups vinegar
¼ teaspoon celery seed
½ teaspoon dry mustard

Peel and core pears. Grind coarsely or chop finely. Grind or chop peppers and onions. Tie pickling spices loosely in a bag.

Mix all ingredients and bring to a boil. Reduce heat and simmer for about 30 minutes. Remove spice bag. Pack hot into hot sterilized jars. Seal.

Hayden Salad

This recipe, or a variation of it, can be found in almost all community-prepared cookbooks.

Mix and bring to a boil 1 gallon chopped cabbage, 1 cup chopped green pepper, ½ gallon chopped green tomatoes, 6 to 8 chopped large onions, ½ gallon vinegar, 2 pounds sugar, 4 tablespoons salt, 2 tablespoons celery seed, 2 ounces cinnamon, 2 ounces allspice, 1 ounce cloves, 2 tablespoons mustard seed, and 1 ounce black pepper. Pack in glass or stone jars.

Green Tomato Relish

12 green tomatoes
4 green sweet peppers
2 red sweet peppers
3 large onions
1 cup flour
5 cups sugar
2 tablespoons salt
4 cups cider vinegar
2 tablespoons celery seed
2 tablespoons turmeric
1 jar (9 ounces) prepared mustard

Cut the stems from the tomatoes. Cut peppers in half and remove seeds and membrane. Peel onions. Put tomatoes, peppers, and onions through a food chopper.

Mix flour, sugar, salt, vinegar, celery seed, turmeric, and mustard. Blend well. Add to tomato mixture and bring to a boil. Reduce heat and simmer for 10 minutes. Pour hot into sterilized jars. Seal.

Tomato Soy

This name is applied to a pickle made from sliced green tomatoes.

Soak the tomatoes in weak salt water overnight and then boil in alum water "just tinged" with vinegar. After scalding in plain water, add a spiced vinegar and boil until the slices are clear. Seal in jars.

Beet Relish

1 pint chopped boiled beets
1 cup chopped celery
1 tablespoon horseradish

Dash of red pepper
⅛ teaspoon white pepper
½ teaspoon salt
¾ cup sugar
½ cup beet juice
1 pint chopped cabbage
1 medium chopped onion
¾ cup vinegar

Mix all ingredients and bring to a good jumping boil. Pack in sterilized jars and seal.

Artichoke Relish

Artichoke relish and pickle are especially popular in the eastern part of the state. This recipe came from Mrs. Julian Lane of Wilson.

½ peck artichokes
24 large onions
3 pints vinegar
2½ cups granulated sugar
2 tablespoons mustard seed
1 teaspoon turmeric
½ teaspoon red pepper
2 tablespoons celery seed
4 teaspoons salt

Grind artichokes and onions coarsely. Mix with remaining ingredients and simmer for ½ hour. Bring to a boil and remove from heat. Seal in sterilized jars.

• • • • •

PRESERVES

APPLE BUTTER

In the apple country of western North Carolina—the region of Alleghany, Avery, and Watauga counties—it is customary for folks to make their apple butter in big pots outdoors. The picture-postcard beauty of the green hills of that area is tantalizing in itself. Add to that the tantalizing aroma of simmering spicy apple butter for a sensory treat.

Making the apple butter is an all-day process. In the old days cane molasses was used to sweeten apple butter. Some cooks made it with apple cider as the liquid. Today, some use oil of cinnamon and oil of cloves to give a light-colored, clear apple butter. Others prefer powdered ground spices, which make a darker product.

Several neighbors "make together," for the process takes a lot of stirring. The big pots are stirred almost every minute with a long wooden paddle, sometimes called a horse's head. Regular makers have a big brass pot for the purpose. Others use a scoured-out black wash pot. Both are used outdoors with a fire built underneath. Some of the pots stand on iron racks, whereas others are supported by big rocks.

Pear Butter

Peel and core keiffer pears. Slice and place in a heavy kettle. Add a small amount of water. Simmer until the pears become a pulp. Mash to make a smooth mixture.

Measure and add 1 part sugar to 2 parts pear pulp. (Brown sugar gives more flavor.) Add spices as desired and the juice of 1 lemon.

Cook the mixture, stirring frequently, until smooth and thick. Pour hot into hot sterilized jars and seal at once.

JELLY

The old-fashioned way of making jelly was to combine equal portions of prepared fruit juice and sugar and allow them to simmer in a big kettle until a spoonful placed in a saucer turned to jelly when cool. During the simmering, the scum was removed from the top of the mixture and discarded. On a jelly-making day, there was always just enough left over to provide a good sampling but not quite enough to fill another jar. That freshly made jelly served with hot biscuits for supper was always the best of the batch.

For special occasions, some jelly makers made *scented jelly* by pouring a light jelly such as apple on top of a rose geranium leaf in the bottom of each jelly glass. Others used sprigs of lemon verbena or mint. The most popular jellies are dewberry, blackberry, apple, and grape. Modern jelly makers follow the instructions of the North Carolina Agricultural Extension Service, test for pectin content, add sugar accordingly, and cook with a thermometer, thereby assuring a uniform product.

OTHER FAVORITES

Wonderful Strawberry Preserves

Wash 1 heaping quart of berries. Dry thoroughly and cap. Place in a large saucepan with a tight-fitting lid. Add 1 tablespoon vinegar. Cover and bring to a boil. Boil for 1 minute. Remove cover and add 4 cups sugar. Stir gently to mix sugar with berries.

Bring to a boil, reduce heat, and simmer for 20 minutes uncovered. Remove from heat and pour into a platter, bowl, or enamelware container to cool.

Pour cold into jars and seal the next day. Process the packed jars for 5 minutes at the simmering point to prevent the formation of mold. If there is leftover syrup, can it to serve over pancakes or let it boil down until thick and pour over preserves.

Sun-Cooked Strawberry Preserves

Wash, cap, stem, drain, and measure the strawberries. Allow an equal weight of sugar for fruit. For every 2 pounds of berries, measure ¼ cupful of berry juice and heat with the sugar. Cook and pour over the whole berries in shallow trays. Stand in the sun for 3 or 4 days, bringing indoors each night. Dampness is a great foe to successful sun cookery.

Allow the fruit to remain in the sun until it is well plumped and the syrup is thickened almost to a jelly. If the sun fails to shine, keep the preserves in a cool oven. Pack in sterilized jars and seal.

Fig Conserve

5 cups chopped figs
1 orange
1 lemon
4 cups sugar
1 cup chopped dates
1 cup chopped pecans

Figs may be skinned or left unskinned, as desired. Chop orange and lemon finely, peeling and all. Mix with figs and sugar. Bring to a boil in a thick-bottomed kettle and cook slowly until clear and transparent—about 25 to 30 minutes. Stir frequently to prevent burning.

Add nuts about 5 minutes before canning. Pour hot into hot sterilized jars and seal.

Pear Conserve

4 pounds prepared firm keiffer pears
4 pounds sugar
1 cup seedless raisins
1 tablespoon grated orange rind
1 tablespoon grated lemon rind
1 cup orange juice
⅓ cup lemon juice
1 cup nuts

Peel pears; quarter and core. Cut into thin slices. Arrange slices and sugar in alternate layers in an enamel kettle or bowl and allow to stand overnight.

Add raisins, rinds, and juices. Cook until pears are clear and tender. Add nuts. Heat thoroughly and pour hot into hot sterilized jars. Seal.

Pear Honey

8 pounds peeled and cored keiffer pears
1 can (20 ounces) crushed pineapple, undrained
Sugar
Juice of 1 lemon

Put pears through a food chopper. Add pineapple and measure. For every cup of fruit, add 1 cup sugar. Add lemon juice. Boil until thick and clear.

Pear and Pineapple Conserve

This is Mrs. T. W. Church's recipe from the cookbook *Out of the Kitchen*, published in 1949 by the Elkin Junior Woman's Club.

4 cups diced peeled keiffer pears
1⅓ cups sugar
½ tablespoon powdered ginger
Grated rind and juice of ½ lemon

1 cup crushed pineapple, drained
⅔ cup chopped walnut meats

Combine pears, sugar, and ginger. Let stand for a couple of hours. Bring to a boil, reduce heat, and simmer until the fruit looks clear.

Add lemon rind and juice and pineapple. Cook over low heat until thick. Add nuts and heat thoroughly. Pour hot into hot sterilized jars and seal.

Peach Honey

Mash peeled ripe peaches to a pulp. Add 2 cups sugar for each cup of peach pulp. Simmer for 30 minutes or until thick and clear. Pour into hot sterilized jars and seal at once.

Spiced Grapes

Use thick-skinned grapes. Pulp 6 pounds of grapes and boil skins until tender. Cook pulp separately and strain through a sieve and add to skins.

Add 2 cups vinegar, 3 pounds sugar, ½ teaspoon ground cloves, and 2 teaspoons each of cinnamon and allspice. Boil thoroughly. Pour into jars and seal.

Spiced Blackberries

3 pounds brown sugar
1 pint vinegar
2 ounces cinnamon
½ ounce cloves
7 pounds blackberries

Scald together brown sugar, vinegar, and spices. Pour over fruit. Let stand for 24 hours. Boil until fruit is tender. Skim it and boil vinegar sugar mixture until thick. Pour over fruit and set aside in jars.

Mincemeat

Mincemeat that tastes like this cannot be found on the commercial market.

5 pounds lean raw beef, cooked and finely chopped
1 pound beef suet, finely chopped
5 pounds apples, peeled and finely chopped
4 pounds sultana raisins
2 pounds currants
1 pound citron, sliced thin
¼ pound each of orange and lemon peel, sliced thin
2 tablespoons mace
2 tablespoons cinnamon
2 tablespoons salt
1 tablespoon each of cloves, allspice, and nutmeg
1 pint molasses
3 pounds brown sugar
2 quarts boiled cider

Cook all ingredients together. When cold, add 1 pint brandy and 1 pint sherry.

Spiced Grapes

5 pounds thick-skinned black grapes
3 pounds sugar
2 teaspoons ground cinnamon
2 teaspoons ground allspice
½ teaspoon ground cloves
½ cup vinegar

Pulp the grapes. Boil the skins until tender. Cook the pulp and strain out seeds. Add sieved pulp to skins with sugar, spices, and vinegar—for a more tart relish, add more vinegar. Cook, stirring occasionally, until thickened. Pour into jars and seal.

Candied Figs

Cover fresh figs with water and simmer for a few minutes, or until tender. Lift out figs and use water to make syrup.

For the syrup, mix 2 cups sugar, 1 cup liquid or water, and ⅓ cup light corn syrup. Bring syrup to a boil and cook until it spins thread or reaches 234° on a candy thermometer. Add figs and simmer until clear and transparent—do not have figs too crowded in the syrup.

Lift figs from syrup and place on a rack to dry until they are no longer sticky. Roll in granulated sugar.

Tutti Fruitti

This is an old treat.

Start with a stone crock—the kind used for making sauerkraut and pickles. It should have a tightly fitting lid. Wash, scald, and cool the crock.

Pour 1 pint brandy into crock. Add 1 quart freshly washed capped strawberries and 1 quart sugar. Stir gently to dissolve sugar.

Store in a cool, dark place like the cellar. Add cherries, peaches, and apricots as they come into season. Add a quart of each with an equal portion of sugar. Stir gently each time. [In addition to the above fruits, one recipe listed the following: blackberries, pears, currants, pineapple, bananas, nuts, ground oranges, and lemons.]

The mixture will be ready to serve on ice cream or sponge cake a week after the last fruit has been added.

Brandied Peaches

One old recipe gave these directions for brandied peaches:

Get the largest peaches you can, but do not let them be too ripe. Rub off the lint with a cloth, and then run them down the seam with a pin skin deep, and cover them with French brandy. Tie a bladder over them, and let stand a week. Then take them out, and make a strong syrup for them. Boil and skim it well, then put in your peaches, and boil them till they look clear; then take them out and put them into pots or glasses. Mix the syrup with the brandy, and when it is cold, pour it on your peaches. Tie them so close down with a bladder, that no air can come to them, otherwise they will turn black, and be totally spoiled.

Brandied Peaches without Brandy

These peaches brandy in ten to fifteen days but are best if left until Thanksgiving or Christmas. During the process, the peaches shrivel and the liquid becomes potent. A woman who had been using this recipe for thirty years claimed: "One teaspoon of the syrup makes me laugh my head off."

Use either openstones or clings that are not too ripe. Wash. Sprinkle granulated sugar about ¼-inch thick in the bottom of a half-gallon fruit jar or crock and add a layer of peaches. Fill crevices around peaches with sugar. Continue until the jar is full. Place lid on, or cover crock, tightly. Tie the jar in a paper bag and store in a dark place.

Peach Mangoes

The old folks used to cut large, firm freestone peaches in half and remove the stones. They stuffed the cavities with chopped candied fruits and nuts and then sewed the two halves back together with a needle and thread. The filled peaches were packed into jars and covered with a mixture of vinegar and sugar, allowing a cup of vinegar to a pound of sugar.

The following version, created by Mrs. Plato T. Durham, appeared in *The Twin-City Housewife* in 1920:

One gallon freestone peaches, one-half gallon cider vinegar, three pounds brown sugar, one cup white mustard seed, one-half cup celery seed, one teaspoon each allspice and ground mace, two small onions, two tablespoons turmeric, six slices fresh horseradish.

Drop peaches into strong salt water for 24 hours. Remove, dry and stone. Boil for 20 minutes in vinegar to which have been added the sugar, mustard seed, celery seed, allspice and mace.

When cold add onions, turmeric and horseradish.

Dinner Cherries

Pour 1 pint vinegar over 3 pounds pitted cherries and let stand for 24 hours. Drain off vinegar, pour 3 pounds sugar on fruit, and let stand until the sugar is dissolved, stirring every day. The sugar will be gone in about 3 or 4 days. Put into jars and seal.

Blackberry Acid

This makes a refreshing drink.

Sprinkle 5 ounces tartaric acid over 12 pounds blackberries. Add 1 gallon of water and let stand for 48 hours. Then strain without mashing the berries. Discard berries. To each pint of juice add 1 pound sugar. Stir well and then bottle.

When ready to serve, use ¼ cup juice to ¾ cup water. Serve cold.

The Best Tomato Juice
(Tested)

1 gallon (4 quarts) unpeeled ripe tomatoes
16 whole cloves
2 bay leaves
4 onions, chopped
6 teaspoons salt
4 teaspoons sugar
½ teaspoon black pepper
¼ teaspoon cider vinegar

Cut tomatoes into quarters, discarding core and hard spots; place into kettle, preferably a white enamel one. Add cloves tied in a bag, bay leaves, onions, salt, sugar, and pepper. Bring to a boil; reduce heat and simmer for 1 hour.

Strain or put through a food mill. Add vinegar. Reheat juice until it is almost but not quite boiling. Pour hot into hot sterilized jars, leaving ¼-inch head space. Adjust caps. Process pints for 10 minutes, or quarts for 15 minutes, in a boiling water bath. Makes about 3 quarts.

Sauerkraut

This method, which once worked perfectly, now often molds in the process. I blame the mold on "something in the air." I suggest using a recipe from *The Ball Blue Book* or the North Carolina Agricultural Extension Service.

Shred or finely chop cabbage. Pack into quart jars. Put a teaspoon of salt on top of each jar. Add boiling water to cover. Place caps on jars but do not screw down. After about 7 days, when the kraut finishes "working," or fermenting, screw caps on tightly.

FOURTEEN

"Y'all Come"

The standard greeting among friends and relatives on parting after a planned or chance meeting is "Y'all come." There are, of course, quite a few occasions when a number of individuals get together for the purpose of eating. These are the events where food is highlighted: barbecues and pig pickings, oyster roasts, clam bakes, fish fries, fish stews, fish roasts, lawn parties, chicken stews, "workin's" and "threshin's," church suppers, family reunions, Sunday school picnics, and wiener roasts. In addition to these occasions, food plays a part at weddings, funerals, football games, and hunt breakfasts and balls.

• • • • •

BARBECUES AND PIG PICKINGS

Barbecues and certainly pig pickings are synonymous with the word *party*. Fans of barbecue eat it in barbecue restaurants and also take it out to eat at home, but generally a big barbecue means gathering a group of people.

A person who does not like barbecue or does not have a tremendous capacity to consume it might by some stretch of the imagination get elected governor of North Carolina, but it is highly unlikely. Politicians joke about the need to like barbecue; in fact, the setting in which it is served makes for good casual conversation that often includes political talk.

Barbecue is a food we grew up on, along with pimento cheese and tomato sandwiches, fried chicken, and baked hen. People who live in or near Lexington eat Lexington barbecue. If you live in Goldsboro, you go to Scott's. If you live in Rocky Mount, you go to Bob Melton's. In Wilson, you go to Parker's. When a woman who lives in Raleigh is having company, she calls up Bob Melton's and says: "Ride me a party." That means Melton's will put barbecue and fixings on the bus for her.

Our barbecue gained new status at the summit of world leaders in Williamsburg, Virginia, in 1983. Craig Claiborne, the *New York Times* food critic, selected barbecue king Wayne Monk of Lexington to prepare the Saturday night meal for President Ronald Reagan and his guests— among them, British Prime Minister Margaret Thatcher and French President François Mitterand.

In the *New York Times* for February 14, 1983, columnist Tom Wicker wrote:

> We North Carolinians, of course, know—we are not taught, we are born knowing—that barbecue consists of pork cooked over hickory coals and seasoned with vinegar and red pepper pods. No serious Tar Heel barbecue chef would disclose his or her preferred proportions of the latter ingredients; "season to taste" is the proper commandment.
>
> But here's a tip: you want 1½ quarts of vinegar, seasoned to taste with red pepper, for a 65-pound pig—and that's been handed down to me through generations of pig fanciers.

Craig Claiborne, in a May 1984 article entitled "Tar Heel Barbecue: Delectable Controversy," noted that no other cooking in this country engenders the strong opinions, lively discussions, and regional chauvinism that barbecue does. He went on to mention the various types of meats, sauces, accompaniments, woods, basting, and slicing or chopping. According to Claiborne, "If barbecue is America's most controversial food, then North Carolina must be its barbecue controversy capital." He pointed out that some fans claim that the true barbecue is cooked only in Lexington, while others declare that only the barbecue "down east" around Goldsboro is authentic. The food critic came to the state to find answers to the controversy. His first stop was Wayne Monk's Lexington Barbecue in Lexington.

Monk prepares barbecue by cooking pork shoulders, which have been sprinkled with a little salt, slowly to an internal temperature of about 180 degrees over the hot coals of hickory or oak. The meat cooks for eight to ten hours. He uses a vinegar-based sauce containing salt, sugar, red and black pepper, ketchup, and water. Monk does not baste but rather adds the sauce later. Actually, the meat is so moist and tasty it does not need a sauce; adding it is a matter of choice. The barbecue is served with crisp hush puppies and "red" cole slaw, which is made with the same (or a similar) sauce that is used on the meat, rather than mayonnaise.

At the first annual Carolina Barbecue Cook Off held in Raleigh in 1985, a team from Havelock, headed by Willis Peaden and Jim Elder, won the top prize for the best barbecue in the state. Peaden said that his sauce starts with a gallon of good vinegar: "a good cider vinegar is best."

Willis Peaden's Barbecue Sauce

1 gallon vinegar
¾ cup salt
Black pepper to taste
2 tablespoons red pepper
3 tablespoons red pepper flakes
1 cup brown sugar, packed, or ¼ cup molasses

Combine all ingredients. Allow to stand for 4 hours. Makes about 1 gallon.

The comparison of various methods of preparing barbecue continued at the Carolina Bar-Be-Cue Championship Cook Off held in Garner in the autumn of 1986. The winners were Roger and Dave Lambert of D. &. R. Ole Timey Barbecue in Franklinville and Greensboro. Roger Lambert said that the meat has to be cooked over hickory wood.

The Lambert brothers and their two sons, Todd and Eric, cooked only pork shoulders for the contest. In another cooker—behind the one with the shoulders—they barbecued a whole hog the way it is done for a pig picking in order to provide the extra meat needed to feed onlookers. As for sauce, Roger Lambert said: "I don't ever baste mine or put any sauce on it." He does offer sauce on the side: "It's nothing but ketchup, vinegar, Texas Pete, salt and pepper, wet mustard, and a few prayers." Another Lambert brother said that their sauce has ketchup, white vinegar, sugar, salt and pepper, mustard, A-1 Sauce, and Worcestershire sauce, but he would not give the proportions.

As winners of the 1986 contest, the Lambert brothers received a huge trophy and a check for two thousand dollars. But the best prize, of course, was bragging rights.

The controversy about North Carolina barbecue and accompaniments boils down to the use of ketchup and vinegar in the sauce, hush puppies or corn sticks, and red slaw with ketchup or white slaw with mayonnaise. Eastern barbecue is usually made from whole hogs. It is most often cooked over charcoal, gas, or electricity and basted with a thin sauce made of only vinegar, red pepper, and salt. The meat is ordinarily minced and served with corn sticks, boiled potatoes, and white slaw.

Western and Piedmont barbecue generally consists of pork shoulders that have been cooked ever so slowly over hot coals burned down from hickory wood. When the barbecue is cool enough to handle, it is chopped by hand (with cleavers) into small chunks. If the meat is cooked correctly, it is moist enough without any sauce. If a sauce is offered, it is served on the side; it is sweet, tart, smoky, spicy hot, and tomatoey. The barbecue is served with hush puppies and either red or white slaw.

$$\bullet \quad \bullet \quad \bullet \quad \bullet \quad \bullet$$

OYSTER ROASTS

Along the coast around Wilmington, an oyster roast is as important to natives as a clam bake is to New Englanders. Some restaurants feature oyster roasts, but in most cases an oyster roast is a private party.

A "brush" roast is the old-fashioned way to do it. A crackling brush fire is built on stones in a hole. An iron rack or thick mesh is placed over the fire. The rack is filled with oysters, which take but a few minutes to cook—they actually steam in their own juice. Oysters may also be roasted over a large can with fire in the bottom and grating over the top or over a regular outdoor fireplace.

One man usually has the job of opening the oysters. When there is a crowd, he really stays busy, for each person consumes dozens of oysters.

OYSTER ROAST AND CLAM CHOWDER AT ORTON PLANTATION

An excellent example of a fine oyster roast was staged in 1979 at historic Orton Plantation on the North Carolina coast near Wilmington. The hosts were James L. Sprunt and his wife, the late June Sprunt, owners with other Sprunt brothers of the plantation. The 12,000-acre plantation, one of the prettiest places in the world, has what has been described as "the finest colonial residence in North Carolina." The gardens attract thousands of tourists each spring. (The house is not open to the public.)

The following is an account of the Sprunt's oyster roast, starting with the man who did the roasting:

Roasting oysters is one of the main jobs of Richard Davis, who has been at Orton for years. He builds a wood fire with hefty logs in a big outdoor fireplace with metal grill and brick chimney.

For each person, he turns about one peck of oysters in the shell out onto the grill. The oysters are covered with several thicknesses of wet newspaper and an upturned metal plate over each pile.

No one dares dispute Davis about when the oysters are hot enough to make the shells open slightly. When he says, "They ain't ready," they *ain't ready*.

When they are indeed ready he turns the hot oysters out on long wood picnic tables with benches on each side. Guests, wearing bulky white gardening gloves to protect their hands, go at the shells armed with an oyster knife—an implement with a plump wooden handle and rounded blade about 3 inches long.

Hot oysters are opened from the muscle end, meaning the plump end as compared to the sloping end, which is cracked when opening raw oysters to serve on the half shell. Use the knife to free the oyster.

The roast oysters, flavored by the briny deep and by the wood smoke, taste more like mussels than oysters. One drinks the oyster liquor from the empty shell.

What do you serve with roast oysters?

A saucepan of pure butter melted over the wood fire and slaw heavy with celery seed were served from a wooden salad bowl bigger than a bushel basket.

Guests were cautioned to discard any oyster that was the slightest bit "suspicious" because, "Nothing makes you sicker than one bad oyster." The conversation included statistics about the number of oysters guests consume. Did they say one man ate 240 oysters?

For an indoor oyster roast, bake oysters in a 350- to 375-degree oven for 15 to 20 minutes or until shells open. Test to tell when.

The ideal appetizer for an oyster roast is lox, followed by clam chowder served hot in paper cups. Mrs. Sprunt makes the spread by putting about half a pound of lox (smoked salmon) in a food processor with a stick of butter melted and a bit of lemon juice. Process and stir in about one carton sour cream. Chill and serve topped with drained capers and with crackers or beaten biscuits which she also makes in the food processor. . . .

The perfect dessert, according to the people on the coast, to serve at an oyster roast is a bite-size orange blossom as the flavor of orange is what is needed after oysters. They are right. An orange blossom is an orange-flavored cup cake dipped in an orange glaze.

June's Clam Chowder

1 pound bacon (the best quality)
2 to 3 fairly large onions, sliced or diced
1 bag (1 pound) frozen hash-browned potatoes
1 cup or more water
5 cans (10 ounces) minced clams
3 cans (10 ounces) New England clam chowder (the best brand)
2 quarts half and half (half milk, half cream)
Salt to taste
Freshly ground black pepper

Fry bacon in a heavy skillet; drain bacon and pour off about half the drippings. In remaining drippings, cook onions until golden. Add potatoes and about 1 cup water; simmer until done, adding more water as needed.

Drain clams and add juice to potatoes, cans of chowder, half and half, and butter. Heat. Add clams and crumbled bacon. Season to taste with salt and add "a copious amount of freshly ground pepper." Heat. Makes 16 servings.

· · · · ·

CLAM BAKES

A North Carolina clam bake does not assume quite the proportions of a New England one but, nevertheless, it is a delightful culinary occasion along the coast where the clams are available. The clams are baked or roasted over an open fire and served with roasted ears of corn.

· · · · ·

FISH FRIES, STEWS, AND ROASTS

An outdoor fish fry used to be held just about any time there was a mess of fish to be cooked. Most often these days, the fish is fried in frying pans on top of an iron grill in a regular outdoor fireplace. In other frying pans, corn dodgers are fried. Cole slaw is the usual accompaniment.

Fish stews that feature fish muddle are favored along the coast. (For muddle recipes see Chapter 9.) In the Currituck area and elsewhere on the coast, fish roasts are popular. Most often, the fish is mullet. Once the fish has been cleaned and the heads have been cut off, the pointed end of a stick is stuck into each fish. Meanwhile, a fire has burned down to hot coals in a long shallow trench. The sticks are stuck in the ground at an angle along the trench, permitting the fish to slowly cook over the hot coals to flavorful goodness. The sticks are rotated during the cooking and when they are done, there is quite a feast. The accompaniments are similar to those served at an oyster roast or fish fry.

· · · · ·

LAWN PARTIES

Lawn parties are infrequent these days but in years past, there was seldom a Saturday night in summer when some church in the community, especially in the smaller communities, did not sponsor a lawn party. Light was provided by Japanese lanterns strung across the lawn. Homemade ice cream was hand-cranked in giant freezers, and ladies of the church provided a vast variety of luscious homemade cakes. The fare usually included lemonade.

Young men were dashing in their white wool flannel trousers. Young women tended to wear white skirts and pullover tops or dresses made of popular warm-weather fabrics such as voile and linen, and they often tied a ribbon in their hair.

. . . . .

CHICKEN STEWS

In times past a chicken stew might be held at a church, at a school, or in other buildings, but typically they took place at tobacco barns. Before oil was used to cure tobacco, someone had to stay at the tobacco barn all night to keep the fires stoked with wood. This presented an occasion for having a chicken stew, which provided entertainment and food for the person stoking the fires as well as for friends and relatives. It was customary to make the stew in a big iron wash pot over an open fire. This traditional black pot looked like a king-size witches' cauldron.

The stew was prepared by cutting plump chickens into pieces and simmering them in boiling salted water until tender. Butter was dropped into the pot by the half-pound cake, and the broth, seasoned with salt and pepper, was thickened with a paste of flour and water. The stew was served in soup bowls.

"Rosen," or roasting, ears of corn were tied with a wire and hung down the tobacco flue to cook, or they were placed on the end of a sharpened stick and held near hot coals to roast. In addition to the stew and corn, there was white bread, crackers, and pickles. To top off the meal, a watermelon was cut and served with an array of homemade pies and cakes.

For anyone who wants to see a tobacco barn, there is one on the Dixie Classic Fair grounds in Winston-Salem.

. . . . .

"WORKIN'S" AND "THRESHIN'S"

Food for these occasions is provided in the same manner as in other parts of the country. The "wimmin-folks" of the men doing the work gather and prepare a big spread.

CHURCH SUPPERS, FAMILY REUNIONS, AND PICNICS

Church suppers, like Sunday school picnics, are simply another way for a group of people to share food and fellowship.

The family reunion, which continues to this day, although with less frequency than in past years, is not only another way to share food and fellowship but also a means of highlighting the importance of family. Some family reunions held earlier in this century were planned like commencement exercises at colleges or universities, with speeches, music, singing, parades, printed programs, and extensive menus.

In the years when eating out in restaurants was rare, picnics and other excursions were popular because a meal was provided in a different setting from the home.

WIENER ROASTS

The wiener roast is, of course, a modern phenomenon and enjoyed throughout the country. Certainly, it has been a popular form of entertainment for teenagers in this state.

FOOD AT WEDDINGS

The festivities include the traditional wedding breakfast and the reception after the wedding. Another custom that seems to be rather distinctive in this state—and undoubtedly in this part of the country—is that of cutting the cake after the rehearsal the night before the wedding. The cake cutting may take the place of the reception or may be in addition to the reception. It is given by the bride's parents, members of either family, or friends. The procedure followed is the same as that for a reception, with the cake cutting as the main event. Today, the cake cutting it more often part of the reception after the wedding.

FOOD AT FUNERALS

The neighborly thing to do when someone dies is to offer a gift of food as well as calling on the family and sending flowers. Neighbors in this state provide food in great abundance. When family and friends gather in the home before and after a funeral service, the display of cakes, pies, and other dishes can look like the lineup at a county fair.

FOOTBALL FOOD

Because the football games at the University of North Carolina in Chapel Hill, North Carolina State University in Raleigh, Wake Forest University in Winston-Salem, and Duke University in Durham are in the central portion of the state, attendance is a pleasant experience for much of the state's population. Going to football games during the season is just the thing to do.

The residents of these places really have a landslide of company on football weekends. The food is usually served informally in a help-yourself manner. It is planned to include friends of friends.

The kitchen gets a mention along with the state's favorite football song. Whenever a group of Tar Heels get together during the football season, this song is heard dozens of times:

> Rah, Rah, Carolina, Lina
> Rah, Rah, Carolina
> I'm a Tar Heel born
> And a Tar Heel bred
> And when I die
> I'll be a Tar Heel dead.
> For, it's Rah, Rah, Carolina, Lina
> Rah, Rah, Carolina.

For some reason, on the heels of that popular song, comes this one:

> Summons in the kitchen with Dinah,
> Summons in the kitchen, I know
> Summons in the kitchen with Dinah

Strumming on the ole ban-jo.
Fe, Fi, Fiffly-I-Oh
Fe, Fi, Fiffly-I-Oh.

• • • • •

HUNT BREAKFASTS AND BALLS

North Carolina is famous for its fox hunts. The centers of organized hunts are Southern Pines, Tryon, and Sedgefield. The season lasts from fall until early spring. Among the festivities—and for some the most enjoyable parts of this traditional event—are the hunt breakfasts and balls.

FIFTEEN

The following menus, presumably for luncheons, are from the late Jessie Payne, a well-known caterer in Lexington.

Ham
Potato Salad
Peas
Perfection Salad
Cheese Soufflé
Devil's Food Cake with White Icing

Chicken Salad
Cheese Straws and Tomato Aspic
Scalloped Potatoes
Coconut Cake

Fried Chicken
Corn Pudding
Buttered Asparagus on Toast
Strawberry Tart

Deviled Crab
Tomato Aspic or Sliced Tomato
Potato Salad or Rolled Toasted Cheese Sandwich
Peas in Bread Cups or Rosettes
Lemon Tarts or Lemon Pie

In addition to luncheons, Tar Heels enjoy giving teas, coffees or Kaffee-klatsches, and Coke parties.

Teas with great numbers of guests were once a favorite way to entertain. Occasionally, a hostess would get the house all cleaned up and schedule a tea from early afternoon until dark. There were also times when a tea was scheduled for three days in a row, with different guests each day. A tea was judged to be the ideal way to launch a bride both before and after her wedding.

The food for these occasions included an assortment of fancy sandwiches and cakes or cookies. There was always the strong possibility that there would be ham biscuits—tiny baking powder biscuits buttered while they were hot and filled with thinly sliced baked country ham—or tiny pieces of fried country ham.

• • • • •

PARTY BEVERAGES

In warm weather, the popular beverage is a fruit punch such as ginger ale poured over lime sherbet. In cold weather, by far the most popular party beverage is Russian tea served spicy and hot in the best thin china cups. There are dozens of recipes for it. The following one is mine.

Russian Tea
(Tested)

1 cup sugar
1 quart water
1 stick (3 inches) cinnamon
1 teaspoon whole cloves
3 tablespoons dry tea
1 cup orange juice
1 can (12 ounces) pineapple juice
½ teaspoon grated orange rind
½ teaspoon grated lemon rind

Mix sugar, water, cinnamon, and cloves in a saucepan. Bring to a boil and simmer for 10 minutes. Add tea and heat through. Remove from heat. Cover and let stand for 5 minutes.

Strain tea mixture and add remaining ingredients. Heat but do not boil. Serve hot. Makes about 8 measuring cups.

Syllabub

Punch cups of syllabub (or sillabub) appear around Christmas and New Year's. Syllabub is nothing more than softly whipped cream flavored with wine and, in some cases, brandy. According to one old recipe, "You should froth the whites of 4 eggs, then froth the milk which has been flavored and sweetened and pour the milk over the eggs, stirring lightly."

The custom was to whip the cream in a syllabub churn, producing soft, drinkable mounds of cream rather than the stiffer mounds produced by an egg beater. Sometimes the syllabub churns were attractive hand-painted china containers that were used right at the table. Or the churn might be a handmade tin affair with a small wooden dasher or a glass one with a beater made of thin wires.

To prepare syllabub, mix 1 pint heavy cream with ½ cup light cream. Add ½ cup sugar and ½ cup wine. Churn or whip lightly with an egg whip until foamy. Serve cold as soon as it is made.

• • • • •

PARTY FOODS

Chess tarts or cakes are often found at teas (for recipes see index). Cheese dreams are another favorite. They are made from an extremely short dough of the cheese straw type.

Cheese Dreams

The late Marvel Carter Campbell, of Winston-Salem, who specialized in these delicious tidbits, prepared them to ship all over the country. They were about the size of a 25-cent piece and had just enough cayenne in them to give a tiny peppery bite.

Mrs. Campbell's recipe for cheese dreams remained her secret, but the recipe here turns out a tasty batch.

2 cups butter
1 pound sharp cheese

4 cups sifted flour
½ teaspoon salt
Cayenne pepper
Paprika

Cut butter and cheese into flour. Add salt and cayenne pepper. Roll or pat out to a thickness of about ¼ inch. Cut into tiny shapes as desired.

Place on an ungreased baking sheet and sprinkle the tops with paprika. Bake at 325° for about 15 minutes, or until done—do not allow to brown.

Another preference is snowballs—hunks of angel food or other type of cake covered with white boiled frosting and coated with freshly grated coconut.

These are some of the cookies you might find on the lace-covered table.

Tea Cakes or Sugar Cookies

This is a plain cookie but a good one. It may be decorated with fruits or nuts or even coated with a thin layer of colored frosting.

About 2 cups sifted flour
1½ teaspoons baking powder
¼ teaspoon salt
½ cup butter, margarine, or shortening
1 cup sugar
1 egg
1 teaspoon vanilla
1 tablespoon milk

Sift 1½ cups of the flour with baking powder and salt. Cream butter and add sugar, egg, vanilla, and milk. Mix well. Add flour mixture. Add enough of the remaining flour to make a dough just thick enough to roll. Chill.

Place dough on a lightly floured board and roll out to a ⅛-inch thickness. Cut with cookie cutters. Place on an ungreased cookie sheet and sprinkle with sugar. Bake in a moderate oven (about 375°) for 8 to 10 minutes. Makes about 5 dozen cookies.

Note: You can make the cookies without chilling the dough but it works much better if chilled.

Refrigerator Cookies
(Tested)

This was a favorite recipe of the late Mrs. Benjamin Parham of Oxford.

¾ cup butter
1 cup shortening
1 cup brown sugar
1 cup granulated sugar
3 eggs, beaten
About 5 cups sifted flour
1 teaspoon soda
1 scant teaspoon salt
1 teaspoon cinnamon
1 teaspoon ground cloves
1 cup chopped nuts

Cream butter and shortening together; add sugars gradually, continuing to cream until light and fluffy. Add eggs; blend thoroughly.

Sift together 3 cups of the flour, soda, salt, and spices; add dry ingredients to creamed mixture. Add just enough of the remaining 2 cups of flour to make a dough stiff enough to handle. Blend in nuts. Form dough into long rolls about 1¼ inches in diameter. Wrap in foil or heavy waxed paper. Chill in the refrigerator overnight.

Cut into thin slices with a sharp knife, and bake on a greased baking sheet in a 400° oven for 8 to 10 minutes, or until lightly browned.

Scotch Shortbread

With the Scottish ancestry of much of the population in the vicinity of Red Springs, Scotch shortbread is widely popular. Mrs. Tom Cameron of Raeford claimed that this is the genuine shortbread recipe from Scotland.

With the hands, pound 3 ounces of brown sugar into a mixture of 1¼ pounds butter and ¾ pound pure lard. Work in 3½ pounds flour. Pack into square tins. Have dough ½-inch thick. Score all over with a fork. Bake in a slow oven until light brown.

Scotch Shortbread

(Tested)

This is my recipe.

1 cup soft butter
½ cup plus 2 tablespoons sugar
2½ cups sifted flour

Cream butter; add sugar gradually while creaming. Stir in flour. Mix thoroughly with hands (it takes the hands to do the job). Chill.

Roll out dough between 2 pieces of waxed paper about ¼-inch thick. Cut with small fancy cutters and make designs on the top with the tines of a fork. Place on an ungreased baking sheet and bake in a moderate oven (about 375°) for 20 to 25 minutes. The shortbread "cookies" are not supposed to be brown.

Cheese Shortbread

There is always the need for an accompaniment for a salad plate. Cheese shortbread is a delicious tidbit to serve with a fruit salad. I have had better luck with this recipe than the one for cheese dreams.

1 stick butter
½ pound sharp cheddar cheese, grated
1 cup sifted flour
Pinch of salt
Paprika

Cut butter and cheese into flour and salt with a pastry blender. Blend well. Form into a roll about 1½ inch in diameter. Wrap in aluminum foil and chill in the refrigerator for several hours.

Slice thin with a wire cheese cutter or with a piece of thread held tightly. Sprinkle with paprika. Place slices on an ungreased baking sheet. Bake at 350° for 15 minutes, or until they get ready to brown—do not allow to brown.

"Shortnin' Bread"

This delicious product is a lot like Scotch shortbread.

2 cups sifted flour
½ cup light brown sugar
1 cup (½ pound) butter

Mix flour and sugar. Cut in butter with a pastry blender until mixed. The mixture will be crumbly. Turn into an ungreased 8-inch square pan and press down mixture firmly with the back of a spoon.

Bake in a 350° oven for 25 minutes, or until lightly browned. Cool and cut into squares. Makes 25 squares.

German Scones
(Tested)

In looking through *The Wilson Cook Book*, compiled by the Woman's Society of Christian Service of Wilson and published in 1941, I ran across a recipe for German scones. It was contributed by Lula H. Ruffin. I tried it and discovered a perfect accompaniment for coffee or tea. I used North Carolina dewberry jelly on top. This is the recipe.

2 tablespoons sugar
1½ cups sifted flour
¼ pound (½ cup) butter
½ cup finely chopped pecans
1 teaspoon vanilla
Jelly
Sugar

Mix sugar and flour and cut in butter. Add pecans and vanilla. Work with hands until the dough is inclined to hold together. It will be crumbly.

Pinch off pieces about the size of a marble and roll gently in the hands to make a little ball. Place on an ungreased baking sheet. With the handle of a knife, make a small dent in the top of each ball. Fill the dent with a dab of jelly. Sprinkle with sugar. Bake at 375° for 20 minutes, or until lightly browned. Makes about 3 dozen scones.

Sand Dabs or Pecan Fingers
(Tested)

I do not believe I have run across a single cookbook published by a North Carolina church or club that fails to include this recipe or a version of it. This is not a sweet cookie; its goodness lies in its shortness.

1½ sticks butter
2 cups sifted cake flour
2 tablespoons powdered sugar
Pinch of salt
1 teaspoon vanilla
1 tablespoon ice water
1 cup chopped pecans
Additional powdered sugar

Cut butter into flour, which has been sifted with the powdered sugar and salt. Add remaining ingredients and mix well. The mixture will be rather crumbly, but it can be molded into finger shapes with the hands. Place on a greased cookie sheet and bake in a moderate oven (about 375°) for 20 to 25 minutes. Roll in additional powdered sugar. Makes about 30 fingers.

Himmel Futter

This recipe came from Mary E. Johnston, of Sylva, a home demonstration agent of Jackson County. The recipe is German in origin; translated, it means "Heavenly Food." This confection is especially popular around Christmastime.

Mix 1 cup nuts, ½ cup flour, 1 teaspoon baking powder, 2 eggs beaten together quickly, 1 cup chopped dates, ½ cup sugar, and ⅛ teaspoon salt. Bake in a flat pan. When done, turn out and sprinkle with powdered sugar.

Note: If desired, add homemade citron made from watermelon rinds. This makes the Himmel Futter more moist.

Bourbon Balls
(Tested)

3 cups crushed vanilla wafers
1½ tablespoons cocoa
1 cup powdered sugar
1 cup chopped nuts
3 tablespoons dark corn syrup
6 tablespoons bourbon

Work all ingredients together. Roll small balls of the mixture in additional powdered sugar. Allow to stand for several hours before serving.

Orange Sticks
(Tested)

This distinctive cookie is the specialty of Evelyn Ripple.

2 tablespoons butter
1 cup brown sugar, firmly packed
2 eggs
2 tablespoons grated orange rind
2 tablespoons orange juice
1¼ cups sifted flour
½ teaspoon baking powder
½ pound orange candy (the kind that looks like orange sections),
cut into small pieces
⅓ cup chopped nuts
Juice of 1 large orange
4 tablespoons granulated sugar

Cream butter and brown sugar. Add eggs and mix well. Add orange rind and blend.

Sift together flour and baking powder. Mix with orange candy and nuts. Add to creamed mixture with 2 tablespoons orange juice. Pour into an 8½- × 11-inch pan that has been greased with waxed paper. Bake at 350° for about 30 minutes, or until done. Turn out.

Mix juice of large orange with granulated sugar and pour over hot cake. Cool and cut into fingerlike pieces. Roll in additional granulated sugar.

Black-Eyed Susans
(Tested)

1 stick butter
1 pound grated sharp cheddar cheese
2 cups sifted flour
Dash of cayenne pepper
Dates stuffed with pecan halves

Cut butter and cheese into flour and cayenne pepper. Roll out thin. Cut into small rounds and squeeze each around a stuffed date. Bake at 325° until they begin to brown.

Black Walnut Drop Cookies
(Tested)

These squares are rich and make luscious use of full-flavored black walnuts.

½ cup shortening
½ cup butter
2½ cups dark brown sugar
2 eggs
2½ cups sifted flour
¼ teaspoon salt
½ teaspoon soda
1 cup crushed black walnuts
⅛ teaspoon walnut flavoring

Cream shortening and butter. Add brown sugar and mix well. Add eggs and mix.

Sift flour with salt and soda and add to creamed mixture with walnuts and flavoring. Do not add any more flavoring because ⅛ teaspoon gives a fine walnut taste.

Drop by half teaspoons onto a greased cookie sheet. Bake in a moderate oven (about 350°) for about 10 minutes, or until lightly browned. Makes about 5 dozen cookies.

Black Walnut Refrigerator Cookies
(Tested)

These cookies are worth making if only for the black walnut odor that fills the kitchen as they bake. But there are other reasons, too—the crispness and the taste.

1¼ cups butter
⅔ cup granulated sugar
1 cup brown sugar, packed
1 teaspoon vanilla
2 eggs
3¼ cups sifted flour
1 teaspoon baking powder
¼ teaspoon soda
1 teaspoon salt
1½ cups chopped black walnuts

Cream butter. Add sugars and cream together until light and fluffy. Add vanilla and eggs, one at a time. Beat well.

Sift flour, baking powder, soda, and salt and add to creamed mixture with walnuts. Shape into rolls about 1½ inches in diameter. If the dough is sticky [mine was], chill a little before shaping into rolls.

Wrap in aluminum foil and chill well. To bake, cut in ¼-inch slices with a sharp knife. Place on an ungreased baking sheet. Bake at 400° for 6 to 8 minutes, or until light brown. Remove from baking sheet and cool. Makes about 5 dozen.

Black Walnut Bread
(Tested)

Make this bread several days ahead of time. Wrap well and age for 2 or 3 days. Slice thin and make into tiny sandwiches with soft butter as the filling.

3 cups sifted flour
4½ teaspoons baking powder
½ cup sugar
1 teaspoon salt
1 cup chopped black walnuts
2 eggs, beaten

1 cup milk
¼ cup melted shortening

Sift together flour, baking powder, sugar, and salt. Add walnuts. Mix eggs and milk and add to flour mixture. Stir only until well mixed. Add shortening and blend. Turn into a greased loaf pan and bake in a moderate oven (about 350°) for about 1 hour, or until done.

Old-Fashioned Oatmeal Cookies
(Tested)

Many a variation of this recipe was tested to find one to produce a spiced-just-right cookie that will remain pliable after baking.

1 cup sifted flour
½ cup sugar
2 teaspoons baking powder
½ teaspoon salt
2 teaspoons soda
1 teaspoon cinnamon
½ teaspoon nutmeg
¼ teaspoon cloves
2 cups quick rolled oats
⅔ cup melted shortening
1 egg, beaten
½ cup molasses
3 tablespoons milk

Sift together flour, sugar, baking powder, salt, soda, and spices; add oats. Combine slightly cooled shortening, egg, molasses, and milk and blend with an egg beater. Pour over dry ingredients and oats. Mix well.

Drop by the tablespoonful on a greased baking sheet, leaving room for spreading. Bake in a 350° oven for 12 minutes, or until done. Do not overbake. For best results, store in a single layer.

Bishop's Bread

The legend, according to Mrs. DeLeon Britt, is that this bread originated in Kentucky and was served to visiting circuit-riding bishops. Mrs. Britt said that she liked to present it hot out of the oven, with or without butter, with a pot of coffee after an evening of bridge.

1¼ cups sifted flour
1 teaspoon salt
3 eggs
½ cup sugar
1¼ cups (½ pound) mixed candied fruits, chopped
1¼ cups chopped nuts
1 cup (6 ounces) chocolate bits
1 teaspoon vanilla
1 teaspoon orange extract

Sift together flour and salt. Beat eggs until light. Add sugar to eggs gradually and beat until very thick.

Combine flour mixture, fruits, nuts, and chocolate bits. Fold in egg mixture, vanilla, and orange extract. Spread in a greased and floured loaf pan, 10 × 5 × 3 inches. Bake in a 325° oven for 50 minutes, or until done.

Benne Seed Cookies
(Tested)

Benne seeds and sesame seeds are the same thing. Sesame seeds can be easily grown in North Carolina soils. Benne seed cookies originated in South Carolina but they are often served in this state. This is a wafer-thin version that I developed.

½ cup benne seeds
½ cup sifted flour
¼ teaspoon baking powder
⅛ teaspoon soda
¼ cup dark corn syrup
¼ cup brown sugar
¼ cup butter

Set oven at 400° and turn benne seeds into a shallow pan. Toast until a shade darker than golden. Watch closely to prevent burning. Remove from oven.

Reduce heat to 350°. Sift together flour, baking powder, and soda. Mix corn syrup, brown sugar, and butter in a saucepan. Bring to a gentle boil and boil for 1 minute. Remove from heat. Dump flour mixture and benne seeds into syrup. Stir until well blended. Let stand until slightly cooled—they are easier to drop that way.

Drop by the half teaspoon on a greased cookie sheet, leaving room for spreading. Bake at 350° for 8 minutes. Remove from oven and cool for ½ minute. Then begin running a spatula under the cookies to loosen from pan.

Scratch Back Cookies

Mix 1 cup butter, 2 cups sugar, 3 eggs, 1 teaspoon soda in 2 teaspoons hot water, 1 cup black walnuts, 1 teaspoon salt, 2 teaspoons cinnamon, 3½ cups flour, and 1 cup raisins. Drop on a cookie sheet and bake in a moderate oven.

THE EDENTON TEA PARTY

With its distinctive old buildings, Edenton is one of the charming cities in North Carolina. Furnishings in some of the buildings include old cooking equipment. The town is also distinguished as the site of the Edenton Tea Party. On October 25, 1774, fifty-one indignant Edenton ladies gathered at the home of Mrs. Elizabeth King to plan their protest against the British tax on tea. The spot where her house stood is marked by a large bronze teapot mounted on a Revolutionary cannon.

The group resolved in this fashion: "We the Ladys of Edenton do hereby solemnly engage not to conform to that pernicious practice of drinking tea, or . . . wear of any manufacture from England, until such time that all acts which tend to enslave this our native country shall be repealed." The names of the signers of the pact are inscribed on a plaque at the courthouse.

Edenton Tea Party Cakes

The story goes that during their meeting the ladies sipped on a beverage made of dried raspberry leaves and ate these tea cakes. The cakes are still made in Edenton on special occasions, such as when the old homes are open for a garden pilgrimage.

Cream ¾ cup butter with 2 large cups brown sugar. Add 3 eggs and blend. Stir 1 teaspoon soda into a small amount of hot water. Cool slightly and add to creamed mixture with ½ teaspoon salt and enough flour to make a stiff dough. Flavor with vanilla.

Chill. Roll out thin, cut with cookie cutters, and bake in a hot oven (about 400°) until done.

Mayonnaise Chicken
(Tested)

Mayonnaise chicken is a favorite dish for luncheons. This recipe came from Mrs. B. G. Campbell.

4 tablespoons plain gelatin
1 cup water
2 cups chicken broth
4 cups chopped chicken (1 hen)
3 cups diced celery
1 cup slivered, toasted almonds
2 cups green peas, cooked or canned
1 cup boiled salad dressing (recipe follows)
1 cup mayonnaise
2 cups pickle relish or chowchow, well drained

Soften gelatin in cold water. Heat broth to boiling and use to dissolve gelatin. Cool. Blend in remaining ingredients and pour into a large mold or individual ones. Congeal and serve on lettuce. Makes 16 to 20 servings.

Boiled Salad Dressing
(Tested)

Boiled salad dressing is not boiled.

2 tablespoons flour
½ teaspoon salt
½ teaspoon dry mustard
2 teaspoons sugar
Dash of paprika
2 egg yolks, well beaten
1¼ cups milk, scalded
⅓ cup vinegar
4 tablespoons butter

In the top of a double boiler combine flour, salt, mustard, sugar, and paprika; add egg yolks and mix well. Stir in milk gradually (scalded means heating to the boiling point but not allowing to boil). Place over hot water and cook for 7 to 10 minutes, or until thickened, stirring constantly.

Remove from heat. Add vinegar and butter. Stir until butter is melted and mixture is blended. Chill. Makes about 1½ cups.

Pressed Chicken Loaf

1 stewing chicken (4 to 5 pounds), cleaned and cut up
1 teaspoon salt
1 small carrot, peeled
1 small onion, peeled
1 envelope unflavored gelatin
¼ cup cold water
1 cup finely chopped celery
2 tablespoons chopped canned pimento, drained
2 tablespoons chopped parsley
1 teaspoon lemon juice
Dash of cayenne pepper or hot pepper sauce
4 hard-cooked eggs, finely chopped

Put chicken pieces in a large kettle; barely cover with water. Add whole carrot and onion. Bring to a boil, cover and reduce heat, and simmer for 2½ to 3 hours, or until tender.

Cool chicken for 1 hour in the broth. Remove skin and separate meat from bones. Discard skin, bones, and fat. Put meat through a coarse food grinder. Strain broth; skim off fat and discard.

Boil broth down rapidly to 2 cups. Soften gelatin in the cold water, then dissolve it in the hot broth. Combine broth with chicken, celery, pimento, parsley, lemon juice, cayenne pepper, and eggs. Mix well and taste for seasoning.

Turn into an oiled loaf pan, 8 × 5 × 3 inches. Chill until firm. Unmold on a platter. Garnish as desired. To serve, slice about ½ inch thick. Makes 6 to 8 servings.

Toasted Pumpkin Seeds

To 2 cups seeds, add 1½ tablespoons melted butter and 1¾ teaspoons salt. Mix well. Spread in a shallow pan and bake in a 350° oven until crisp and brown.

SIXTEEN

Dinner to Go

Carrying your own lunch is an old custom with North Carolinians. Children used to eat their lunch at school from a dinner pail, which was nothing more than an empty lard can—the kind that came with a handle. And often Papa and the hands took their dinner pails to a far-away field. Most often these dinner pails were filled with little more than sausage biscuits and maybe some fried pies.

Then came the commercial dinner pail, made from shiny tin in much the same shape as the lard bucket minus the lard label. The tin dinner pail was eventually streamlined into the workman's lunch box, with its rounded lid built to hold a thermos jug. The latter innovation, providing an easy way to carry a beverage, came along about the same time that hot and cold running water became routine in most homes.

In the 1920s, when grammar school girls wore big hair ribbons and panties made of the same materials as their dresses, small, rectangular, gaily painted tin boxes with handles were the vogue.

• • • • •

PICNICS

Oh, what wonderful memories the word *picnic* evokes—picnics on those leisurely, lazy summer days before instant foods. The best way in the world to become the target of the town's gossip was to take a skimpy picnic basket to a church supper, a family reunion, or "an all day meetin' with dinner on the grounds."

How Grandmother would load that old picnic basket with fried chicken, country ham, potato salad, home-packed pickles, tarts, pies, and always a luscious layer cake. She never tried to put out her meal when no one was looking but was one who made a great flourish of arranging her offerings. And when a woman of Grandma's dimensions (180 pounds and five feet tall) flourished, that was quite a flourish.

Today picnics, like many other things, are not what they used to be. Many Sunday school groups have discontinued the tradition of a picnic, for the baskets became so skimpy there was scarcely enough food to go around. Those who belong to the stable and football sets have adapted the picnic idea for their tailgate meals at football games and at fox hunts. This is a meal served from the tailgate of a station wagon or other vehicle. Here is the menu for a traditional southern picnic:

Fried Chicken
Ham Biscuits
Tomato Sandwiches
Pimento Cheese Sandwiches
Potato Salad
Deviled Eggs
Jar of Pickles
Homemade Cake and/or
Brownies and Chess Tarts

• • • • •

BOX SUPPERS

Box suppers were another old southern custom. A box supper party was both a money-making and a beau-getting scheme. The young ladies of the church or community packed suppers for two in boxes. The boxes were auctioned off to the highest bidder. The young man who bought the box was entitled to eat it in the company of the girl who packed it. That is how many a young lady was snatched from spinsterhood and found herself cooking for that young man for the rest of her life—but without another penny's pay for it.

COVERED-DISH AND POTLUCK MEALS

The covered-dish supper is a loose term that seems to mean, *Come and bring whatever you have but put a lid on it.* The identification of a potluck supper is a little nebulous, too. Sometimes it means, *Come share what I have in my pot.* Other times it means, *I'll bring my pot and share it with you.* Most often it means, *You're in luck if you like what's in the pot.*

SEVENTEEN

"Feelin' Rite Peert"

"YARBING"

Gathering herbs, or "yarbing," was once widely practiced in western North Carolina, especially in the Avery County area. The bulk of the medicinal herbs used in the United States was collected within an eighty-five-mile radius of Asheville.

When times were bad and money was scarce, many individuals took to the woods in search of herbs and the warehouses bulged. But when times were good and the jobs in town plentiful, only a few people continued to gather herbs. During World War II, when everyone was able to get a job, there was a tremendous shortage of herbs. Today, there are women who learned the art of finding herbs from their mothers and grandmothers. However, those who really know their herbs are diminishing in number.

The price list in Table 1 indicates the vast number of herbs found in North Carolina. The prices from about 1950 are given only for comparative purposes. The mere names of the herbs fascinate me.

• • • • •

LULU RUCKER, HERB WOMAN

A typical herb woman was the late Lulu Rucker, who for over twenty years prior to 1950 rarely missed taking her wares to the city curb market in Winston-Salem each Saturday. She would sit behind her collection, piled on four planks on a wooden sawhorse, smiling at her customers as

TABLE 1

North Carolina Herbs and Price per Pound, ca. 1950

Herb	Price per Pound	Herb	Price per Pound
Adam and Eve Root	.20	Calamus Root, natural	.01
Agrimony Herb	.01	Catnip Herb, leafy	.12
Angelica Roots, whole or split	.30	Catnip Leaves	.35
Arbor Vitae Leaves	.02	Chestnut Leaves	.04
Balm of Gilead Buds, green	.45	Cleaver Vine	.10
Balmony Leaves, true	.25	Corn Silks, dry	.10
Bamboo Briar Root	.01	Cotton Root Bark	.06
Bayberry Root Bark	.15	Cranesbill (Alm) Root	.10
Beeswax, yellow cake	.35	Crawley Root	.45
Beth Root, clean	.12	Culvers (Black) Root	.15
Birch Bark, rossed	.01	Dandelion Root	.10
Bitter Root, east and west	.08	Deer Tongue Leaves	.12
Bittersweet Root Bark	.05	Elder Flowers	.15
Black Alder Bark, natural	.03	Fringe Tree Bark of Root	.28
Blackberry Root Bark	.09	Garden Sage	.25
Blackberry Roots	.04	Gelsemium (Yellow Jasmine Root)	.10
Black Cohosh Root, clean	.08	Ginseng Root	(Highest market)
Black Haw Bark of Root	.40	Golden Seal Herb	.30
Black Haw Bark of Tree, natural	.18	Golden Seal Root, dry, clean	(Market)
Black Haw Bark of Tree, rossed	.20	Gravel Plant	.02
Black Walnut Hulls, dry	.01	Ground Ivy Vine	.02
Black Willow Bark, not rossed	.02	Haircap Moss, clean	.02
Black Willow Buds	.12	Hellebore Root	.20
Blood Root, natural	.30	Horehound Leaves	.05
Blue Cohosh Root	.08	Horsement Herb, cut up	.03
Boneset Herb	.01	Horsenettle (Bullnettle) Roots	.25
Boneset Leaves	.02	Huckleberry Leaves	.10
Bugleweed Herb	.06	Hydrangea Root	.05
Burdock Root, clean	.03	Indian Physic Root	.10
Butterfly (Pleurisy) Root	.20	Indian Turnip Root, sliced	.05
		Ironweed Root	.05
		Jersey Tea, bark of root	.20
		Jerusalem Oak Seed	.05

Herb	Price per Pound	Herb	Price per Pound
Jimson Weed Leaves	.05	Sampson Snake Root	.60
Lady Slipper Root	.35	Seneca Snake Root	.75
Lemon Balm Leaves	.10	Serpentaria (Black Snake) Root	1.50
Life Root Plant, clean	.05		
Liverwort Leaves	.15	Shonny Haw Root Bark	.30
Lobelia Herb, no roots	.10	Shonny Haw Tree Bark, natural	.18
Maiden Hair Fern	.12		
Mayapple (Mandrake) Root	.15	Shumac [Sumac] Berries, dry, no stem	.01
Maypop (Passion Flower) Herbs	.08	Sinkfield Vine	.04
		Skunk Cabbage Root	.05
Milkweed (Silkweed) Root	.10	Slippery Elm Bark, rossed, white	.10
Mistletoe Leaves and Tops	.02	Solomon's Seal Root	.10
		Spearmint Leaves, clean	.10
Motherwort Herb, young	.08	Spikenard Root, clean	.15
Mullein Leaves, dry	.05	Squaw Vine, bright, clean	.17
Peachtree Leaves	.04		
Pennyroyal Herb	.04	Star Grass Root	.40
Pennyroyal Leaves	.10	Star Root, grub	.50
Peppermint Leaves	.15	Stickweed Leaves	.01
Pipsissowa (Evergreen) Herb	.12	Stilingia (Queen) Root	.05
		Stinging Nettle Leaves	.02
Plantain Leaves	.01	Stone Root, clean, dry	.06
Poke Berries, dry	.10	Strawberry Leaves	.07
Poke Root	.03	Sumac Bark of Root	.04
Poplar Bark, rossed	.01	Tansy Leaves and Tops	.06
Prickly Ash Root Bark	.05	Turkey Corn (Pea Root)	.25
Pumpkin Seed, white, dry	.06	Wahoo Root Bark, clean	.65
		Wahoo Tree Bark, natural	.15
Queen of Meadow Root	.05		
Raspberry Leaves	.08	Walnut (Black) Leaves	.02
Ratsbane (Striped Wintergreen)	.12	White Oak Bark, rossed	.02
		White Pine Bark, rossed	.05
Rattleweed Root	.08	White Pond Lily Root, sliced	.05
Red Clover Tops, bright	.15		
Sarsaparilla Root, white	.15	White Walnut Bark of Root, clean	.03
Sassafras			
Root Bark, not rossed	.18	White Willow Bark	.01½
Root Bark, select	.25	Wild Cherry Bark	
Tree Bark, not rossed	.01	Thick, not rossed, no wood	.02
Tree Bark, rossed	.02		

Herb	Price per Pound	Herb	Price per Pound
Thick, rossed	.08	Wintergreen Herb, dry	.06
Thin, slick, not rossed, natural	.06	Wintergreen Leaves	.10
		Witch Hazel Bark	.03
Thin, slick, rossed, no wood	.11	Witch Hazel Leaves, bright, no nuts or twigs, dry	.07
Wild Ginger Root	.20		
Wild Indigo Root, bone dry	.10	Yarrow Herb, bright, cut up	.02
Wild Lettuce Leaves	.16	Yellow Dock Root	.03
Wild Plum Bark, natural	.06	Yellow Parilla Root	.08
Wild Yam Root, natural, bone dry	.04	Yellow Root	.08

if her herbs were jewels. To her, they were. People would not be "allus ailin' effen they doctored with yarbs en stayed 'way from them doctors," she claimed. When she ran down the list of her leaves, roots, and sticks, tied in neat bundles, the sound was for the world like that of a tobacco auctioneer.

Mrs. Rucker believed in herbs and used them. In the spring, she made up a quart of liquid from a combination of six or eight herbs. "I drink it 'til it's gone. Then in the fall, I make another quart 'en drink it 'til it's gone."

Never was there a patent medicine that would cure as many ills as Mrs. Rucker's herbs. Just listening to her tell what was good for what and just how to chew, brew, simmer, or stew it was most entertaining. If one of the herbs was for a rather delicate condition, she would lean across the planks and speak of it in a whisper. These were some of her remedies:

- Rabbit tobacco is good "fer life everlastin', fer colds en fer the athme."
- Asthma sufferers have a choice of medications. For adults there is the hunt leaf, and for children, the sourwood stick [sourwood as in honey].* [At the mention of the sourwood stick, she would reach down under the counter and pull up a stick about eight feet long: "What

*A sourwood tree provides flowers with nectar, which attracts bees.

ye do is measure 'em while they sleep en then ye never let 'em see the stick."]

- Sarsaparilla or "sassperilly" [though known to some as a beverage] is a treatment for "the rheumatise."
- For measles, make spicewood into a liquid [called measles tea].
- Hunt leaf is also for the weak heart.
- Horehound [also used for making candy] is splendid for colds and cough syrup. [The horehound leaves were brewed into a strong, bitter liquid, which reportedly would take care of a cold overnight.]
- Angelica is needed by the whole world, times being what they are. "It's for when ye git all shook up inside. Ye ken jist be so nervous, ye can't hardly hold still en then chew on a little angelico en jist get calmed right down." [Angelica smells like celery and tastes good, too.]
- Make tender young catnip shoots into a tea for anemic infants. The devil's shoestrings go into tea for the nerves.
- Silkweed root is good for the "indigestion, the weak heart, en the rheumatise." Calamus root helps "the indigestion en is good for the high blood."
- Wild cherry bark made into a syrup will take care of a hacking cough before you have the opportunity to hack twice.
- "Septnight" [whatever that really was] will tackle a cold or treat "the sugar dibeetees."
- Blood root, black haw, and "pennyroy" [pennyroyal] all "build up her blood."
- Star grass "will clean yer cold out" and is especially advisable in the spring after winter colds, the flu, and grippe.
- "Yaller root" helps kidney trouble and puts a new lining in "the ulcerated stomach." Ratsbane is another treatment for kidney trouble.
- [Of mullein leaves, Mrs. Rucker had this to say]: "Ye take mullen leaves en ye make a ooze outen 'em. Ye use it on sweelin's like 'round yer ankles."

Adam and Eve root was probably Mrs. Rucker's most fascinating herb. According to her, the root portion offered "encourgmint to men" and the leaf portion offered "encourgmint to wimmin." The exact nature of that encouragement seemed too delicate to investigate further.

Mrs. Rucker spent the week roaming the countryside around her home gathering her sticks, roots, bark, and leaves. When Saturday came, she headed for her stand in the city market. As she observed: "They's times when I'd like to stop comin' but then I git to thinkin' 'bout folks a-ailin'. They's people that say they can't git along lessen they git ther yarbs. So I jist keep on acomin'. I feel like I'm doin' the Lord's will."

Mrs. Rucker finally stopped going to the market many years ago.

• • • • •

OTHER OLD REMEDIES

Flora MacDonald, former home demonstration agent of Moore County, had quite a collection of old remedies. Here are some of the choice ones she found:

- Cure the itch by bathing in water from boiled poke root.
- Wild cherry bark tea takes care of a sore throat.
- Blackberry wine, beat-up fire coals in water, or the inside bark of a blackjack tree when chewed are fine treatments for dysentery or flux.
- To treat a cough, try wild cherry bark tea, a teaspoon of sugar with a drop of kerosene or turpentine, chopped onion and sugar mixed together, cinders in whiskey, or sumac tea made from the red velvety berries and sugar. Or make a cough syrup by mixing honey, vinegar, and butter or cherry bark, alum, and honey.
- To make the measles break out and to treat hives, make a tea from sheep testes (goat testes will not do). Fodder tea is another treatment.
- Catnip tea is good for the colic and for soothing the nerves. Maypop is another colic treatment.
- In the spring, sulfur and molasses will purify the blood, as will wild cherry bark boiled in water to make a thick syrup. [Bleeding was another treatment for strong blood in the spring. To bleed a person, a vein was cut in the elbow. The knives to make the cut were put together like our measuring spoons—the big knife was for the horses and the little ones were for people.]
- To stop a cut from bleeding, put soot on it.
- For rheumatism, try prickly sage root tea and whiskey three times a day, or white ash root tea with whiskey.
- For a headache, put your feet in a bucket of hot water.

Some others are these:

- Sassafras tea helps anemia. For heartburn, chew mustard seed mixed with a little soot. Sumac tea will help kidney trouble, while yupon tea will treat liver conditions.
- Juniper tea made by steeping cedar "straw" will give immunity from malaria [once widely used in the swamp section of eastern North Carolina].
- Raw onion slices tied flatly against the bottom of the feet will draw out fever.
- Cobwebs gathered in dark old barns will produce sleep [used by early settlers].
- A brew of prickly ash bark helps the elderly to ease aches and pains.
- An infusion of dried peach leaves and boiling water will treat children suffering from whooping cough.
- Roasted figs stuffed with ginger will cure hoarseness.
- Dandelion wine is a fine tonic for older people.
- Treat the hiccups by chewing caraway seeds.

• • • • •

WINES AND OTHER BREWS

Wine making was once a common household activity. Scuppernong and other grape wines, blackberry wine, and cherry wine were the most popular. From time to time, efforts have been made to produce wine commercially; there are now several successful producers in the state.

Grape Wine

Discard all imperfect and green grapes. Crush ripe grapes and let stand for 12 hours. Drain off the juice and add 2 pounds of sugar to every gallon of juice.

Pour half the quantity of water as you had juice over the crushed grapes and let stand for 24 hours. Draw off and add 2 pounds of sugar to the gallon. Repeat and let stand for 48 hours. The last wine drawn off is the best.

Grape Wine

Get out the stone crock. Stem grapes. Place 10 pounds grapes in crock and mash. Add 2½ quarts boiling water. Tie cloth over the top.

Allow to stand for 3 days. Strain through a cheesecloth bag. Hang bag and allow juice to drain out. Pour juice back in crock and add 2½ pounds sugar. Cover crock and let stand until fermentation ceases. Remove scum. Strain, bottle, and seal.

Blackberry Wine

Make just as you would grape wine.

Pokeberry Wine

The old folks often made pokeberry wine when the berries were fresh and ripe. They claimed that nothing else was so good for rheumatism.

Persimmon Beer

A peck of full, ripe persimmons is enough for a 10-gallon cask. Mix up a little bran with persimmons. Add warm water and mash well. Put in a tub or barrel with straw in the bottom and let stand in a warm place.

When the beer is fermented enough for use, the persimmons will rise to the surface. Then draw off the clear brew and add brown sugar or molasses if not sweet enough. Cork and bung [whatever that may mean] tightly or put in corked demijohns, jugs, or bottles. The beer is light, lively, and pleasant to taste.

Locust Beer

Some of the old makers would start with a layer of straw in the bottom of a keg. When the beer was drawn out through the bottom, the straw acted as a filter.

Gather the long black locust pods and cut away the hard part. Break the remaining portion into pieces and place in layers in a stone crock or wooden keg together with a few crushed ripe persimmons or dried apples.

Cover with hot water and place a weight on top. Let stand in a warm place for several days. The beer does not ferment. Drink soon as it does not keep too well.

Seed Beer

It seems that old-timers swapped what is called beer seed, a starter for a refreshing soft drink. A starter of the seed, which was once available from a man in Mathiston, Mississippi, had the odor of hops and vinegar.

To make the seed into a beverage, place it in 1 quart water. Then add ½ cup sorghum molasses and let stand until it works good. Renew as needed. When the weather is cold, let the seed stay in sweetened water. Do not throw away.

Dandelion Wine

Boil 3 pounds dandelion blooms (no stems), the grated rind and juice of 3 oranges and 3 lemons, and 2 gallons water for 20 minutes. Set aside overnight. The next morning strain and add 3½ pounds sugar and 1 cake yeast. Put in a crock and tie a cloth over the top. Leave for 2 weeks and then bottle.

Ginger Pop

Add 2½ pounds sugar, the juice and rind of 2 lemons, 2 heaping table-spoons ground ginger, and ½ teaspoon cream of tartar to 2½ gallons boiling water. Let boil. Cool and add 1 cake of yeast. Bottle after it ferments.

Blackberry Cordial

Boil ripe berries and strain. To every gallon of juice, add 2 pounds sugar, 2 ounces allspice, 2 ounces cloves, and ¾ ounce cinnamon. Boil a while. When cold, add ½ pint brandy.

Metheglin

Make this beverage from fermented (not distilled) honey and water. It is of Welsh origin.

Bishop's Punch

The aroma of this drink is almost as good as the flavor.

Stick an orange full of cloves and roast it in front of the Yule log (or in the oven) until soft and brownish. Cut it in quarters, pour over it a quart of hot port wine, and simmer for half an hour. Serve in punch glasses.

Switzel Tea

This beverage was made by the early settlers.

To 1 gallon cold water, add 1 cup cider vinegar, 2 cups sugar, and 1 tablespoon grated nutmeg.

●　●　●　●　●

MOONSHINING

At one time North Carolinians in some sections of the state were famous, or infamous, for their moonshine-making and bootlegging activities. As the old saying goes, "Those hills are full of stills." But as a result of raids and "revenoors," today those stills are almost nonexistent.

Corn liquor was, of course, the main product of moonshining. It was made by distilling a mash of corn, sugar, water, and sometimes sorghum. The first run of this mash could equal 110 to 140 proof. Corn liquor, which is about as white as water, was traditionally bottled in fruit jars. That is how the expression, "I grew up with a ring around my nose," originated. The ring or impression of a ring supposedly was from drinking corn liquor from a fruit jar.

In addition to corn liquor, stills turned out apple brandy, some of which was of excellent quality.

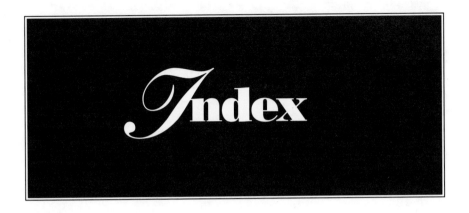

Index

dilly, 308
green, and new potatoes, 159
pickled, 307–8
Beef, 26–27, 124–25
Brunswick stew, 112
corned, 125
cured, 56
dried, 56
jerky, 56
mincemeat, 319
spiced, 125
Beer
locust, 362–63
persimmon, 362
seed, 363
Beet relish, 313–14
Belle femme (strawberries in wine), 4
Benne seed cookies, 347–48
Berries: in North Carolina, 34–36
sauce, 230
Beverages, 322, 336–37, 361–64
Bird's nest pudding, 225
Biscuit break (machine), 187
Biscuits, 183–86. *See also* Buns; Rolls
beaten, 186–88
buttermilk, 183, 184
as pie pastry, 233
cornmeal, 206
dessert, 184
egg, 184
ginger, 185
ham, 212
naple, 184
sausage, 212
soda, 183
sugar, 90
sweet potato, 185
Bishop's bread, 347
Bishop's punch, 364
Blackberries, 34–37
acid, 322
cordial, 362
jam cake, 279–80
pie, 235
pudding, 228

roll, 229
sack dumplings, 230
sauce, 230
sonker, 233
spiced, 318
wine, 362
yum yum pie, 241–42
Black cake, 293
Black-eyed peas, 60
Danny's, 169
fried, and onions, 170
Hopping John, 159
Black-eyed Susan cake, 275
Black-eyed Susan cookies, 344
Black John cake and filling, 267
Black walnut(s). *See also* Walnuts
bread, 345–46
drop cookies, 344
pie, 248
refrigerator cookies, 345
shoe box cake, 288–89
Blood loaf, 65
Blueberries, 35
yum yum pie, 241–42
Bluefish, 132
Boars, wild, 30
Boiled pot dinner, 123–24
Bonney clabber, 53
Bottle trees, 6
Bourbon balls, 343
Brains scrambled with eggs, 120
Brandy
peaches, 320–21
peaches, without brandy, 321
tutti fruitti, 320
Bread(s). *See also* Biscuits; Rolls
bean, 62
bishop's, 347
black walnut, 345–46
cheese loaf, 196
chestnut, 62
chicken, 185–86
corn, 62
corn, steamed, 208
corn lace, 207

rolled gingerbread, 89–90
sugar biscuits, 90
Cole slaw, 97
hot, 160–61
Moravian (Dutch), 97–98
Collard greens, 21–22
Comforts, 91
Company pickle chunks, 302
Composition cake, 293
Conch stew, 147
Cookies
benne seed, 347–48
black-eyed Susans, 344
black walnut drop, 344
black walnut refrigerator, 345
bourbon balls, 343
comforts, 91
crullers, 91
deceptions, 90
Edenton tea party cakes, 349
fried cakes, 92
German scones, 341
ginger nuts, 83
heifta cakels, 92
Jackson cakes, 84
love drops, 83
Moravian Christmas, 79–84, 89–90
molasses, old-fashioned, 231
oatmeal, old-fashioned, 346
orange sticks, 343
pecan fingers, 342
pepper nuts, 84
refrigerator, 339
sand dabs, 342
scones, German, 341
scratch back, 348
seed cakes, 84
shortbread, 339, 340
shortbread, cheese, 340
Shrewsbury, 82–83, 84
springerles, 82
strumbundles (strumbendles), 91
strumpfbenled, 91
such cakes, 92
sugar, 338

tanglebritches, 91
tea cakes, 84, 338
White Christmas cakes, 81
wonders, 92
Cooking methods
for fish, 138
for meat, 108–9
Cooks, 11–13, 15–18
Coots, 29
Core Sound oyster stew, 147
Corn, 162–65. See also Green corn
all-corn muffins, 203–4
bread, 62, 202–8
crackling, 203
cush, 204
steamed, 208
bread dressing, 110
cakes, 17
and chicken soup, 129
creamed, 162–63
custard, 163–64
dodgers, 62, 205
crackling, 203
dried, 59–60, 65
fried, 163
fried pepper and, 163
grilled, 165
grits, 180
fried, 180
gritted bread, 63
lace bread, 207
on-the-cob
dried, 65
grilled, 165
pone, 205–6
pone bread, 208
preservation of, 59–60
pudding, 164
green, 164–65
sour, 59
stewed, 163
sticks, 204
Corned beef, 125
Cornmeal, 45
all-corn muffins, 203–4

apple johnny cake, 90
ash cakes, 205
biscuits, 206
corn bread, 62, 202–8
    crackling, 203
corn cakes, 17
corn dodgers, 62, 203, 205
    with cracklings, 123
corn lace bread, 207
corn pone, 205–6
corn sticks, 204
dumplings, 124
griddlecakes, 155
hoe cakes, 205
hog head mush, 122
hush puppies, 204
mush bread, 204
pie (pudding), 223
Scotch bannochs, 206
soul bread, 21
spoon bread, 206–7
    green corn, 207
as thickening agent, 25, 94
yeast rolls, 201
Cosmopolitan shrimp, 145
Cottage cheese. See Clabber
Country ham
    baked, 116
    fried, 115
    with redeye gravy, 116
Country-style steak, 124
Crab(s)
    bisque, sea, 150
    blue, 140
    cakes, baked 140
    -meat dressing, 141–42
    -meat stew, 149
    shrimp and, combination, 140
    soft-shell, 140
    stew, 149
Crackers, soda, 211
Cracklings, 24
    in corn bread, 203
    in corn dodgers, 123, 203
Cranberries, 35

Cream cheese sandwich loaf, 212
Croaker, 135
Crullers, 91
Crumb cake, 87–88
Cucumber(s). See also Pickles
    catsup, 98
    fried, 96
    pickles, 301, 302
Currants, 36
Cush, 204
Custard(s)
    boiled, 218
    corn, 163–64
    egg, 17–18
    pies, 243–46
        coconut, 245
        coconut, deluxe, 245
        egg, deluxe, 244
        pumpkin, 237
        strawberry egg, 244–45
        sweet potato, 240

Dairy products: in North Carolina,
        51–54
Damson plum(s), 40
    pie, 241
Dandelion wine, 363
Date(s)
    hermit cake, 285
    and nut cake, 286–87
    orange date nut cake, 265–66
    Queen Elizabeth's cake, 266–67
Deceptions, 90
Deer, 29. See also Venison
Desserts, 215–97
Devil's food cake, 270–71
Dewberries, 35
    pie, 235
    roll, 229
Dewey's Bakery (Winston-Salem), 71
Dinner menus, 105–6
Dinner rolls. See Rolls
Dip (boiled custard), 218
Dixie relish, 310
Dolly Varden cake, 281

for Queen Elizabeth's cake, 266
seafoam, 296–97
seven-minute butter, 295
white, for brown front cake, 276
Fruit cake
dark, 283–84
dried apple, 290
farmers, 289–90
Japanese, 284
layer, 291
light, 282
raised, 290
stack, 287
Fruit(s): in North Carolina, 32–40, 179–80. *See also* names of specific fruits
Frying: as cooking method, 108
Fudge frosting, 296

Game: in North Carolina 27–30, 126–28
Geese: parboiling of, 108, 126
Giblet gravy, 110
Gingerbread, 262–63
rolled, 89–90
trainer's, 88
Golden orange frosting, 275–76
Goobers. *See* Peanut(s)
Gooseberries, 36
Grains: in North Carolina, 44–46
Grape(s), 37–38
-leaf pickles, 300
pie, muscadine, 237
spiced, 318, 319
wine, 361, 362
Grasshoppers: fried, 64
Gravy
chicken cream, 109
cream, with fried fatback, 118
giblet, 110
redeye, 115, 116
sausage, 118–19
Gravy sponge, 185
Green beans and new potatoes, 159
Green corn
pudding, 164–65

spoon bread, 207
Green onions, fried, 168
Green pepper(s). *See also* Sweet red pepper(s)
chowchow, 311
Dixie relish, 310
fried, and corn, 163
green tomato relish, 313
Hayden salad, 312–13
pear relish, 312
pickled stuffed, 304–5
scalloped, 170
vegetable relish, 311–12
Greens, 165. *See also* Collard greens
parboiling of, 109
pot liquor of, 166
washing of, 165
Green tomato(es)
pickled, 303
pie, 240–41
relish, 313
tomato soy, 313
vegetable relish, 311–12
Griddle cakes. *See also* Pancakes; Waffles
buckwheat, 210–11
cornmeal, 155
flannel, 210
grits, 211
light hot, 210
Gristmills, 45
Grits, 180
fried, 180
griddle cakes, 211
hominy bread from, 206
Gritted bread, 63
Groundhogs, 28
Grouper, 135

Half-moon pies, fried, 242–43
Ham(s)
baked country, 116
biscuits, 212
corned, 120
country, boiling of, 116

Pike, 137
Pimento cheese, 213
  cooked, 214
  sandwiches, 212–14
Pineapple
  and pear conserve, 317–18
  in pear honey, 317
Planting, customs, 77
Plums. *See* Damson plum(s)
Pokeberry wine, 362
Poke stalk(s), 170
  pickles, 309
Pole beans. *See* Beans
Pomegranates, 40
Pone bread, 208
Pon-haws, 94
Pork, 24–26, 115–24. *See also* Ham(s)
  backbones, 117, 121
  barbecued spareribs, 117
  cake, 293
  fried fatback with cream gravy, 118
  salting of, 56
  sausage, 25, 118
    preservation of, 56
    and sweets (sweet potatoes), 118
  tenderloin, preservation of, 56
Possums, 27–28, 126–27
Potato(es), 31, 170–73. *See also* Swamp
    potato meal; Sweet potato(es)
  boiled, 170
  bread, 191–92
  cakes, 170
  creamed, 170, 171
  mashed, 171
  new, 170
  new, and English peas, 169
  new, and green beans, 159
  noodles, 96
  pancakes, 96
  pudding, 223
  puffs, 90
  salad, 172–73
  soup, 130
  stewed, 171–72
  surprise, Albemarle, 172

Pot dodgers, 208
Pot liquor, 166
Poultry: in North Carolina, 23–24. *See
    also* Chicken; Game; Geese;
    Turkeys
  roasting and stuffing, 75–76
Pound cakes. *See* Cake(s)
Preservation. *See* Food preservation
Preserves, 314–22
Prince Albert cake, 280–81
Prince of Wales cake, 280–81
Pudding(s), 217–28
  banana, 228
  bird's nest, 225
  blackberry, 228
  carrot, 226–27
  corn, 164
  green corn, 164–65
  hypocrite, 242
  Jeff Davis, 226
  kiss, 225
  liver, 25
  meringue crumb, 225–26
  persimmon, 218–19, 220
  queen of, 220
  rice, 221
  snow cream, 217
  suet, 97
  sweet potato, 176–77
  tipsy, 227
  tomato, 178
  whim wham, 224
Pumpkin
  baked, 237
  blooms, fried, 181
  custard pie, 237
  dried, 65
  pie, 238
  pie, eggless, 238
  seeds, toasted, 351

Quail, 29
  broiled, 128
  fried, 128
  smothered, on toast, 128

Queen Elizabeth's cake and frosting, 266–67
Queen of puddings, 220

Rabbit(s), 27, 128
  in Brunswick stew, 112
  fried, and peckerwood dressing, 111–12
Raccoons, 29
Railroad cake, 294
Rail (mud hens), 29
Rainbow trout, 136
Raisin
  nut chess pie, 252–53
  pie, 253
Ramps, 32
Raspberries, 35
Red pepper(s). *See* Sweet red pepper(s)
Red snapper, 136
  Morehead-style, 136
Refrigerator cookies, 339, 345
Relishes, 310–14
  artichoke, 314
  beet, 313–14
  chowchow, 311
  Dixie, 310
  green tomato, 313
  Hayden salad, 312–13
  pear, 312
  pickle, 22
  sweet red pepper, 311
  tomato soy, 313
  vegetable, 311–12
Rhubarb
  pie, 236–37
  pie, candied, 236
Rice, 46
  chicken and, 115
  fish, 97
  Hopping John, 159
  pudding, 221
Riffles, 193
Rivels, 193
Robert E. Lee cake, 269–70

Rochester cake and filling, 293
Rockfish, 136
  muddle, 146
  Murfreesboro, muddle, 146
Rock garden pudding. *See* Meringue crumb pudding
Rocky Mountain filling, 297
Roe, 153–55
  canned, cakes, 155
  creamed shad, 153
  dried, 154
  herring, and scrambled eggs, 155
  menhaden, 154
  mullet, 153
  sautéed shad, 153
Rolls, 198–202. *See also* Biscuits; Bread(s); Buns
  buttermilk, 200
  cheese refrigerator, 201–2
  cornmeal yeast, 201
  icebox, 199
  rich yeast, 198–99
  sour dough, 199–200
  yam yeast, 202
Rotation cake, 260
Rucker, Lulu, 355, 358–60
Ruffed grouse, 29
Russian tea, 336–37

Salad(s), 157
  boiled, dressing, 350
Salat, 157
Salem tarts, 93–94
Sally Lunn breads, 197–98
Sally White cake, 289
Salmon (smoked) spread, 329
Sand dabs, 342
Sandwich(es), 212–14
  banana, 212
  cream cheese, loaves, 212
  ham biscuits, 212
  pimento cheese, 212–14
  sausage biscuits, 212
  tomato, 212
Sangaree, 70